BEASTLY BUGS

by **Adam Hibbert**

Contents

Clever Clogs Books

Copyright © 2006 **ticktock** Entertainment Ltd.

http://www.ticktock.co.uk

BUG OLYMPICS

Creepy-crawlies are some of the world's most astounding athletes. Relative to their size, bugs of various descriptions are record-breakers in weightlifting, the long jump, sprinting and all sorts of other physical feats. They may be ugly, but they're champions of the world!

BUGS QUIZ

How fast can the fastest insect go?

a) 30 km/h
b) 45 km/h
c) 58 km/h

How far does the call of the loudest insect travel?

a) 15 metres
b) 150 metres
c) 1.5 km

If we could jump as high as a flea, how high could we jump?

a) on to an elephant
b) over St Paul's Cathedral
c) over Mount Everest

(answers on page 32)

BEEFY BEETLES

The scarab beetle family reigns supreme in the beetle kingdom. It includes the heaviest beetle in the world, called a goliath beetle, and the strongest weightlifter, the rhinoceros beetle. A third scarab record-breaker is the dung beetle, which can move balls of manure hundreds of times heavier than its own weight.

Three-horned rhino beetle

The rhinoceros beetle can bear 850 times its own weight, making it 50 times stronger than us!

SO LONG, SUCKER!

Cat flea

The blood-sucking common flea is the world's most amazing jumper. At an average 1.5 mm long, the flea can jump as far as 33 cm, or 220 times its own length. If we could jump so well, we would need much bigger sandpits for the long-jump – around 400 metres long, in fact!

ROACH RUNNER

Cockroaches may look chunky and heavy, but don't be fooled, they are actually very fit. Scientists have worked out that at least one kind of cockroach can run at 5.5 km/h, covering a distance 50 times its own body length every second. If you could do that, you'd be sprinting at 330 km/h!

IN A FLAP

Some insects are record-breakers whether or not you allow for their size. The world record-holder for the fastest muscles is a tiny midge which beats its wings 62,760 times a minute (or 1,046 times a second). Its wing muscles have to flex back and forth at a phenomenal speed.

INCY WINCY

Spiders are among the world's most successful predators, with a 300-million-year track record. They are not true insects, but arachnids; their closest cousins are scorpions. Almost all spiders use venomous fangs to bite their prey, and some also use their sticky silkthreads to make traps.

Raft spider

RAFT RAIDER

Very few spiders live underwater, but some catch fish! The raft spider spreads its legs out over the surface of a pond, to feel the vibrations of passing prey. When a little fish or tadpole comes in range, the raft spider plunges into the water, grabs the fish, and takes it back onto dry land to eat.

Tarantula

HAIRY HUNTER

Tarantulas are well-known for their big bodies and fat-looking, hairy legs. Almost all of them scavenge at night, sometimes chasing smaller insects, mice and even snakes. In South America, there are tarantulas which spin webs big enough to catch small birds and bats.

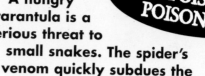
A hungry tarantula is a serious threat to small snakes. The spider's venom quickly subdues the snake – ready for the kill!

STUCK ON YOU

For some spiders, spinning sticky threads is less important than being able to spit. Spitting spiders have developed a special glue, which they make in the glands other spiders use for venom. When they see prey, or an enemy, they spit the glue at it, sticking it to the spot!

DINNER DATE

Spiders are incredibly skilful at catching insects. The bolas spiders of America, Africa and Australia simply dangle from a thread and snatch passing moths out of the air. Baffled scientists finally realised that these spiders imitate the 'scent' of a female moth to lure male moths within reach.

BUGS QUIZ

The Trobriand Islanders use the giant wood spider's webs for...

a) fishing nets
b) silk underwear
c) shopping baskets

How many different kinds of silk does a garden spider make?

a) 2
b) 4
c) 6

Why was the real Little Miss Muffet scared of the big spider that sat down beside her?

a) she was just shy
b) the spider bit her hand
c) her father made her eat spiders

(answers on page 32)

I MARRIED A CANNIBAL!

BUGS QUIZ

Why do some people call the praying mantis 'mule killer'? Is it because:

a) very hungry mantises eat mules
b) mantises scare mules to death
c) if a mule ate a mantis, it would die

How does a male orb spider tell a female not to eat him when he steps onto her web?

a) he plucks the web like a guitar
b) he whistles
c) he carries a pink rose

Why does one type of firefly imitate the mating signals of another firefly species?

a) to tease them
b) to make her mates jealous
c) to eat the male

(answers on page 32)

A DINNER DATE

Male black widow spiders have to make a quick getaway after mating. If they fail, the female eats them for dinner

The female black widow spider likes to make a meal of her mate. Males attempt a variety of tricks to get away, including bringing something to distract the female, and stroking her to calm her down. But they don't always succeed, and that's the end of them!

Jumping spider

SPIDER SNACK

It's tricky for male spiders to get away, because spider mating is complicated. Males make a silk pouch filled with sperm. They have to place the pouch into the female and squeeze it to release their sperm. Perhaps baby wolf spiders pick up their mother's nasty habit: they often eat their brothers and sisters.

MUNCHED MANTIS

The female praying mantis is the most dangerous mate in the world. She likes nothing better than feasting on her partner after mating. The male is adapted to cope with the danger of being eaten before completing the task and his body will continue to mate with a female even after she has bitten his head off.

MY MATE, MY DINNER

Male bugs often provide dinner for their mate: unfortunately for them, they're the ones on the menu! By doing this, females benefit from having a handy snack just as their eggs are growing. Males also benefit in a way, by making it more likely that their offspring will have a healthy mother.

PRAYING OR PREYING?

Praying mantises take their name from the special way in which they hold their forelegs in front of their head. When any prey comes close, the mantis quickly shoots its legs out to grab it. These creatures are ferocious carnivores from the very start: their newly-hatched offspring often eat each other.

Praying mantis

STRENGTH IN NUMBERS

On their own, not many bugs are a match for humans. But when insects join forces, they can achieve amazing things. Ants are one example of insects that work together to help their queen reproduce successfully, even though most of them will never breed. Bees and termites do the same.

Bulldog ant

BULLDOG BITES!

Because they are born to do different jobs, ants in the same nest can be all sorts of different shapes and sizes. The longest worker ants in the world are the bulldog ants of Australia, which can be up to 3.7 cm long. They come equipped with a very painful pair of pincers, and a stinging tail which can kill people who have allergies.

If we were as strong as ants, we could carry a blue whale calf weighing 3 tonnes!

AWESOME ANT-MAN

SLAVE DRIVERS

All sorts of ants take advantage of other species, making them work as slaves. Some species attack other ants' nests, stealing eggs, and bringing up the young ants as workers. One queen ant in Africa lets enemy ants drag her into their nest, where she kills their queen and takes over!

ON THE MARCH

Army ants form columns up to 100 metres long and 1 metre wide, marching around South America, eating everything in their path. Some villages make army ants welcome, moving their farm animals away, letting the ants gobble up all the village's mice and other vermin.

Ant army

SEW CUTE

Some ants use their larvae (grubs) for building nests. The weaver ant larva is specially-shaped for this job, and produces silk in a long strand. The adult weaver ants use their grubs as needles and thread, poking them through the edges of leaves to stitch them together, making a cosy nest.

NOW YOU SEE IT, NOW YOU DON'T

No amount of disguise can hide the Hercules emperor moth – it's as big as a dinner plate!

Insects make a tasty snack for birds, lizards, snakes and small mammals. Some try to hide from these predators while others rely on a quick getaway. But many are masters of disguise, blending in with their surroundings to escape notice.

INVISIBLE VANDALS

The buffalo treehopper looks exactly like a new leaf emerging from a twig. Less than 1 cm long, it can do serious damage in orchards, particularly to young apple trees. Egg-laying females cut into the protective bark of the tree, letting fungi and diseases attack the tree from inside.

Buffalo treehopper

MOTH FASHION

In the middle of the nineteenth century, British moth experts noticed that the peppered moth, which had been light grey with dark spots, was becoming dark grey in parts of the country. The moths were adapting their colours to match tree bark which had been blackened by soot from new factories.

FIERCE FLOWER

Although all praying mantises are good at hiding among leaves, the flower mantis is champion. With a bright pink coat, and knobbly growths over its body, the flower mantis can lurk inside a flower, or even just pretend to be one on its own. Insects arriving at the 'flower' for a snack are in for a surprise!

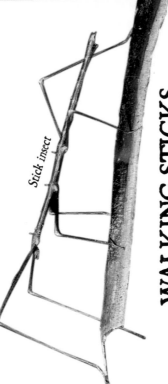

Stick insect

WALKING STICKS

Stick insects are so good at pretending to be twigs on a plant, birds are more likely to try to perch on them than eat them. Unlike many camouflaged bugs, which have to stay completely still to blend into the background, stick insects bend their knees rhythmically, pretending to sway in the breeze.

THIS SUCKS!

There are at least 300 different types of leech in the world, from pond-dwellers to land-lurkers. Some of them are the world's most specialised bloodsuckers, and their peculiar talents have even earned them a role in medicine.

BUGS QUIZ

How do leeches breathe?

a) they suck oxygenated blood from animals
b) through their skin
c) through their nose

How do aquatic leeches get into their victim's nostrils?

a) they hide in handkerchiefs
b) via drinking water
c) they lurk under your fingernails

What's a favourite place for a meal for a sea-going marine leech?

a) a penguin's beak
b) the gills of a fish
c) the eyeball of an octopus

(answers on page 32)

DOCTOR LEECH

Leeches were a popular tool for early medical practitioners. Doctors believed that some illnesses were caused by high blood pressure, and carried a jar of leeches wherever they went, to drain patients of their excess blood. The patients often decided that they suddenly felt much better, rather than go through the treatment again!

Medicinal leech

NOSE BLEED

Some unlucky birds and cattle are killed by leeches, but not because they lose too much blood. There are types of leech which climb inside their victim's nostril to suck blood. As they swell with blood, the nose can be blocked and the animal suffocates.

LEECH LUNCH

Not all species of leech are bloodsuckers. They can be accomplished swimmers and crawlers, hunting down and eating slow-moving prey, such as snails, worms and insect larvae. Their eggs are laid in a cocoon of slime, and hatch out into fully-formed miniature leeches.

DRIPPING BLOOD

The slimy, bloodsucking leeches of the world have three jaws which make a Y-shaped cut in your skin. Their saliva is specially developed to soothe the pain, and to stop your blood from clotting. You may not notice a leech bite until the leech has gone, fat with your blood and leaving behind a cut that won't stop bleeding.

HUNGRY HERBIVORES

Creepy-crawlies aren't just troublesome because they bite us. Swarms of them can also be a serious threat to plant life, threatening starvation for plant-eating creatures. Even in high-tech countries, farmers can have their businesses ruined by ugly bug armies.

FLYING PIG

Polyphemus moth caterpillars eat 86,000 times their weight in 2 months. If a human baby ate that much, it would get through 36 elephants!

Cabbage white caterpillar

SLOW SLURPER

Even the harmless slug can cause serious crop damage. Using its rasping tongue, a slug can chomp through important foodstuffs such as potatoes, wheat, sugar beet and green vegetables. Slugs in the UK alone are thought to eat as much as 36,000 tonnes of potatoes each year.

STOMACHS WITH WINGS!

Locust

Locusts can be a deadly pest, massing in huge swarms. The desert locust of Africa and the Middle East moves in swarms of up to 50,000,000,000, eating in one day the annual food requirements of half a million people. Locust swarms cause car accidents by covering roads in a squishy, slippery coating of squashed locust bodies!

CABBAGE CARNAGE

The caterpillar of the European cabbage butterfly is a real nuisance for anyone who wants to grow a cabbage. The white butterfly adult was once unknown in the Americas, but was accidentally transported to North America in around 1860, causing heavy losses to cabbage farmers.

BUGS QUIZ

One swarm of locusts in North America in 1872 covered an area as big as...
a) 20 sq km
b) 2,000 sq km
c) 5,200 sq km

How tall can a desert locust swarm become?
a) 400 metres
b) 900 metres
c) 1.5 km

If all the offspring of one aphid survived and reproduced for a year, what would they weigh?
a) 1 tonne
b) 1,000 tonnes
c) 822 million tonnes

(answers on page 32)

HAIR THEY ARE

Even if you don't have a single dust mite in your home, you probably have other mites living in your skin. Follicle mites, about 0.3 mm long, like nothing better than the cosy little gap around the roots of hairs, and are especially fond of eyelashes. Scientists aren't sure what they eat there, but they seem harmless.

BUGS QUIZ

To kill bedbugs it's probably best not to introduce the masked bedbug hunter. Why not?

a) hunting in a mask is bad manners
b) it bites humans, too
c) it stays up late playing loud music

Does the earwig have anything to do with ears?

a) no, nothing
b) yes, it eats ear wax
c) not really — it just likes hiding in small spaces!

Why would anyone want to sleep with a dish of warm sheep's blood under their bed?

a) to trap fleas
b) to distract vampires
c) to keep their toes warm

(answers on page 32)

TINY MITE

Dust mites are harmless enough, foraging through the fibres of your mattress, cushions, carpet, and anywhere else that flakes of old skin might collect. Unfortunately, their droppings are so tiny that they can float in the air in just the same way as pollen grains, causing some people to have a reaction like hayfever.

EGGS-AUSTING!

A well-fed female bedbug can lay 600 eggs in your bed every year!

MICRO MONSTERS

You might think that you haven't met a beastly bug yet today, but you certainly have; you just didn't notice it. In every house there are millions of bugs too small to see with the naked eye, from dust mites that feed off flakes of skin trapped in the carpet, to dried-up tardigrades waiting for rain.

Prostigmatid mite

BLOWING IN THE WIND

If you're reading this on a dry day, you've probably already breathed in a few tardigrades, or water bears. Less than 1 mm long, these moisture-loving minibeasts dry up and blow around in the wind until they find a nice, moist new habitat. So there's another good reason to use a handkerchief!

Bedbug

THAT REALLY BUGS ME

The most annoying housemate you are likely to meet is the bedbug, but it's usually up and about long before you are. The bedbug uses its pointy beak to saw through your skin, and suck your blood while you're asleep. Don't worry, though, it's tiny.

SUPER SLIMY

Snails and slugs are gastropods, meaning 'stomach foot'. Most slugs and snails browse on plants, but some will chew anything! There are some gastropods that live in ponds and rivers, and even under the sea. They are also divided into those which have shells, and those that don't.

BUGS QUIZ

What's the average speed of a garden snail?

a) 0.048 km/h
b) 0.48 km/h
c) 4.8 km/h

How old is the oldest snail?

a) 5 years
b) 10 years
c) 20 years

The largest snails in the world live under the sea near Australia. How heavy are they?

a) 1 kg
b) 10 kg
c) 18 kg

(answers on page 32)

CUPID'S ARROWS

With most slugs and snails, there are no males or females. When two of a kind meet and decide to reproduce, they inject each other with little darts. The darts contain sperm, which find their own way to the unfertilised eggs in each slug or snail.

African giant snail

YELLOW SLUGMARINE

Slugs have glamorous relatives that live in the sea. Sea slugs have gills for breathing under water, and specialise in eating poisonous animals such as jellyfish. They use the poisons to make themselves nasty to eat, and look every bit as dangerous as they are, with bright yellow, pink and red colouring.

Thick-horned aeolid

D.I.Y. HOUSE

Snails are born in tiny shells, but they need more space as they grow. To build an extension to the shell, they have to find calcium and other minerals. Because calcium can be hard to find, snails are less widespread than their naked cousins, the slugs, who don't bother building a house.

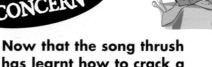

A CRACKING CONCERN

Now that the song thrush has learnt how to crack a snail's shell using a stone, understandably snails are pretty worried!

GIGANTIC GASTROPOD

The African giant snail is the largest land snail, growing up to 40 cm long, with a 20-cm shell, and weighing up to 900 g. Some scientists think these snails could be farmed as a staple food for humans. They are very cheap to farm and very meaty!

BUGS QUIZ

What does the Latin name for centipedes and millipedes, *Myriapoda*, mean?

a) many feet
b) beautiful nose
c) shiny shoes

How fast can the fastest centipede run?

a) 5 cm a second
b) 15 cm a second
c) 50 cm a second

Why is one European centipede called Electricus?

a) it eats wiring
b) it glows in the dark
c) it is used for manufactuing lightbulbs

(answers on page 32)

MILD-MANNERED

Millipedes don't have fangs, preferring fruit and leaves to meat, but they can be just as poisonous as centipedes. They are equipped with poison glands down the sides of their body, which are used to discourage predators (including centipedes) from biting them. Some even use the glands to squirt cyanide!

FANG MONSTER

Centipedes are all equipped with poisonous bites for slowing or killing their prey, and many have claws which can give humans a nasty nip. Most are too small to notice, but the Malayan centipede, a bright blue monster with red fangs, can cause months of illness with a single bite.

Giant millipede

750 FOOT INSECT!

Millipedes can be distinguished from centipedes by their round bodies (centipedes are always flat), and by their two pairs of legs on each segment of their bodies (centipedes only have one pair). But don't believe their name – millipedes can have anything from 24 to 750 feet!

LOADS OF LEGS

When you do a lot of rummaging around under rotting leaves and through the tiny spaces in the soil, it's a great help if you're long and thin and have lots of legs.

Centipede

OLD TIMER

Centipedes have been hunting around on land for as long as any other animal. The oldest fossilised land animal so far discovered was a centipede. It was found in a rock estimated to be 414 million years old. Tracks found in rocks 50 million years older than that also appear to belong to centipedes.

Millipedes may win a leg competition, but centipedes would win a length competition – they can grow up to 33 cm, in fact!

LONG vs LEGGY

SMALL BUT DEADLY

Rat flea

Some quite harmless insects are made deadly by the diseases they can spread. So don't worry about venomous spiders, angry scorpions or exotic poisonous centipedes. More of a threat are the tiny mosquito, the humdrum housefly or the fearsome flea.

FILTHY FEET

In the past, if a housefly landed on your food, it may have left behind any of 30 deadly diseases.

SWAT SENSATION

Diseases spread by houseflies can be dangerous. Killing flies can stop the spread of diseases such as cholera, typhoid, leprosy, diphtheria, smallpox and polio. In 1933, the citizens of Tokyo in Japan rallied round for 'Haotor', or National Fly-Catching Day, and killed 117,500,000 of the little pests.

FLEA FEAR

There are many different kinds of flea, from the common flea to a giant flea found in the nests of mountain beavers in North America.
The only really deadly flea, as far as humans are concerned, is the oriental rat flea, the most effective carrier of bubonic plague, or Black Death.

PLAGUE PANIC

In the fourteenth century, over a quarter of the population of Europe was wiped out by the Black Death, carried by fleas on black rats. Luckily for Europe, black rats have now lost ground to brown rats, and only live in the tropics. Brown rats carry different fleas, which don't much like human blood.

How many people die each year from mosquito-related illnesses?

a) 10,000
b) 100,000
c) over 1,000,000

How many people died in the 14th century from the bubonic plague?

a) 2.5 million
b) 25 million
c) 250 million

How long does the average male housefly live?

a) 10 days
b) 20 days
c) 3 months

(answers on page 32)

MOZZIE MENACE

You wouldn't mind the occasional bite from a mosquito, if it wasn't for its filthy table manners. The mosquito jabs its snout through your skin, and then spits into the wound.
The spit is meant to stop the blood from clotting, but it can also contain killer diseases and parasites!

Yellow fever mosquito

23

STING IN THEIR TAIL

The arachnid family is famous for its spider members, but the deadliest, ugliest, and altogether weirdest of the bunch is the scorpion, with claws, scuttling legs, and a very nasty sting at the end of its tail.

BUGS QUIZ

How long was the longest live scorpion ever measured?

a) 9.5 cm
b) 18.7 cm
c) 29.2 cm

How big was the biggest prehistoric scorpion, which lived 300 million years ago?

a) 40 cm
b) 86 cm
c) 1.2 m

How long will a dog survive after being stung by the northern African fat-tailed scorpion?

a) 7 hours
b) 24 hours
c) 1 week

(answers on page 32)

DEADLY DANCE

The scorpion male has to be extremely careful when approaching a mate. Grasping the female by the claws, it 'dances' her around, sometimes for hours. Then it places a parcel of sperm on the ground and pulls the female onto it. Many males fail to get away again, and are eaten alive.

POISON PARENTS

Despite their poisonous reputation, scorpions can be some of the most caring mothers in the world of creepy-crawlies. The female scorpion gives birth to live young, rather than laying eggs. She protects them by carrying them around on her back, feeding them until they've grown enough to fend for themselves.

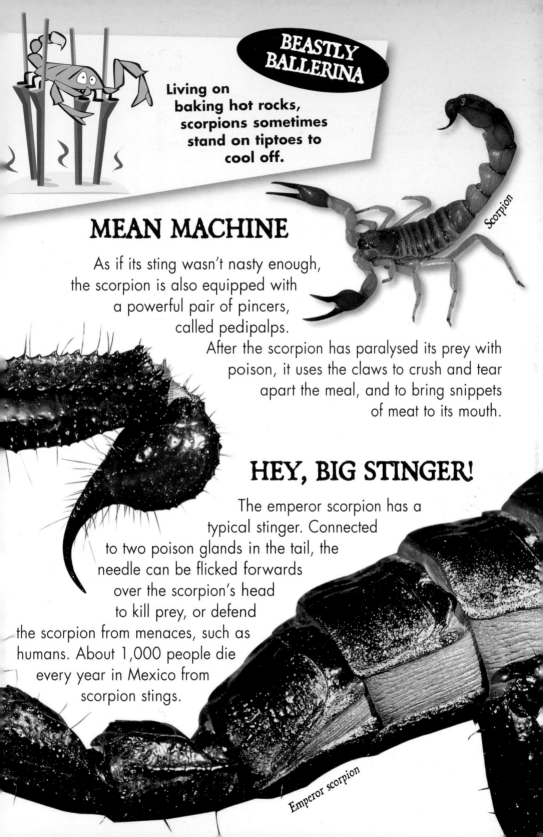

Living on baking hot rocks, scorpions sometimes stand on tiptoes to cool off.

Scorpion

MEAN MACHINE

As if its sting wasn't nasty enough, the scorpion is also equipped with a powerful pair of pincers, called pedipalps.

After the scorpion has paralysed its prey with poison, it uses the claws to crush and tear apart the meal, and to bring snippets of meat to its mouth.

HEY, BIG STINGER!

The emperor scorpion has a typical stinger. Connected to two poison glands in the tail, the needle can be flicked forwards over the scorpion's head to kill prey, or defend the scorpion from menaces, such as humans. About 1,000 people die every year in Mexico from scorpion stings.

Emperor scorpion

BUGS QUIZ

An insect's suit of armour needs regular, careful cleaning, otherwise it...

a) rusts
b) upsets the insect's mother
c) gets attacked by fungus

How do beetles replace their armour when they need a bigger suit?

a) trade it in at a flea market
b) strip off their old one and grow another
c) spray themselves with concrete

How hot is the jet of chemicals from a bombardier beetle's bottom?

a) 50°C
b) 75°C
c) nearly 100°C

(answers on page 32)

SNAPPY STAG

Sometimes called a pinching bug, the stag beetle is smaller than the rhino beetle, but has proper pincers which can draw blood if they clamp hold of your finger. They only attack if provoked, preferring to forage for sap to suck among rotting wood.

FLAME THROWER The **bombardier beetle** uses an amazing 'flame-throwing' technique to fend off enemies: it squirts a boiling jet of noxious vapour from its bottom!

Stag

RHINO RAGE

Despite their fearsome appearance, rhino beetles aren't all that aggressive, and can't use their 'horns' to hurt humans. The horns are used to show off to females.
If two males are competing for one female, they will use their horns for wrestling, trying to topple their rival onto his back.

ARMUUR PLATING

Beetles are the tanks of the insect world. Some have developed thick armour plating, which allows them to fight, hunt quite dangerous creatures and avoid being eaten themselves. The hard shells are made of a protein called chitin, and have to be replaced whenever the beetle grows bigger.

INSIDE OUT

Beefier beetles, such as rhinoceros beetles, have very strong armour. As with all insects, this is so tough that they don't need a skeleton; they use their casing as an external skeleton, or 'exoskeleton', with muscles and internal organs attached to it from the inside.

Rhino beetles

The male minotaur beetle brings a rabbit dropping to its mate for the beetle grubs to eat.

FIG FEAST

Despite their name, dung beetles don't just eat pooh. Scientists in Borneo recently caught a 5-mm long dung beetle cutting itself a chunk of fig, which it buried to feed its offspring. This species of dung beetle was thought to be rare, until scientists learned to look for it near fig trees.

MOBILE HOME

Dung beetles range in size from 5 mm to 3 cm, gathering and burying animal dung to eat. In this way they act like nature's own muck-spreaders, enriching the soil. Some dung beetles are very hard workers, fashioning dung into a ball and rolling it some distance to their burrow.

WONDER WORM

Dung beetle

Another contributor to fertile soil is the common earthworm. On a damp night you can catch worms dragging leaves down into their burrows. By chewing on rotting leaves and the like, worms fertilise the soil. Their burrows also bring water and air below, helping bacteria do their work.

RECYCLING BUGS

Insects and other creepy-crawlies are the biggest and most vital part of the ecosystem (the network of animals and plants which makes life on Earth possible). Insects and worms help to turn dead animal and plant tissue into soil and nutrients, which other organisms can use to grow.

ESCAPE FROM MOLEDITZ

When a mole is full, rather than leaving an earthworm alone, it will bite the worm's head off and leave it in a 'larder'. The worm doesn't die, but can't go anywhere without a head. However, if the mole doesn't come back quickly enough, the worm grows a new head and slinks away.

BUGS QUIZ

How many of the Earth's 1,200,000 species so far identified are insects?

a) 50,000
b) 500,000
c) 1,000,000

In which of these places would you be most likely to find an Australian dung beetle?

a) a Sydney sewer
b) a wallaby's bottom
c) a kangaroo loo

How long can a giant earthworm grow?

a) 67 cm
b) 1 metre
c) 6.7 metres

(answers on page 32)

SMELLY BUGS

Shield bug

If you're a creepy-crawly without an armour shell, you could always try putting off predators with a nasty niff. It works nine times out of ten, but not always: the grey meerkat likes to munch stinky millipedes. No one knows why – even the meerkat looks disgusted while it chews!

BIG NOSE

You might think that the female emperor moth is the smelliest insect in the world. In 1961, scientists discovered that the male moths can smell them from up to 11 km away. But it's just that the males have very sensitive 'noses' – their antennae can detect a single molecule of the female's scent.

BUGS QUIZ

How many chemicals does the African milkweed butterfly make for its scent?

a) 21
b) 124
c) 214

What is the name of the shield bug that feasts on Colorado beetle grubs?

a) *Podisus*
b) *Spudicus*
c) *Pongitus*

What shape are an emperor moth's feelers?

a) nose-shaped
b) feather-shaped
c) balloon-shaped

(answers on page 32)

PONGY PEST

Some shield bugs are real pests for farmers. Because they are so stinky most birds won't eat them, which means they can suck the sap from a cabbage all day without being eaten. But others are helpful; one type likes to munch on the larvae of the Colorado beetle, a major potato pest.

STINKY SHIELD

Some leaf-dwelling bugs look a little like the shields medieval knights used to carry, so they are called shield bugs. But because they are horribly smelly, they are also called stink bugs. Some kinds can grow up to 5 cm long, and one can spit its stinky slime as far as 30 cm!

Beetle larvae

BEETLE BUTTY

Fancy something more pongy than old cheese? Some people prefer a stink bug sandwich!

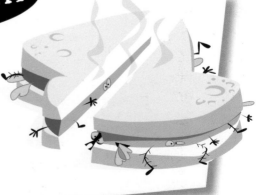

Index

Quiz answers

- **Page 2** c, 58km/h; c, 1.5 km; b, over St Paul's Cathedral.
- **Page 5** a, fishing nets; c, 6; her father made her eat spiders.
- **Page 6** c, if a mule ate a mantis, it would die; a, he plucks the web like a guitar; c, to eat the male.
- **Page 9** b, it eats the frazzled insects; b, 100,000; c, 12.8 metres.
- **Page 11** a, its larvae are transparent; b, caddis fly larva; a, stick insect.
- **Page 12** b, through their skin; b, via drinking water; b, the gills of a fish.
- **Page 15** c, 5,200 sq km; c, 1.5 km; c, 822 million tonnes.
- **Page 16** b, it bites humans, too; c, not really – it just likes

hiding in small spaces!; a, to trap fleas.
- **Page 18** a, 0.048 km/h; c, 20 years; c, 18 kg.
- **Page 20** a, many feet; c, 50 cm a second; b, it glows in the dark.
- **Page 23** c, over 1,000,000; b, 25 million; b, 20 days.
- **Page 24** c, 29.2 cm; b, 86 cm; a, 7 hours.
- **Page 26** c, gets attacked by fungus; b, strip off their old one and grow another; c, nearly 100 °C.
- **Page 29** c, 1,000,000; b, a wallaby's bottom; c, 6.7 metres.
- **Page 30** c, 214; a, Podisus; b, feather-shaped.

Acknowledgements

Copyright © 2006 **ticktock** Entertainment Ltd. First published in Great Britain by ticktock Media Ltd.,
Unit 2, Orchard Business Centre, North Farm Road, Tunbridge Wells, Kent TN2 3XF, Great Britain.

A CIP catalogue record for this book is available from the British Library.
ISBN 1 86007 951 2 Printed in China.
Picture Credits: t = top, b = bottom, c = centre, l = left, r=right, OFC = outside front cover, OBC = outside back cover, IFC = inside front cover
Ann Ronan @ Image Select; 12c. Oxford Scientific Films; 4/5, 5b, 6b, 7b, 8b, 10/11t, 12/13, 14b, 18/19, 23b, 26/27t, 26/27b, 28b, 28/29, 30/31.
Planet Earth Pictures; 1, 2b, 2/3, 8/9, 11b, 14/15, 16/17, 17b, 19t, 20, 20/21, 25b, 25t, 31c. Science Photo Library; 22/23. Telegraph Colour library; OFC (main pic).

Contents

Some words are printed in bold, **like this**. You can find out what they mean by looking in the glossary.

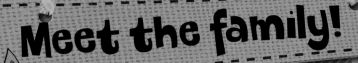

I'm Angus. I'll be introducing you to the different parts of my family. I'm a Shetland pony – a very ancient type of horse. You can find out more about me on page 8.

There are lots of different shapes and sizes of horse.

Horses and people

No one really knows how horses and humans started living together. It is likely that humans caught young horses and **tamed** them. The horses worked for the humans, and in return were fed and looked after. Horses were very useful, so their popularity spread quickly. Soon, people throughout Europe and Asia were keeping horses.

Horse jobs and breeds

Horses can do all kinds of jobs. Big, strong horses can pull or carry heavy loads. Smaller horses are fast and can change direction quickly. They are good for riding. Large, long-legged horses can run faster than any other, and love to race.

Humans used these characteristics to create different types of horse, called **breeds**. For example, they encouraged big, strong **mares** and **stallions** to mate. This produced horses that were useful for carrying heavy loads.

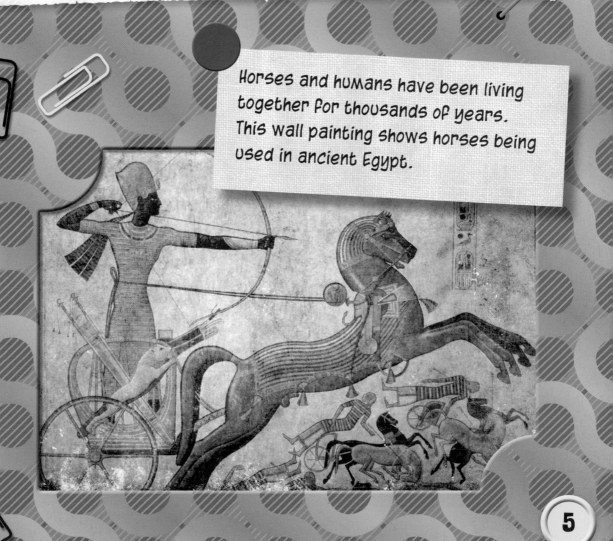

Horses and humans have been living together for thousands of years. This wall painting shows horses being used in ancient Egypt.

Wild at heart

My family includes top athletes, hard workers, and grandstand performers. But we all have lots in common with our wild **ancestors**.

Wild horse herds are normally led by a female. Herds also include other females, foals, a **stallion**, and sometimes a few young males.

Wild horses live in **herds**. As herd animals, all horses need company. Horses that are left alone all the time become hard to manage. Fortunately, they can become friends with humans and animals such as dogs, not just other horses.

Horses are able to fall half asleep standing up. They are resting, but ready to run if danger threatens.

FAMILY SECRET

Horses need to lie down for a proper sleep – but just a few minutes each day is often enough!

Eyesight and hearing

In the wild, horses live mostly in grasslands. They have to keep a sharp lookout for predators creeping up on them. Because of this, horses have good eyesight and hearing.

Food and living conditions

Wild and **feral** horses eat mainly grass. **Domesticated** horses need to eat similar food. Horses can survive in most areas where there is food and water, but they do not like to be very cold or very hot.

Ponies

Most small horses are called ponies. A lot of pony **breeds** developed in the wild. Having to survive in the wild made us clever and tough. We rarely get sick or go **lame**.

Shetland ponies are among the smallest horses. They are no more than 117 centimetres (46 inches) tall.

Shetland pony

Shetland ponies are incredibly strong for their size, and surprisingly fast moving. They are great fun to ride, as long as you're not too big! Shetlands are brave and gentle – though they can be stubborn, too. This breed is at least 2,000 years old.

Pony of the Americas

This pony has a gentle, friendly character and runs very smoothly. It is very popular as a children's pony. The Pony of the Americas first appeared when Appaloosa horses were **crossed** with Shetland ponies. It is often used for trail riding, jumping, and racing.

The Pony of the Americas was developed in the United States, in the 1950s.

Little and large

Sometimes, the family album surprises even me! Comparing the smallest and biggest horses, it's amazing to think that we're all part of the same family.

The Falabella, standing with its doggy friend, is from a breed named after the family who developed it.

Falabella

Lots of people think the Shetland pony is the smallest horse, but they're wrong. It is actually the Falabella. It is no more than 86 centimetres (nearly 3 feet) tall – about the size of a big dog! Falabellas are brave, friendly horses. People keep them as pets, or sometimes use them to pull tiny carriages and carts.

Shire horse

The Shire horse is the world's tallest, strongest horse **breed**. In fact, the biggest horse ever was a Shire called Mammoth. He was 2.2 metres (more than 7 feet) tall, and weighed about 1,500 kilograms (3,300 pounds). That's about the same as 18 fully grown men! Shire horses are gentle giants. They were bred for pulling things, such as a plough or a wagon, for hours on end.

FAMILY SECRET

The heights of horse family members are traditionally measured in "hands". A "hand" is about 10 centimetres (4 inches).

Like all horses, this Shire horse's height is measured from the ground to the **withers**.

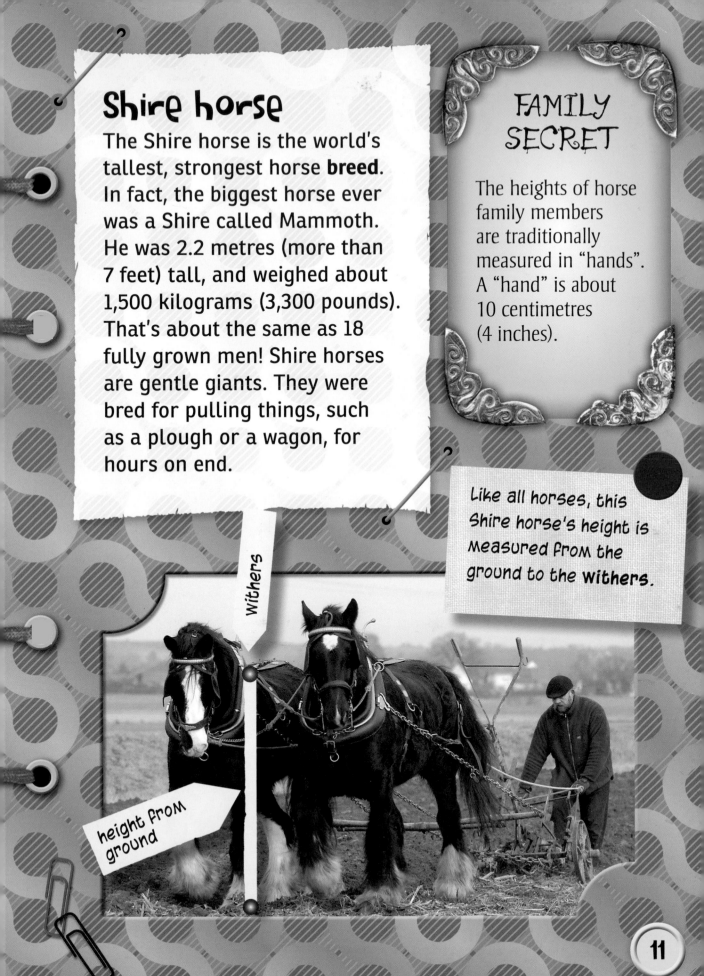

Withers

height from ground

Arabian horses were bred to be both tough and beautiful.

Now it's time to meet the boy (and girl) racers of the family. These are the horse equivalent of Formula One cars.

Arabian

The Arabian horse has a tough, fiery character. It originally came from the desert lands of Arabia. The most famous type is probably the Bedouin, which is named after the tribe that first bred it. Arabians are not as fast as Thoroughbred racehorses, but are able to travel much further.

Thoroughbred

If you want to ride the fastest **breed** of horse in the world, you need to climb on board a Thoroughbred! Some of these large horses are racehorses. Others compete in **dressage** or show jumping. Thoroughbreds need an experienced rider, as they can be hard to control.

Lots of money can be won at horse racing. Because of this, Thoroughbreds are the world's most valuable horses.

Percheron

Imagine being an English soldier at a battle in France, hundreds of years ago. The French knights are charging towards you – scarily fast! Their horses are large, strong, intelligent, and brave. They are Percherons. Later in history, Percherons began to be used for **towing** and carrying loads. It was less heroic, but much safer!

In the past, many horses have had to work hard for their whole lives – sometimes in very dangerous situations.

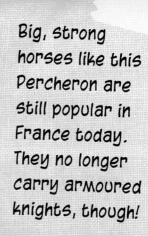

Big, strong horses like this Percheron are still popular in France today. They no longer carry armoured knights, though!

14

Clydesdale

Clydesdale horses were originally bred for the mining industry, but you would struggle to fit one down a mine! Instead, these big, strong horses were used for towing wagons along cart tracks. They can pull heavy loads all day. Today, Clydesdales are mainly seen in show rings and in parades. They look very smart, with their **manes** brushed and the long hair around their **hooves** (called feathering) swishing through the air.

These parading Clydesdales look very smart and proud.

Circus and rodeo horses

Let me introduce you to some of the showbiz members of the family. These two **breeds** love getting dressed up and taking part in a parade — or even better, a circus.

If you close your eyes, you can feel an Appaloosa's spots with your fingertips.

Appaloosa

Appaloosas are small, fast-moving, brave, and fearless. These spotty horses can be very exciting to ride, and are often used as circus or parade horses. The Nez Percé Indians of North America originally developed the Appaloosa breed. It wasn't long before European settlers saw what good horses they were, and began riding them as well.

Australian Stock Horse

Australian Stock Horses are lively, clever horses. They are **descended** from Arab, Spanish, and Thoroughbred horses. The Australian Stock Horse can do all kinds of jobs, including rounding up sheep or cattle, playing **polo**, and taking part in riding contests.

FAMILY SECRET

Australian Stock Horses are sometimes called Walers. It's because the breed originally came from New South Wales in Australia.

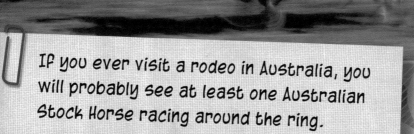

If you ever visit a rodeo in Australia, you will probably see at least one Australian Stock Horse racing around the ring.

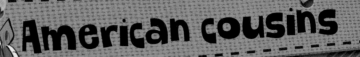

You've already met some of my American relatives, and here are two more. These come from among the most famous branches of the whole family.

The Quarter Horse is the world's fastest horse over short distances.

The Quarter Horse

The Quarter Horse got its name from its amazing speed in races held over a quarter-mile (400-metre) course. The Quarter Horse can also be ridden for long distances. When the western United States began to be used for cattle farming, the Quarter Horse was popular with cowboys. It is now the most common **breed** of horse in the United States. There are more than 2 million Quarter Horses living there.

18

Morgan

This whole breed is **descended** from just one **stallion**, called Figure. Figure could do everything. He ploughed fields, dragged fallen trees, won races, and **towed** carriages and carts. Figure became known as "Morgan's Horse", after the man who owned him. He was such an amazing horse that he ended up being bought by the US Army. They kept him as a **stud horse**. He had many **foals**, who were all very like him.

Morgan horses can be used for riding, towing carriages, or pulling loads.

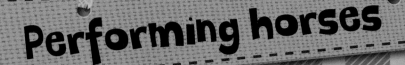

This branch of the family is very different from mine. They're tall and long-legged. They learn amazing tricks, such as fancy backward walks. When I try those, I always trip over!

Saddlebreds walk with a smart, high-stepping style.

Saddlebred

The Saddlebred is one of the cleverest members of the horse family! It holds its head and tail up high, and its long neck and legs give it a very snooty appearance. Despite looking like horse royalty, Saddlebreds are friendly, helpful horses that are comfortable to ride.

Lipizzaner

Lipizzaners are the ballet dancers of the horse family. They can remember amazing steps in the show ring. At their home in Austria, only **stallions** that have performed to the highest standard are allowed to breed. Lipizzaners are also bred in Hungary. There, they are sometimes used for pulling a light carriage.

FAMILY SECRET

Lipizzaners are born dark-coloured, but almost all turn light grey by the time they are seven years old.

This Lipizzaner stallion is performing in a **dressage** competition.

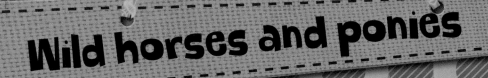

Wild horses and ponies

My wild cousins are some of the cleverest horses in the whole family. They have to be, to survive in the wild without any humans to look after them!

American Indians captured Mustangs to ride. They were also used by cowboys for rounding up cattle.

Mustang

Mustangs were not originally wild horses. Their **ancestors** went to America with the first Spanish settlers, hundreds of years ago. Some escaped, and began to roam free. Eventually they spread through the land. Not long ago, wild Mustangs almost died out. Today, though, they are able to live in specially protected areas.

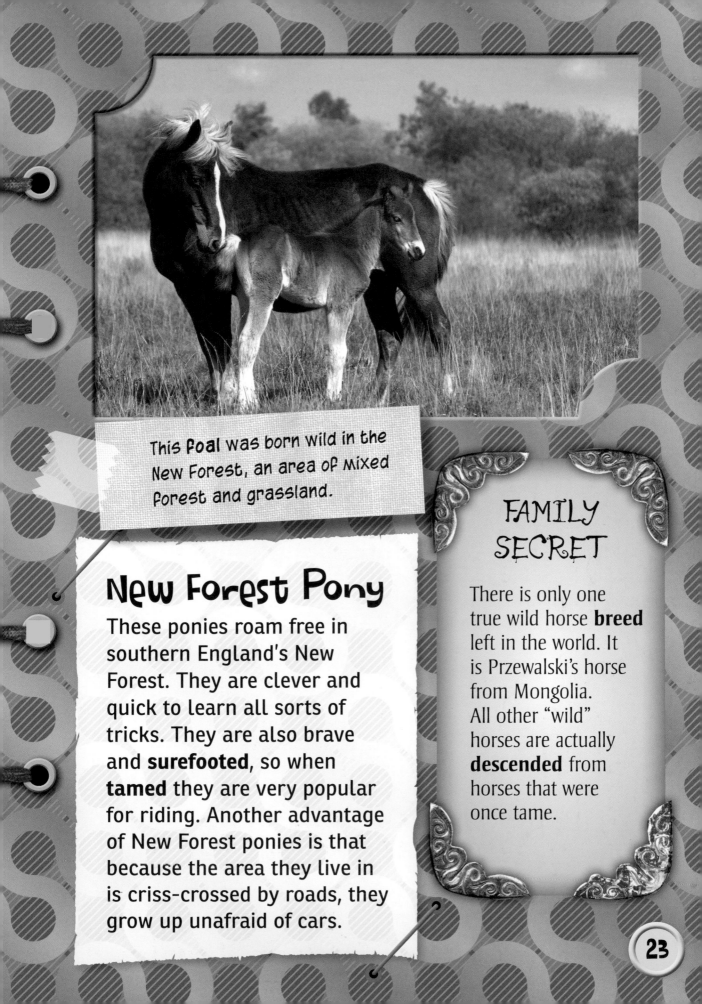

This **foal** was born wild in the New Forest, an area of mixed forest and grassland.

New Forest Pony

These ponies roam free in southern England's New Forest. They are clever and quick to learn all sorts of tricks. They are also brave and **surefooted**, so when **tamed** they are very popular for riding. Another advantage of New Forest ponies is that because the area they live in is criss-crossed by roads, they grow up unafraid of cars.

FAMILY SECRET

There is only one true wild horse **breed** left in the world. It is Przewalski's horse from Mongolia. All other "wild" horses are actually **descended** from horses that were once tame.

Distant relatives

Zebras are wild, stubborn animals that are almost impossible to tame.

Donkeys and zebras are my most distant relatives, and hardly ever send me Birthday cards. Still, they're part of the family, so they get a place in the album!

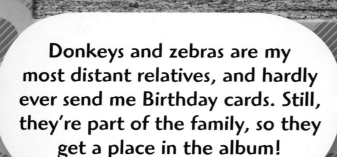

09

Zebra

Once in a while, someone manages to **tame** a zebra – but not very often! The chances of persuading one to carry you or **tow** your cart are practically zero. The three main types of zebra all have stripy hair. Some experts think horses also once had stripy hair.

Donkeys are strong, long-lived animals. They can be ridden, or used for carrying loads or pulling carts.

FAMILY SECRET

The Kiang is a wild donkey from Tibet, in China. The Kiang has an unusual skill – it is a very good swimmer!

Donkey

Unlike zebras, donkeys are happy to live with humans. They can be stubborn, though! Trying to persuade a donkey to do something it doesn't like is almost impossible. Donkeys enjoy company, and become lonely if they are kept alone all the time. They are happiest when kept with other donkeys.

A new horse or pony

Hardly anything is cuter than a knock-kneed foal! Of course, like all babies, foals take a lot of looking after. Many humans prefer to get an older, experienced horse.

Most foals are able to stand and run within a few hours of being born. When they are born, their legs are almost as long as those of a fully-grown horse.

Foals

A young horse less than a year old is called a **foal**. Foals are looked after by their mothers and drink their mother's milk. Later, they start to eat solid food. Foals are still too young to work or be ridden. They begin to get used to humans, though, by having their coats groomed or their **hooves** trimmed.

FAMILY SECRET

Not all horses and ponies belong to a **breed**! Horses are often bred for a special purpose, such as riding across rough, muddy countryside, by combining breeds.

Older horses and ponies

Most people who get a horse either buy or **adopt** an older one. These range from young horses of six months to older, fully grown animals. Some people give a new home to a horse that has been abandoned or treated cruelly.

Horses need a lot of space and plenty of grooming and exercise, so they're not the pet for everyone.

What type of horse are you?

You're not a horse, of course – you're a human. Maybe your personality is similar to some horses', though? This simple quiz will give you some ideas about what kind of horse you might be.

1. During a fireworks display, do you...

a) Get really annoyed about the noise and race over to complain

b) Not notice it, as you have a lot of housework to do

c) Enjoy the show (though it would probably be improved if you were in it)

2. What is your favourite form of exercise?

a) Running, especially if it's in a race of some sort

b) Carrying loads of shopping home is really good exercise!

c) Dancing! No, jumping around! No – both!

3. When was the last time you were not well?

a) Last week, when you pulled a leg muscle

b) Last year: you hardly ever get ill

c) A month ago you caught a nasty cold, standing backstage waiting to go on

4. How good are you at learning and remembering things?

a) Not that good, as you don't usually like being told what to do

b) Quite good, because you're happy to practise a new thing all day, for weeks

c) You LOVE learning new tricks!

5. Do you like fancy dress?

a) Once in a while you like a bit of brightly coloured satin

b) Not really. You can't wear fancy dress to work!

c) Not unless you count velvet, leather, feathers, and bright clothes as fancy dress. You do? Then yes!

Answers

Mostly a: with your love of running fast and your slightly hot temper, you must be a Thoroughbred or an Arab.

Mostly b: your friendly character and willingness to work hard means you would be a good work horse, such as a Clydesdale or Shire Horse.

Mostly c: what a drama queen! There's no doubt that a performer like you would be a circus or parade horse, such as an Appaloosa.

Glossary

adopt take over the care of something or someone

ancestor relative that lived long ago

breed particular type of one kind of animal. For example, an Appaloosa is a particular breed of horse. All the members of a breed are a similar size and shape, and they look alike.

crossed mixed together. In the animal world, when two different breeds mate, their young are known as a "cross-breed" or "crossed".

descended related to an ancestor

domesticated used to living with humans

dressage sport in which a horse is trained to perform difficult steps and movements

feral once domesticated, but now living in the wild

foal young horse, less than one year old

herd group of animals

hoof (more than one: **hooves**) hard material at the end of a horse's leg, which touches the ground when it walks or runs

lame unable to walk or run properly

mane long hair on the neck of a horse

mare female horse of at least four years old

polo team sport played on horseback. Riders try to score goals by hitting a small ball with a mallet.

stallion male horse of at least four years old, which is able to breed

stud horse horse that is kept for breeding

surefooted steady and well balanced, and so unlikely to stumble or slip

tame make an animal less frightened of humans, and easier to control

tow pull along with a rope or chain

withers place where a horse's neck meets its back

Find out more

Books

Horse and Pony Handbook, Camilla La Bedoyere (Miles Kelly, 2009)

Kingfisher Illustrated Horse and Pony Encyclopedia, Sandy Ransford (Kingfisher, 2010)

The Usborne Complete Book of Riding and Pony Care, Gill Harvey and Rosie Dickins (Usborne, 2009)

Websites

www.bhs.org.uk
The British Horse Society has everything you need to know about riding, caring for a horse, or working with horses.

www.horsetrust.org.uk
The Horse Trust is a charity based in the Chiltern Hills, where they run a sanctuary for retired or rescued horses, donkeys, and ponies.

www.rspca.org.uk/allaboutanimals/horses
The RSPCA website is full of interesting facts about horses and how to care for them.

www.ypte.org.uk/animal/zebra-grevy-s-/199
Grevy's zebras are in danger of dying out. Learn more about these amazing horse relatives on this website.

Index

CONTENTS

Words that appear **in bold** are explained in the glossary.

Copyright © **ticktock Entertainment Ltd** 2008
First published in Great Britain in 2008 by **ticktock Media Ltd**,
Unit 2, Orchard Business Centre, North Farm Road,
Tunbridge Wells, Kent, TN2 3XF
ISBN 978 1 84696 778 8 pbk
Printed in China

We would like to thank Penny Worms, and the National Literacy Trust

Picture credits: t=top, b=bottom, c=centre, l-left, r=right
Alamy: 6-7, 11c, 14-15, 17c, 24b, 31. Corbis: 4-5, 8, 9, 10-11, 12-13, 16, 17b, 20-21, 25, 26t, 27, 28, 29, 32.
Oxford Scientific Photo Library: 18-19. Superstock: 22-23.

Every effort has been made to trace the copyright holders, and we apologise in advance for any unintentional omissions. We would be
pleased to insert the appropriate acknowledgements in any subsequent edition of this publication.

THE GRASSLANDS OF AFRICA

Huge numbers of animals live on the grasslands of Africa.

Their lives are not easy. Sometimes there is heavy rain. At other times, it is as dry as a desert.

Antelopes and zebras eat the tough grass. Giraffes feed on the thorny trees.

Many **predators** live in this **habitat**, such as cheetahs, leopards, and the largest grassland predator – the lion.

THE WORLD OF THE AFRICAN LION

African lions live on grasslands in the red areas on the map.

AFRICA

AFRICA

Atlantic Ocean

THE PRIDE

A family of lions is called a pride.

The pride may have many females, called lionesses, but only between one and four males.

When young male lions are two to four years old they will leave their pride. Sometimes they will stay together in male groups.

When they are old enough, male lions look for a pride of their own.

MALE LIONS

Male lions are bigger than females, and their **manes** *make them look even bigger.*

Adult male lions are in charge of the pride. They guard the pride's **territory** and keep the group safe.

Males leave their scent on trees and rocks, and roar loudly to warn other lions to stay away.

A male lion will lead his pride until a younger and fitter male fights him and takes over.

All lions have black hairs at the end of their tails.

LION CUBS

Lionesses will have two to four cubs at one time. They give birth in a den, hidden away in rocks or long grass.

Cubs feed on their mother's milk until they are six months old. When they are about six weeks old they will start to eat some meat caught by their mother.

The females in a pride share the job of looking after the cubs.

MUMS AND BABIES FACT

Lionesses carry their cubs in their mouths.

11

HUNTING FOR FOOD

Lions will hunt at any time, but they prefer to hunt at night.

The lionesses do most of the hunting. Male lions are big and heavy and not as fast as the females.

Lions get some of their food by **scavenging**. They look for animals that have died, or have been killed by another predator.

NIGHT VISION

Lions can see in the dark six times better than a human!

13

MAKING WAY FOR PEOPLE

Life is becoming tougher for the lions of Africa. They are having to make way for people.

Some of these people are miners looking for **minerals** and metals in the ground.

When the miners find valuable minerals, large areas
of grassland can be destroyed or polluted.

Local lions may be seen as a danger
to workers and are shot.

LIONS AND FARMERS

*In the African countries where lions live, human **populations** are growing.*

Towns are spreading and more and more of the grasslands are turning to farmland.

Without the grasslands, **prey animals**, such as zebra and antelopes, will disappear. Hungry lions will attack farm animals if they have no prey animals to hunt.

Many lions are shot by farmers who do not want lions killing their cattle.

TROPHY HUNTING

Hunting lions as sport is allowed in some places in Africa. Hunters kill the animals, especially males, so they have a trophy.

THE ASIATIC LION

If the African lions are not helped they could be in as much danger as their cousins in Asia.

Around 200 years ago, the Asiatic lion was found from India all the way to Europe.

Now, because of hunting and habitat destruction, there are fewer than 300 Asiatic lions left in the world.

The only place they live wild is in the Gir National Park in India.

ASIA

AFRICA

Gir National Park

Asiatic lions are smaller than African lions. The males have smaller manes.

A SAFE HOME FOR LIONS

The best way to make sure that lions have a future is to find them a safe place to live.

In Africa, some countries have set up wildlife reserves. It is against the law to hunt animals in the reserves.

Wardens protect the animals and make sure that there is enough grassland to feed prey animals, such as antelopes and zebras.

Lions can be brought into the reserves from places where they are not safe.

21

DO LIONS HAVE A FUTURE?

There are between 17,000 and 23,000 lions living wild in Africa. This is about half the number there were fifty years ago. Their future depends on people.

Allowing **tourists** into the wildlife reserves to see the lions brings in money. It must be done carefully, but lions soon get used to visitors.

Tourism also creates jobs for people who live in or near the reserves. This makes protecting the lions and other wild animals important to local people.

Farmers who live in the area also understand that they must share the reserve with the lions.

GLOSSARY

habitat A place in the wild that suits a particular animal or plant.

manes The long hair around the necks of male lions.

minerals Valuable substances, such as gold or platinum, found in the earth.

populations The people who live in places or countries.

predators Animals that kill and eat other animals.

prey animals Animals that are hunted by predators for food.

scavenging Looking for meat that other predators have left, or animals that are already dead.

territory The area in which an animal or family of animals lives.

tourists People who are on holiday.

wardens People whose job it is to look after protected reserves and the animals that live there.

INDEX

Dolphin Boy

Julie Bertagna

Illustrated by **Chris Chapman**

mammoth

First published in Great Britain in 1999
by Mammoth, an imprint of Egmont Children's Books Limited
239 Kensington High Street, London, W8 6SA

ISBN 0 7497 3730 1

10 9 8 7 6 5 4 3

A CIP catalogue record for this book is
available from the British Library

Printed in Great Britain by Cox & Wyman Ltd,
Reading, Berkshire

Contents

1 The boy who didn't speak

Mrs Ottley looked helplessly at Amy.

'I'm sorry to drag you out of class yet again, Amy. But Dibs is being a police car and he won't stop.' The teacher sighed deeply. 'I don't know what's upset him but he's disturbing all the other children.'

Amy sighed too. Mrs Ottley hadn't needed to tell her Dibs was being a police car. The moment she heard the noise echoing down the school corridor she knew it was her little brother. Whenever Dibs was upset he pretended to be a police car with its siren on full blast. It was uncannily like the real thing.

Dibs was crouched underneath a table in the corner of the classroom, whooping and wailing at the top of his voice.

'Dibs!' Amy hissed and knelt down beside him. 'Stop that right now. If you stop, I'll

ask Mum to take us to the seaside on Saturday. I'll tell her you've been good this week.'

The police siren began to fade. Dibs quietened until he made just a gentle rumbling noise with an occasional horn beep. It was the exact sound of traffic in the street outside.

'That's better,' said Amy. 'Now remember, you'd better be good or I'll tell Mum and Dad all about this and there'll be *no* seaside trips for ages and ages.'

Dibs flashed a fleeting glance at his sister. Then he fixed his eyes on his shoes.

Amy stood up and forced a smile at Mrs Ottley. 'He's fine now.'

'Thank you so much, Amy,' said the

teacher. 'You seem to be able to work wonders with Dibs. I wish I knew your secret.'

Amy forced another smile, a sweet smile that made her look like an angelic big sister. But Amy knew she wasn't angelic. Her secret was to bribe and threaten Dibs whenever he acted up.

Mrs Ottley wouldn't approve and neither would Mum and Dad. But Amy didn't care. Her secret method worked. It put a stop to Dibs's embarrassing behaviour. And that was all that mattered.

Amy was fed up with Dibs. She was fed up being fetched out of class to make her little brother behave. He was too much trouble. Dibs could imitate the exact noise of a police car, a fire engine, a cat, a dog or even a washing machine. He could copy almost any noise in the world. But he never spoke a single word. Nobody else had a brother who made silly noises instead of talking.

All Amy wanted was an ordinary brother, one who talked and behaved like everyone else.

When she got home from school, Amy stormed upstairs. She slammed her bedroom door and stamped across the room. Then she sat down on her bed and burst into tears.

Why couldn't Dibs be like everyone else? Why didn't he talk? Why did he behave so oddly, so unlike other children? Mum and Dad couldn't tell her because they didn't know why. Dibs couldn't tell her because he couldn't talk. No one could tell Amy why, at six years old, Dib's hadn't spoken a single word in his whole life.

Secretly, Amy was sure Dibs could talk if he really wanted to. She was sure he was clever in an unusual kind of way. But not talking got him lots of special attention, so he just didn't bother.

For as long as Amy could remember there had been special doctors, special toys, even special trips and holidays. All for Dibs. All because he didn't talk. If Mum and Dad heard about something that might help Dibs speak then he got it, straight away.

For weeks and
weeks, Amy had
wanted a pair
of silver roller
blades with a
matching crash

helmet and knee pads. She would have
asked Mum and Dad but they had just
bought an expensive new computer with all
sorts of games and programs. They said it
was for the whole family but Amy knew it
was really for Dibs.

If she asked for roller blades now, Amy
told herself, Mum and Dad would say she
would have to wait until her birthday
because they had spent so much on the
computer. She'd bet they would. So she

wouldn't even bother asking.

Sometimes, when Amy was especially angry with Dibs, she would pretend she didn't have a brother at all. She imagined going to school without the worry of what Dibs might do. She imagined having all of Mum, and Dad's attention and getting all the toys and treats she wanted. Like a pair of silver roller blades . . .

A soft miaowing came from outside Amy's bedroom door. That would be Dibs. Miaowing like a lost kitten was his way of saying sorry.

'I don't care if you're sorry!' yelled Amy. 'Go away and leave me alone. I'm fed up with you, Dibs.'

The miaowing grew louder and more

pitiful until Amy could stand it no longer. She tried wrapping her pillow round her ears but still she could hear it. At long last, she gave in and opened the door.

Dibs was crouched at her feet like a cat. As usual, he wouldn't look at her. Dibs never really looked anyone in the eyes. Mostly, he stared at his feet.

'Listen, Dibs,' Amy told him. 'I've decided I'm not going to bother with you any more unless you start acting like a proper boy.'

Now Dibs started to mewl like a kitten or a tiny baby. He crawled through Amy's legs and pushed his way into her bedroom. Amy could remember when Dibs was just a baby. She had been so pleased and proud to have a little brother. Amy had been too little to say his real name, Douglas. It had come out as Dibs. Somehow the name had stuck and now everyone called him Dibs.

Dibs lay down beside Amy's clutter of felt-pens and paper on the floor. Swiftly, he sorted the pens into a perfect rainbow spectrum. Then he began to draw.

Amy sprawled beside him. Watching Dibs

draw always soothed her. He worked quickly and ever so carefully. In moments the drawing was finished. Dibs placed it on Amy's knee.

It was a beautiful drawing of a fish. Dibs only ever drew things to do with the sea. He was mad about the seaside. It was his favourite place. Dibs stroked the outline of the fish he had drawn, his finger following its long, trailing fins and rainbow-patterned body.

Nobody understood how a boy of six who couldn't speak could draw such amazing pictures. It just proved that he was clever, thought Amy. But it was a cleverness that didn't include being able to talk.

'It's lovely, Dibs,' she said.

Dibs flickered a glance at his sister then looked back at his feet. He purred like a contented kitten, and Amy smiled.

Now that her anger had died, she wished she could hug her little brother. He could be really sweet when he tried. But you couldn't hug Dibs. He hated being touched.

'I'll pin it on the wall, shall I?' Amy asked, knowing he'd like that.

As Amy pinned the beautiful rainbow fish above her bed, Dibs showed just how delighted he was by erupting into a perfect imitation of a jumbo jet on take-off.

Amy couldn't help laughing. Dibs *was* odd. He was a thorough pest a lot of the time. But nobody in the world had a brother quite like him.

2 Dibs finds a dolphin

Dibs had been sitting under the dining table all morning, drawing pictures. He worked at top speed and as soon as he finished one, he would stick it up on the wall then sit down and start right away on another. The living-room walls were now covered in beautiful sketches of seashells and crabs and pebbles and fish. All the time he worked, Dibs made the gentle, shushing noise of a calm sea.

'No more, Dibs,' groaned Dad, as Dibs ran out of wall space and began to stick a drawing to the window. 'Not the windows, too. That's enough.'

Mum looked pleadingly at Amy. 'What do you think, Amy? I know we hadn't planned it, but we could take Dibs for a quick visit to the seaside and still go into town.'

It was just typical, thought Amy. Saturday was pocket-money day and she liked to go to the shops and potter around for ages before choosing what to spend hers on. She hadn't forgotten about her deal with Dibs. She knew she had promised to ask for a trip to the seaside today. But Amy didn't want to go to the seaside. Anyhow, Dibs couldn't talk so he couldn't tell on her, could he? 'It's too *cold* for the seaside today,' said Amy.

Mum glanced out of the window at the wintry, grey sky. 'Amy's right, Dibs. Perhaps we'll go next week.'

Dibs stopped drawing and stared at his feet. He crawled out from under the table and began to rip all his drawings from the walls. Once he had made a great pile of them he tore them into shreds. Then he began to throw handful after handful of his torn pictures at Amy. His police siren was on full blast.

'Stop it, Dibs!' yelled Dad.

Mum gave Amy another pleading glance.

'All right, all right,' said Amy. 'Let's go to his stupid seaside. I kind of said I would go,' she muttered, feeling guilty now as she

looked at the snowstorm of shredded paper all over the floor. Dibs must have been really upset to destroy all his beautiful drawings.

The sea was only a short drive from the

house, which was just as well. Dibs was so excited he spent the whole journey making every animal and engine sound that he knew, at the top of his voice. He finally burst into ear-splitting gull shrieks as the sea came into full view.

'Thank goodness for that!' cried Dad, as Dibs ran out of the car and down on to the sand. 'I doubt if my ears could have taken any more of Dibs and his noise factory.'

He took Amy's hand. 'I'm so glad at least one of you is a nice, quiet creature.' Dad smiled down at her. 'Dibs is very lucky to have such a kind big sister. He's not the easiest brother in the world to put up with, is he?'

'No, he isn't,' Amy laughed. 'Nobody else

had a noise factory for a brother.' She felt warm inside at Dad's words. Then she felt ashamed. She had been horrible to Dibs lately. It wasn't his fault that he was different. It was just the way he was. Amy squeezed Dad's hand and ran off to see what Dibs was up to.

It took a little while to find him. Amy had to search all the rock clusters on the shore before she finally found Dibs crouched over something at the edge of the sea. What had he found?

At first, when Amy saw the curving, grey object with what looked like a rudder sticking out of it, she thought Dibs had found a small, upturned boat. Then she saw that the rudder was a fin.

As Amy drew near, she saw Dibs put his
hands upon the still, grey creature. Tears
streamed down his face and he whimpered
softly.

Dibs never cried. He might scream and
rage but he never cried. And he hated
touching. Yet he was touching this strange
creature, stroking it as if he was trying to

comfort it.

Amy moved closer so that she could see the creature more clearly. It was smooth and rubbery-looking with front flippers and a tail fin. When she saw the creature's kind, gentle face she finally knew what it was.

Amy raced across the sand to find her parents. 'Come quickly!' she shouted. 'Dibs has found a dolphin!'

3 Rescue!

'Is it alive?' Amy whispered.

The dolphin's eyes were shut tight and it lay quite still.

'I don't know,' said Dad. He put his hand over a small opening on the top of the dolphin's head. 'There's air coming out of its blowhole. That means it's breathing.'

'We'd better get help,' said Mum.

'Help from where?' asked Amy. 'Who can help?'

Mum and Dad looked at each other blankly. Dibs was beginning his police siren wail.

'Don't worry, Dibs,' said Mum. 'We'll get help.'

'The police!' exclaimed Amy. 'Phone 999.'

'A stranded dolphin *is* an emergency,' Dad agreed. 'I'll find a phone box.'

Amy knelt beside Dibs as Dad ran to the car. She put out her hand and touched the dolphin. It felt like rubber: cold, dry, rubber. But a dolphin shouldn't be dry.

'It needs water!' Amy cried. 'Help me.'

Mum pulled Dibs away from the dolphin as Amy ran into the sea, cupped her hands and began splashing water. Mum took off her cardigan, soaked it in sea water and draped it over the dolphin's body. At first, Dibs stood at the side siren-wailing, then he

23

stepped into the very edge of the waves and began kicking up splashes.

'Good boy, Dibs!' yelled Amy.

Dad was running back across the beach.

'The police are bringing someone who knows all about dolphins,' he gasped. 'A marine biologist. They'll be here as soon as they can.'

★　★　★

'Well done,' said Kaleb, the marine biologist, once he arrived. He had brought buckets to throw sea water over the dolphin. 'Keeping the skin wet is the best thing you could have done.'

It took a vanload of policemen to drag the dolphin on to a thick sheet of canvas. Then they hauled the canvas into a small tank full of water that sat in the back of the police van.

'The Ocean World centre where I work isn't too far from here,' said Kaleb. 'We can put her in the aquarium there and I can look after her.'

'Can't you put her back to sea?' asked Amy.

Kaleb shook his head. 'This is a very sick little dolphin. See those marks on her skin and the irritation around her eyes? I'd guess she's been swimming in polluted waters around the coast. She's sick on sewage. And she's lost. A little one like this should still be with her mother. We need to get her well first and then see what's best for her.'

All this time Dibs had been standing wringing his hands, staring at his feet. Every so often he would give a small siren wail. Amy saw Kaleb and some of the policemen give Dibs puzzled glances. But she was used to people giving Dibs funny looks.

'Dibs doesn't speak in words,' she said. 'Only sounds.'

'Really?' said Kaleb. 'You can do a lot with sounds, as every dolphin knows.'

Most people did not know what to say when Amy tried to explain about Dibs. They would look away, embarrassed. But Kaleb was looking at Dibs with interest. Now he took a step towards Dibs, but Dibs shied away, wailing louder.

'I just wanted to thank you, Dibs,' said Kaleb. 'This little dolphin is very lucky you found her. If we hadn't got to her when we did she would have died. You saved her life.'

Dibs stopped wailing and flashed one of his fleeting glances at Kaleb. Then he slowly raised his hand and with his fingers closed he made a gentle wavering, wiggly motion with his hand.

'Dolphin?' said Kaleb. 'Is that your sign
for dolphin?'

'He's never done that before,' said Mum,
watching in amazement. 'We've tried to

28

teach Dibs sign language but he won't do it.'

'Well, it looks like he's doing it now,' smiled Kaleb. 'I think Dibs has made up his own sign for dolphin.'

Back at home Dibs made dolphin signs for the rest of the day. He kept up his police siren wail too and only stopped when he fell asleep. But he started again as soon as he woke up on Sunday morning.

'All right, Dibs,' groaned Dad at last. 'You win. I'll phone Ocean World and ask Kaleb if you can see the dolphin.'

Dibs stopped his wailing. But he didn't stop signing.

Dolphin, he kept on, endlessly. Dolphin, dolphin, dolphin . . .

4 Dibs speaks dolphin

The little dolphin swam slowly, backwards and forwards, in the dimly lit blue water of the aquarium. Amy watched her from behind the thick glass window.

'She looks happy enough,' said Dad.

Kaleb shook his head. 'Don't be fooled by that sweet face. She's not really smiling. This little dolphin is missing her mother very badly. She's only a few months old. And whatever pollution she swam into has made her quite sore and sick. I've called her Baby Blue.'

'Her eyes are sad,' agreed Amy. 'And the slow way she swims seems so sad and lonely.'

'Can't you put her back in the sea?' asked Mum. 'Won't she be happier there?'

Again, Kaleb shook his head. 'Somehow she got lost. She would have been just beginning to learn all her dolphin skills so I doubt if she would survive for long on her own out in the ocean. Dolphin calves tend to stay with their mothers for about five years, until they have learned the skills they need to survive all the dangers of the oceans. Putting Baby Blue back into the sea right now would be like leaving a toddler alone in a busy street.'

All this time Dibs had been staring at his

feet. He hadn't looked once at Baby Blue, even though he'd made such a pest of himself about coming. But Amy was sure Dibs was listening keenly to every word that Kaleb said.

'There is one thing I could try,' Kaleb was saying. 'If I could make a recording of Baby Blue's voice, I could send it out into the ocean on the dolphin sound wave. Sound travels huge distances in water and there's just a chance her mother, or another dolphin, might pick it up. A dolphin's sense of sound is far more powerful than ours.'

'How would her mother know it was Baby Blue?' Mum asked.

'The same way any mother knows her baby,' smiled Kaleb. 'Every dolphin has its own unique voice. But I can't do any of that until Baby Blue starts to talk. Just now, she's too sad to talk.'

Everyone stared at Baby Blue. Everyone except Dibs.

'She can't talk?' murmured Amy, glancing from the dolphin swimming in its silent, lonely pool to her little brother.

'Oh, I'm sure she *can* talk,' said Kaleb. 'She just won't. But I hope she will soon. Now, how about a coffee for the big people and some juice for the littler ones?'

'Sounds good,' said Dad. 'Coming, Dibs?'

Dibs had moved over to the aquarium window. Now he was pressed against the thick glass. His face was full of concentration.

'Come on, Dibs,' urged Mum.

Dibs didn't move. He stayed with his cheek pressed hard to the aquarium window, as if he was listening. Yet the

dolphin made no sound.

'I don't mind if Amy and Dibs want to stay with Baby Blue while we have a coffee,' said Kaleb. 'My office is right next door.'

Amy nodded. 'We'll be fine.'

She knew Dibs wanted to be with Baby Blue. He had heard every word Kaleb had said about the lost dolphin. What was he thinking? Amy wondered. For Dibs had found a little dolphin that was just like himself – one that didn't talk.

At home that evening, Dibs began to draw yet another dolphin picture. But now he drew slowly, stopping every so often as if he wasn't sure what he was doing.

When the picture was finished, Amy looked at it. Dibs had drawn Baby Blue exactly, but all round her body he had sketched a delicate pattern of wavy lines.

'What's that?' wondered Amy.

With a fingertip, Dibs traced the rippling wave patterns. Amy was sure Dibs had a good reason for drawing the strange

patterns, but he couldn't tell her what it was.

Kaleb had said they were welcome to visit Baby Blue any time, so Mum took Amy and Dibs most days after school. On the days they didn't go, Dibs would sit wailing, signing dolphin, dolphin, dolphin. It was all he seemed to think about. And he would draw dolphins from the moment he got up till he went to bed.

Little by little the dolphin pictures were changing. After each visit, Dibs would alter the way he drew the wave patterns. He no longer drew them all round the dolphin's body. Now they had become a wide triangle of wavy lines that radiated from the dolphin's head like a beam of light.

Amy took one of Dibs's drawings to show to Kaleb.

'It looks like he's drawn the way a dolphin's sonar works,' Kaleb said slowly. 'A dolphin sends out a high-pitched beam of sound through the bulge in its head that sits just in front of its blowhole. When the sound hits objects and bounces back, the dolphin can tell what lies in its way. Imagine a torch beam in the dark. That's what a dolphin's sonar is:

a beam of sound that lets it "hear" its way through the seas. It's called echo-location.'

'But how could Dibs know that?' wondered Amy.

'He probably saw it in a book,' suggested Kaleb.

Amy shook her head. 'Dibs hates books. No, he found out from Baby Blue. He's been listening to her. That's how he knows.'

Kaleb looked over to where Dibs had his ear pressed against the aquarium window. 'I wonder,' he murmured. 'Is it possible that Dibs is picking up sounds from Baby Blue that we can't hear? It still doesn't explain how he knew the sonar works like a beam coming from her head.'

'I don't know how he knows,' said Amy,

'but in his first pictures he drew wave patterns all round Baby Blue. Then he drew them all round her head. It's only now he's drawn them like a torch beam.'

'That's incredible,' said Kaleb. He went over to Dibs. 'This is a very good picture, Dibs. You have drawn the way Baby Blue uses sound. But can you tell me how you knew? Can you show me how you knew?'

At first Dibs didn't move. Then he turned from the aquarium and took his drawing from Kaleb. He took out the pencil he always kept in his pocket and sketched a small figure in the corner of the page. Then he drew wave patterns all round and inside the body of the little person he had drawn.

'You felt it?' Kaleb asked. 'You felt the

sound waves all over and inside your body?'

Dibs touched the little person he had drawn, tracing the wave patterns. Then he went back to the aquarium window. Kaleb stood close behind him for a while then came back over to Amy.

'This is absolutely amazing,' said Kaleb.

'Amy, when we first met that day at the beach, you told me Dibs didn't speak in words, only in sounds, didn't you?'

Amy nodded. 'You name it, he does it. Aeroplanes, police sirens, lawnmowers, all sorts of animals. It drives us all mad.'

Kaleb nodded. 'Well, now he speaks dolphin. Very, very quiet dolphin. So quiet that none of us heard. But I heard him just now, talking in the gentlest clicks and whirrs and buzzes, exactly like a dolphin. I think Baby Blue and Dibs have been speaking to each other.'

'I heard him making odd little noises like that when he was drawing,' Amy remembered. 'But he makes all sorts of odd noises all the time. I didn't know they were dolphin noises.'

Kaleb smiled at Amy. 'I'd guess that Dibs is a very intelligent boy,' he said. 'The way he mimics sounds and seems to feel sound inside his body as well as hear it – strangely, that's more like a dolphin than a boy. But I believe dolphins are among the most intelligent and sensitive creatures on this earth.'

Amy nodded. She had always known Dibs was clever in a special kind of way. How else could he make such amazing pictures and sounds? But everyone else, including Mum and Dad, had overlooked his special cleverness and treated him as a baby, just because he didn't talk.

Maybe now, thought Amy, they would know.

Kaleb explained to Mum and Dad that Dibs and Baby Blue seemed to be communicating.

'Would you let Dibs help Baby Blue?' he asked them.

'How could Dibs help?' asked Dad.

'Remember I said I wanted to make a voice recording and send it out through the ocean? That way we might get Baby Blue

back to her mother or at least team her up with a passing dolphin. Well, if Dibs can get Baby Blue to make dolphin sounds, loud and clear, then I could try,' Kaleb explained.

Mum looked thoughtful. 'Dibs might like that. What would you want him to do?'

'Would you let Dibs swim with Baby Blue?' asked Kaleb. Mum and Dad exchanged glances.

'I don't know,' said Mum doubtfully. 'He might get hurt. He's only a little boy. I don't want him in any danger.'

'I wouldn't suggest it if I thought Dibs would be in any danger,' Kaleb told her. 'Normally, I would never let anyone swim with a wild dolphin because you never can be sure how either of them will react. But Dibs and Baby Blue have made friends with each other and that's why I'm sure it's safe. In fact, I think they'd both love it.'

'Why not ask Dibs?' said Dad. He put his arm round Mum, who still looked worried. 'Let's see what Dibs thinks.'

Kaleb nodded, smiling. 'Dibs!' he called. 'How would you like to go for a swim with Baby Blue?'

Dibs, who was pressed against the aquarium window as usual, jumped. Slowly, he turned round. Slowly, he lifted his hand and made his wiggly dolphin sign. There was an unusual look on his face.

'Look!' cried Amy. 'Look at Dibs! He's smiling.'

It was a shy, awkward kind of smile because Dibs never smiled.

Amy and Dad hugged each other, laughing. Mum rushed over to Dibs with tears in her eyes, then stopped. There was no point in hugging Dibs. It would only make him cross.

'I'll take that smile as a yes.' Kaleb was laughing too. 'Come on then, Dibs. Let's see if we can hunt down some swimming trunks for you.'

5 A very special swim

Once swimming trunks were found for Dibs, Kaleb took everyone up a flight of stairs and through a door which led to a small pool. Amy peered down into the blue water and saw that one side of the pool was made of glass.

'Is that the aquarium window?' she asked Kaleb.

'That's right,' he nodded. 'Usually we watch Baby Blue from a side window that lets us see under the water. Now we are at the top of the pool. And it's much harder to

see from here, isn't it? Where has that dolphin gone?'

Amy saw a dark shape in the water at the far side of the pool. The little dolphin was frightened, no doubt by their sudden appearance above the surface of her pool.

'Dibs, why don't you speak to Baby

Blue?' said Kaleb. 'I think if you were to talk to her like a dolphin she might come over. She's a bit scared and nervous.'

Dibs stared at his bare feet. But when Kaleb sat down at the side of the pool and dabbled his feet in the water, Dibs did too. He was wailing quietly though, like a distant police siren.

'I think Dibs is scared and nervous too,' said Amy.

Kaleb nodded. 'Well, it's not every day you get to swim with a dolphin, is it, Dibs?'

Dibs was a good swimmer. He loved being in the water. It was even hard to get him out of the bath. Dibs was almost more like a dolphin than an ordinary boy, thought Amy. A kind of dolphin boy. Even though, just now, he was pretending to be a police car revving its siren for an emergency dash.

'Would it help if we left you and Baby Blue alone to talk?' Kaleb suggested.

Dibs's police siren faded.

'All right,' laughed Kaleb. 'We'll stand back.'

'He'll be all right, won't he?' asked Mum. 'That dolphin won't bite him, will it? It has a lot of teeth.'

'Don't worry,' Kaleb assured her. 'I'm right here, just in case.'

Everyone kept quiet and still as they watched Dibs sit paddling his feet at the edge of the pool. After a few minutes he began to make the gentlest clicks. Baby

Blue still kept to the far side of the pool. Then Dibs quietened and leaned towards the water.

'Hear that?' breathed Kaleb, as a small clicking sound came from the pool. 'That was Baby Blue. They're starting to talk.'

Now a long run of clicks erupted from Dibs, followed by the same from Baby Blue. Her smooth, grey body moved through the water and she began to swim all around the pool. Then both Dibs and the dolphin began to chatter in loud bursts of whirrs and buzzes, each taking their turn. Soon the pool room was echoing with dolphin chatter. It was impossible to tell which was the dolphin and which was Dibs.

'What a racket!' Dad laughed. Mum had

her hands over her ears.

'Wonderful,' grinned Kaleb. 'That little dolphin has certainly found her voice.'

All of a sudden Baby Blue burst from the water with a loud *squeak*! She arched high into the air and nosed back into the pool with a great splash that drenched Dibs and scattered water over everyone else.

Dibs sat perfectly still and quiet now, as if frozen in shock.

'Oh dear,' Mum said. 'That gave him an awful fright.' She started to hurry over.

But before Mum reached Dibs the dolphin poked her head out of the water and nudged his bare feet with her long bottlenose. Baby Blue wriggled, threw her head back and opened her smiley mouth.

Then she let out what could only be called a dolphin laugh. It was a wild, joyful sound.

Dibs's body relaxed. He threw back his head just as Baby Blue had done and let out the same wild and happy laughter.

Amy could hardly believe it. For the first time ever she heard her little brother laugh. And he sounded just like a dolphin.

In the days that followed, Dibs learned to swim with Baby Blue by holding on to her dorsal fin. The two of them would course round and round the pool, chattering and laughing together.

'I think he's more dolphin than boy,' Amy told Kaleb one day, as they watched from

the poolside. 'It's partly the way Dibs talks in sounds. But he loves anything to do with the sea. Maybe Dibs should have been a dolphin. Maybe that's what's wrong with him.'

'It *is* curious,' Kaleb agreed. 'But you know, although Baby Blue is very different from us on the outside, you'd be surprised how alike she is on the inside.'

Kaleb explained that a dolphin is a warm-blooded mammal and has a heart, lungs, stomach and many other organs that are very similar to those of a human. Baby Blue had the same five senses, and even a similar size brain.

'It's just that living in water means a dolphin has a highly developed sense of sound. They use echo-location where we use our eyes. And they are very affectionate creatures – though they have a fighting side. But dolphins love to play and touch and nuzzle. They're wonderful mimics too – they've even been heard to copy a human voice.'

'Dibs has a fighting side all right, but he hates to play and he hates anyone touching him. And he's never been heard to talk in a human voice,' said Amy. So Dibs was different from a dolphin in some ways.

'Well, he doesn't seem to mind playing with Baby Blue,' remarked Kaleb, as the dolphin nuzzled into Dibs's neck with her nose and he let out a loud squeak.

'No,' said Amy. And suddenly she was

full of hurt and anger. Dibs would never play games with her. Not ever. He would never even let her touch him. If Amy ever tried to play rough-and-tumble or be the least bit affectionate, Dibs would erupt in a huge tantrum. So she had learned to let him be.

Yet it was different with Baby Blue. Dibs preferred a dolphin to his own sister. And, as usual, it was Dibs who was getting all the fuss and attention. Nobody had once asked Amy if she would like to swim with Baby Blue. Nobody had given her a thought.

It was only Dibs that anyone ever thought of.

That evening as Amy lay in her bed, still hurt and angry, Dibs came into her room.

'Go away, I'm reading,' she told him, even though she was in too much of a bad mood to read.

But Dibs moved closer.

'I said go away,' snapped Amy.

Dibs took a book from the scattered pile beside her bed and put it on her knees. Then he sat on the bed and snuggled up to Amy.

Amy stared at Dibs in amazement. He

never wanted to snuggle up for a bedtime story. Dibs hated books and he hated snuggles.

'You can have a story,' said Amy slowly, 'but only if you talk. Just one word. Say your name. Say "Dibs".'

Dibs moved his lips, but he made no sound. Then he hung his head and turned his face from Amy.

Leave me alone, he was telling her.

But Amy couldn't leave him alone. She was too angry.

'If you can make all those sounds then you *must* be able to talk. You don't even try. Just say your name. Say "Dibs". D-I-B-S.' Amy sounded out the word.

Dibs stayed silent.

Amy slammed the book down on the floor.
'You like that stupid dolphin more than me!
You talk to *her* all the time. Why don't you
go and live in the aquarium with Baby Blue
and have a dolphin for a sister? You're more
like a dolphin than a boy anyway. So go

away and be a dolphin boy. I'm fed up having a stupid brother who can't speak!'

Amy pulled the quilt over her head until she heard Dibs leave her room. She didn't care if she'd upset him. Why should she? Dibs didn't care how much he hurt her by preferring a dolphin. He didn't care that he got all the attention and treats.

Yet Amy could not get to sleep. She lay awake for hours, bothered by all sorts of mixed-up feelings. At last she went downstairs to get a glass of milk and a biscuit.

Mum and Dad were in the kitchen with Dibs.

'Not you too, Amy,' Dad yawned. 'Now we're all up. It's nearly midnight.'

'What's wrong?' asked Amy. Dibs stood at the back door with his anorak on. He was making his wiggly dolphin sign, over and over again and looked so unhappy that all of Amy's anger and hurt turned to shame.

'It's my fault,' she burst out. 'I told him to go away and live with Baby Blue.'

'Amy! Why?' said Mum.

'Because he prefers her to me!' cried Amy. 'And because he gets everything, all the treats, whatever he wants, just because he can't speak. I never get anything. If Dibs wasn't here you might notice *me* for a change.' Amy burst into tears.

'I had no idea you felt like that, Amy,' gasped Mum. 'You're always so good with Dibs.' She sounded really upset.

'But it's true,' said Dad quietly. 'I know you feel left out sometimes, Amy, and it's our fault.' He looked hard at Mum. 'We make so much fuss about getting Dibs to speak that we forget to make a fuss of Amy. We treat Dibs like a baby but we expect

Amy to be grown-up.'

'I didn't realise,' said Mum. 'I really didn't.' She reached out and squeezed Amy's arm. 'I spoil Dibs because I don't know how to help him but I never meant you to feel left out, Amy.' Mum turned to Dibs. 'Never mind Baby Blue just now, Dibs. We want Amy to know she's just as special as you are.'

At Amy's outburst, Dibs had stopped making his dolphin sign. Amy looked at him now as he stared at his feet. He was wearing his slippers, Amy saw, and his pyjamas were under his anorak. The silly boy was going off to live with Baby Blue wearing his night clothes. Amy laughed at the sight of him. All of a sudden she knew what would make her feel special, and it wasn't silver roller blades.

'I just want Dibs to be my friend, like he is with Baby Blue. I don't care if he ever talks or not,' said Amy.

Slowly, Dibs raised his head. He opened his mouth wide and burst out with a wild and happy dolphin laugh that filled the room. It was impossible to hear it and not laugh too.

Maybe Dibs *was* starting to change, thought Amy. After all, he had wanted to read a book with her tonight, something he had never done before. It was as if Baby Blue was teaching him how to play and make friends. It was just a pity the dolphin couldn't teach him how to talk.

But then, as Amy laughed along with Dibs, she had the most wonderful idea.

6 Amy's wonderful idea

When Dibs next swam with Baby Blue, Amy told Kaleb all about her idea.

'Dibs is different since he made friends with Baby Blue. It's as if she's teaching him how to be a boy,' Amy finished, as she watched her little brother swim and chatter with the dolphin. With Dibs holding on tight to Baby Blue's dorsal fin, he and the dolphin were so close and happy they could almost be one creature. A dolphin boy.

Kaleb looked thoughtful. 'I think they are learning from each other. In a strange way,

Dibs has taught Baby Blue how to be a dolphin again. I've made recordings of her voice and any day now I'm going to send her call out into the ocean.'

'When will you put her back in the sea?' asked Amy.

'That depends on whether we get a response from other dolphins. If we want to return her to the wild we can't keep her here too much longer or she'll lose her natural instincts.'

Amy realised there might not be much time to put her plan into action.

'Can we try my idea?' she asked Kaleb.

He smiled at her. 'Why not? Dolphins are very good mimics so Baby Blue might just do it. Let's try it now.'

Kaleb took a fish from Baby Blue's feed bucket. Right away, the dolphin swam over, leaped out of the water, swiped the fish from Kaleb's hand and gulped it down.

'Dibs!' Kaleb called. 'Come on over!'

Dibs swam across and Kaleb leaned over the poolside to speak to him.

'Dibs, remember I told you that Baby Blue will need her sonar skills to look after herself if she returns to the ocean? And you have helped her to be happy and find her voice again. But how would you like it if Baby Blue gave you a reward? Would you like her to speak to you in your own language?'

Dibs raised his head and looked straight at Kaleb. Then he gave a loud and

delighted dolphin squeak.

'I thought so,' smiled Kaleb. 'Well, I can't say whether she will or not, but we can try. The only thing is, you will have to teach her. I don't think she would do it for anyone else. You are her best friend. You are the one she speaks to. Would you like to teach her to talk?'

A very odd look came over Dibs's face. He looked as if he wanted to laugh and cry at the same time. He gave out a dolphin laugh that ended in a siren wail.

'He wants to but he doesn't think he can,' explained Amy.

'Hmm,' said Kaleb. 'Well, there's only one way to find out, Dibs. And that is to try. We'll leave you to it.'

Kaleb motioned to Amy to follow him to the very back of the pool room.

'Shouldn't we help? He won't be able to do it himself,' whispered Amy, as Dibs hung on to the poolside making a loud siren wail.

Baby Blue kept poking her head out of the water to look at him, wondering what was wrong with her friend.

'I'll bet Dibs has had plenty of people trying all sorts of ways to get him to speak,' said Kaleb.

Amy nodded. 'Lots. And it never worked.'

Kaleb was right. The only person who could get Dibs to speak was himself. He really had to want to. And if Baby Blue couldn't make him want to, then nobody could. It was as if, when Dibs first met Baby Blue, he had somehow known that only he could help the lost and lonely little dolphin. And now, only the dolphin could help Dibs.

Amy sat down beside Kaleb and waited.

When Mum and Dad came to collect them, Amy rushed over. She put her finger to her lips.

'Listen!' she whispered, smiling broadly.

From the pool there came the noise of loud chatter.

'I can hear them,' said Mum. 'They're making their usual racket.'

'But it's not their usual racket,' laughed Amy. 'Listen carefully.'

Mum and Dad stood and listened.

The chatter of the two voices, the boy's and the dolphin's, filled the pool room with

so many echoes it was hard to hear clearly. But at last they did hear. There were no clicks or buzzes or squeaks or whirrs or whistles. Only a fast, hard sound.

'Dib-Dib, Dib-Dib, Dib-Dib!' chanted Baby Blue and Dibs, one after the other, over and over again.

Mum and Dad were too amazed to say a single word.

'Dibs taught Baby Blue to say his name!' shouted Amy, jumping up and down with excitement. 'It was my idea and it worked. Dibs taught her by saying it himself. Now he can talk! Dibs can really talk!'

7 Goodbye, Baby Blue

Now that Dibs knew the little dolphin could copy sounds, he began to teach her all his favourite noises. Baby Blue was an excellent mimic and the pool room would echo with the usual dolphin chatter mingled with police sirens, aeroplanes, motorbikes, barking dogs and telephones.

Then Baby Blue would start to call Dib-Dib-Dib and they would begin to say words, too – just a few, simple words that sounded clumsy and babyish. But each day there were new ones. Dibs was really beginning to talk.

One day Kaleb called Dibs out of the pool. He motioned to Amy to come over too.

'I've got some good news for Baby Blue but it's sad for all of us,' said Kaleb. He looked very serious. 'You know I've been sending recordings of Baby Blue's voice out into the ocean on the sound wave used by dolphins. At first nothing happened and I thought it wasn't going to work. There were no replies from other dolphins on the sound sensors I'd anchored on the sea bed. Then, just as I was about to give up, there came another dolphin call. I sent out more of Baby Blue's calls and the other dolphin kept sending back replies.'

'Is it her mother?' asked Amy.

'It's impossible to tell,' said Kaleb. 'But whoever it is wants very much to meet Baby Blue.'

'But Baby Blue is happy here, and safe. You said the sea was a dangerous place for her. And Dibs will miss her so much.' Amy suddenly realised how much *she* would miss Baby Blue. She liked it when the little

dolphin nuzzled her hands and face after a fish reward. She liked to tickle Baby Blue's smooth, rubbery body and play ball with her. Amy had even taken turns at swimming with Baby Blue, though she wasn't nearly as good as Dibs. He and Baby Blue had burst out laughing when she lost her grip and somersaulted through the water.

Now that she had made friends with the dolphin, and Dibs had grown more playful and friendly, Amy no longer felt jealous. She had grown to love Baby Blue too.

'The sea *is* a dangerous place,' said Kaleb. 'But she won't be alone now. And what if that other dolphin is her mother? Or a future mate that she could have a family with once she's grown? Baby Blue might be happy enough now, but she has a long life ahead of her. Will she still be happy swimming round and round a tiny pool ten years from now? Or will it feel like a prison to her? Shouldn't she be free and wild in the sea where she belongs?'

Amy looked at Dibs who was staring sadly at his feet.

'What do you think, Dibs?' Kaleb said gently.

Slowly Dibs raised his hand and made his wiggly dolphin sign. Dolphin, dolphin, dolphin. Then he raised his head and watched Baby Blue as she swam round the pool.

'Bye-bye,' he sighed at last. 'Bye-bye, Baby Boo.'

A coastguard crew helped load the small
tank containing Baby Blue into their boat.
On the seashore, Amy and Dibs watched
with Mum, Dad and Kaleb as the little

dolphin was tipped from the tank into the ocean.

'Oh, Dibs,' whispered Amy, wiping away the tears that streamed down her face. It was so hard to believe they would never see Baby Blue again. Amy couldn't bear to imagine what Dibs was feeling as he watched the silken grey body of the dolphin slip into the sea.

But when Amy looked at Dibs she saw he wasn't crying. He was listening. Then all of a sudden his face lit up and he let out a wild and happy dolphin laugh.

Far out at sea, two dolphins broke from the waves and leaped high into the air. Over and over again they leaped, mirroring each other exactly. 'Goodbye, Baby Blue!' called

Amy, as the dolphins swam out into the
choppy grey ocean.

'Hello,' said a small voice beside her.

'Not "hello", Dibs,' said Amy gently.

'Bye-bye. Say bye-bye to Baby Blue.'

Dibs slipped his hand into his sister's. Amy looked at her little brother in surprise. Dibs never held hands.

'Hello,' Dibs said again.

Amy squeezed her little brother's hand.

'Hello, Dibs,' she said.

If you enjoyed this
MAMMOTH READ try:

Badger Boy

Anthony Masters
Illustrated by Joan-Marie Abley

Barry has withdrawn into his own world.
Now he only has time for the badgers that
live in the nearby wood.

His cousin Kerry is desperate to be his
friend. But how can she get through to him?

Then the new farmer threatens to clear the
wood. Barry's badgers will be homeless.

Is this a battle he can fight on his own?

If you enjoyed this
MAMMOTH READ try:

Hey, New Kid!

Gary Kilworth
Illustrated by Stephen Player

Danny is the new kid in school, again.
(He's been to twelve of them and he's
only thirteen.)
Robbie picks on him but at least he has
one friend, Jacko.

Then a local woman goes missing and the
police enlist Robbie's help to find her.
Danny and Jacko are determined to get to
her first. They want to be heroes.

Will they do it before Danny has to
move again?

Contents

Some words are shown in bold, **like this**. You can find out what they mean by looking in the glossary.

Look but don't touch: Many small mammals are easily hurt. If you see one in the wild, do not get too close to it. Look at it, but do not try to touch it!

What is a mammal?

A mammal is an animal that has hair. Almost all mammals give birth to live young. Only five **species**, or kinds, of mammals lay eggs. All female mammals produce milk to feed their babies.

Three groups

There are three main groups of mammals. One group is called the **monotremes**. These are the few mammals that lay eggs. The second group is made up of the **marsupials**. They give birth to very tiny babies. The babies make their way into their mother's pouch, where they continue to develop. The remaining mammals form the largest group – the **placental** mammals. They do not have pouches and therefore give birth to live young.

This mother shows some features that make her a mammal. She has hair on her body, and she produces milk to feed her baby.

Mammals are **vertebrates**. These are animals that have a backbone. Mammals are also warm-blooded creatures. This means that their body temperature always remains about the same. It does not cool down on cold days or heat up on warm days. Humans are mammals. So are pandas, house cats, dolphins, pigs, and giraffes, to name just a few.

Where's the hair?

All mammals have hair. But it is certainly difficult to find on some animals such as the whale and the armadillo. Dolphins, whales, and **porpoises** do have hair, though. It appears as tiny bristles on their heads, snouts, or around their mouths. In some species, it falls out shortly after birth. Armadillos, on the other hand, have hair throughout their lives. It is coarse (rough) and grows on their bellies.

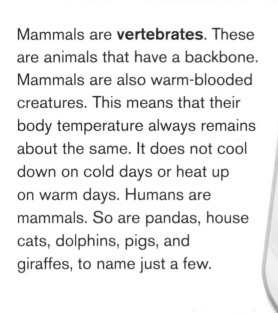

What are the different kinds of mammals?

There are about 5,000 **species** of mammals known today. Scientists believe that many mammals have not yet been discovered. Still, with 5,000 species, scientists need a method for sorting them out.

Scientists have organized the mammals by creating different groups and deciding which ones belong in which groups. The groups are based on similarities – ways in which the animals are alike. For instance, the **primate** group includes monkeys, gorillas, chimpanzees, and humans. The **canine** group includes dogs, wolves, and foxes.

Kingdom, phylum, and class

All mammals belong to one enormous group called the animal kingdom. Scientists divide the animal kingdom into smaller groups, and each one of these is called a **phylum**. In the animal kingdom, there is a phylum for flatworms, one for insects, crabs, and spiders, one for sea urchins and sand dollars, and so on. One phylum has the name **Chordata**. It includes animals that have a bundle of nerves, such as a spinal cord, running down their backs. Mammals, birds, fish, reptiles, and amphibians are members of the phylum Chordata.

Scientists further divide each phylum into classes. The class that includes all of the mammals is called **Mammalia**.

Where do bats fit in?

In ancient times, people thought bats were types of birds. After all, both have wings and are good fliers. However, bats do not have feathers, as birds do. Their bodies are covered with short hairs. Also, bats do not lay eggs. They give birth to live, wriggling little bats. Today, bats are classified as mammals.

Smaller and smaller groups

Scientists divide the thousands of mammals into about 30 groups called orders. One order includes only elephants, one includes all the kinds of rabbits, one has only the armadillos, and so on. Orders are next divided into smaller groups called families. Families are divided into groups called **genera**. And each genus is divided into species. Every species is one particular kind of mammal.

Let's take a look at just one mammal and figure out which groups it belongs to. This is the dik-dik.

Here are a few of the groups in the animal kingdom. Where does the dik-dik fit in? Which phylum, class, and order does it belong to?

Animal Kingdom
Phylum Echinodermata (includes sea urchins and sand dollars)
Phylum Annelida (earthworms)
Phylum Arthropoda (includes insects and spiders)
Phylum Chordata (have a nerve bundle down their backs, usually as a spinal cord)
Class Amphibia (frogs, toads, and salamanders)
Class Reptilia (lizards, turtles, and other animals covered with scales or plates)
Class Aves (songbirds, owls, and others that have feathers and lay eggs)
Class Mammalia (animals with hair)
Order Diprotodontia (animals that have pouches where their young grow)
Order Rodentia (rats, squirrels, and other gnawing animals)
Order Artiodactyla (animals with two-toed hooves, such as giraffes, camels, and cattle)
Order Lagomorpha (includes hares and rabbits)
Order Cingulata (animals that have leathery armour on their bodies)

New discoveries of old animals

Sometimes scientists discover bones of animals that became **extinct** long ago. They still classify these animals, though. If a newly discovered animal is similar to a living animal, it might be placed with it in the same phylum, class, order, family, or genus. If the new animal is totally unique, then scientists will create new groups for it.

How is a mammal born?

Almost all mammals give birth to live young. The babies develop and grow inside the bodies of their mothers. When they are born, many look very much like their parents. For them, it is obvious that the babies and parents belong to the same **species**.

Different plans

Marsupials, however, do not fit this pattern. Their development begins inside their mothers, but they are still very tiny when they are born.

After birth, they creep along the outside of their mother's body, slowly making their way to a pouch on her belly. Once inside the pouch, they latch on to a nipple and begin to drink their mother's milk. Some marsupials spend weeks in the pouch, and others spend months, slowly growing and developing. Kangaroos are marsupials that are tiny, pink, and helpless at birth. After several months in the pouch, they look completely different.

The **monotremes** follow an entirely different plan. They lay eggs. Once the young hatch, they remain close to their mothers. The mothers produce milk from openings on their bodies. The milk leaks out onto their fur, where the babies lick it off. There are only a few monotreme species, and they all live in Australia and New Guinea (see page 11).

Egg layers

The monotremes include the duckbill **platypus** (top) and several species of **echidna** or spiny anteater (bottom). They are found in Australia and New Guinea. The female platypus lays one or two eggs, while the echidna lays only one. Eggs hatch in about 10 days, and the young of both animals are no bigger than jelly babies.

Dependent babies

Some mammal babies are completely helpless when they are born. Of course, tiny marsupial babies could never survive on their own. But many other mammals also start life small and weak. Puppies and kittens are born with their eyes closed. Their little legs are weak, and they can only squirm around. Hamsters are born with no fur, so they must stay close to their mothers for warmth.

These helpless babies depend completely on their parents for food and safety. But some stay with their parents long after they have grown strong. Tiger cubs, for example, will stay with their mother for months, learning how to hunt.

Ready to go

Many grazing animals have babies that are not as helpless. Within hours of birth, little horses, zebras, buffalo, and sheep are standing and walking around. Their spindly legs are almost as long as those of their parents. These babies are ready to get moving shortly after birth. This helps them survive. They are able to travel in the safety of a herd from the very start.

Got hair?

Rabbits and hares are in the same order and they certainly look alike, so are there any differences between them? Yes! One difference is the amount of fur they have at birth. Rabbits are born without fur, while hares are covered with it. You could say that hares have hair!

Shortly after birth,
a baby giraffe begins
to learn to walk.

How does a mammal grow?

All mammal babies start life on a diet of milk. This is the perfect food for them. It is easy to swallow, and they don't have to chew it up. Whales produce milk that is very rich and fatty. It is ideal for large newborns that live in cold water and need lots of nourishment. The milk of harp seals is loaded with fat and protein. These are exactly what the baby seals need. Drinking this rich milk helps them gain almost 2.3 kilograms (5 pounds) a day!

Carnivores

In time, babies begin to feed on other things. Some develop a taste for meat. These are the **carnivores**. Carnivores such as foxes and jaguars begin hunting small **prey** when they are young. In time, they also develop claws for catching their food, and sharp teeth for tearing it.

The wolf is clearly a meat eater. Its long sharp teeth are for piercing flesh.

Herbivores

Plant-eating mammals are called **herbivores**. A herbivore baby develops flattened teeth in the back of its mouth. These teeth are perfect for grinding grass, leaves, and stems. Herbivores also develop long **digestive** systems. They need them to break down those tough plant materials. In horses, for example, the digestive system is more than 30 metres (100 feet) long!

Omnivores

Some babies belong to **species** that eat just about anything. These mammals are called **omnivores**, and they are not picky. They will eat insects, fruit, eggs, frogs, and fish.

This little raccoon is an omnivore. It might grow up to find and eat insects, fish, frogs, lizards, and even food left out for pets!

Living alone or with others

As mammals grow, they take on the habits and behaviours of their parents. Over time, some set off on their own. Others become part of flocks, herds, packs, **pods**, or colonies.

Virginia opossums, woodchucks, and skunks prefer to live **solitary** lives. Except when mothers are tending their young, these animals live alone. Big cats such as cougars and cheetahs keep their babies nearby for months. During this time, the young will chase one another, play, and wrestle. This is preparing them for life on their own, when they will have to chase and bring down prey.

Mammals that live in groups are called social animals. Group life has many advantages. Young that grow up living in a herd find safety among the many adults. They may also find other 'mothers' willing to look out for them. Female howler monkeys, for example, sometimes adopt young monkeys who have lost their mothers.

Safety in numbers

One good thing about living in a herd is that other members offer protection. When musk oxen of the Arctic feel threatened, the adults form a circle. They keep the young and weak oxen in the centre of the ring. The adults face outwards, ready to take on any attacker. This works well for the animals. Not many **predators** want to take on that angry bunch!

This mother is taking her cubs out hunting. At first, the young might actually be afraid of prey. But eventually, they sharpen their hunting skills.

How do mammals move?

Mammals move in all kinds of ways. After all, they must travel on the ground, underwater, through trees, in pitch black caves, and down in burrows. They each have ways to get around in these natural surroundings.

Mammals that spend part of their life underground are built for burrowing. They have strong arms and claws for digging in the dirt. Gophers and moles are excellent burrowers. They have tiny eyes and short hair that does not become matted with soil.

kangaroo

kangaroo rat

Here are just two of the mammals that are good jumpers. What do they have in common that makes them suited for this means of travel?

Herding animals have hooves that can withstand many hours of standing, walking, and running. The hooves are made of hard material that constantly grows as it is worn down. Most herding animals are not fierce fighters. However, they do have ways to escape their enemies. When alarmed, springboks and gazelles of Africa will leap high into the air, then land on all four feet. This spring-loaded method of travel is an excellent way to surprise and outdistance **predators**.

This little **kinkajou** spends most of its time high in the trees of South America. Notice its large, clawed hands, which are good for clinging to branches. The kinkajou can turn its feet backwards. This allows it to run forwards or backwards along a tree trunk or branch. It can also hang from tree limbs by its long tail.

Other ways to travel

Tree-dwelling mammals get around by leaping, swinging, and gliding. Many **primates** live in trees. Some have small, slender, athletic bodies and strong arms and legs. They can quickly scamper up a tree trunk and leap nimbly from limb to limb. Examples are the squirrel monkeys and spider monkeys. Gibbons are primates with incredibly long arms, hands, and fingers. They swing from tree to tree, often sailing through the air to grab the next branch.

Made for the water

Some mammals are built for **aquatic** travel. The otter and the **platypus** are not closely related, but they both spend a lot of their time in the water. They have webbed feet for swimming and muscular tails for steering.

This gibbon knows how to get around. Its fingers are naturally curved into a hook shape. How might this help the gibbon as it travels from branch to branch?

Many mammals spend all of their time in water. These include whales, dolphins, and **porpoises**. Rather than having arms, legs, paws, hooves, and tails, they have fins, flippers, and **flukes**. These structures help to propel (move) them to great depths and back to the surface where they can breathe. Their streamlined bodies can easily shoot through the water, and their large stores of fat provide energy for swimming.

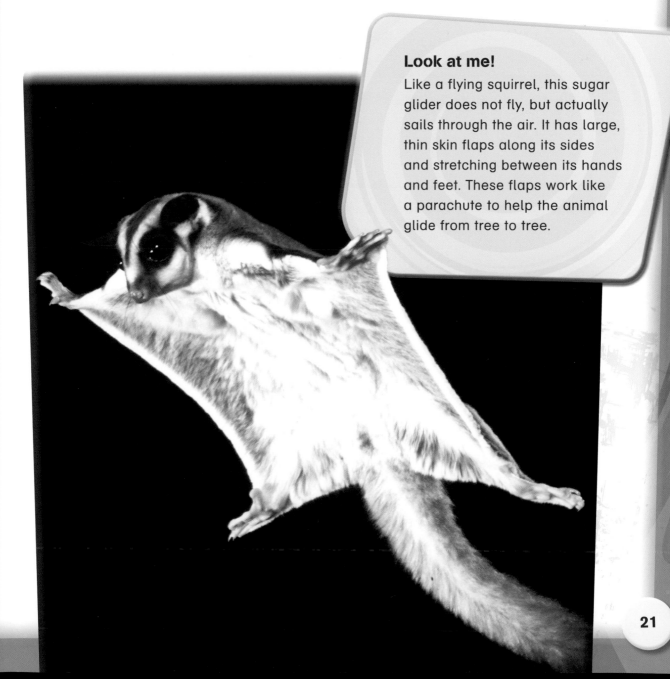

Look at me!
Like a flying squirrel, this sugar glider does not fly, but actually sails through the air. It has large, thin skin flaps along its sides and stretching between its hands and feet. These flaps work like a parachute to help the animal glide from tree to tree.

Migrations

Some mammals spend their entire lives within a small area. Little mammals, such as shrews, may stay within a small section of a field for their entire lives. Other, larger mammals, such as the rhinoceros, might travel within an area the size of a small town. But the greatest travellers of all are those that make long trips every year called **migrations**.

Mammals that make these trips are doing it to survive. They migrate in order to find food for themselves and for their young. Reindeer and gray whales are two examples of migrating mammals.

Reindeer, or caribou, live in northern Europe, Asia, and North America. They feed on spongy plantlike foods called **lichens**. As the weather cools in the autumn, the northernmost lichens begin disappearing and the reindeer head south. Their migrations take them several hundred kilometres to where food is plentiful. When warmer weather returns, the reindeer trek north again. With an abundance of fresh lichens available, they can continue feeding and have their calves.

Up and down

Not all migrations are long, difficult trips. Dall sheep in Alaska simply migrate up and down the mountainsides. They spend their summers in the mountaintops, then move to the valleys in the wintertime. In the lower areas, there is less snow and food is easier to find.

This grey whale is making its annual migration. Grey whales often leap out of the water and fall back with a splash. Scientists are not sure why the whales do this.

A long swim

In the summer months, grey whales live in the northern Pacific Ocean, along the coastlines of North America and Russia. Because of the long, sunny summer days, the waters are packed with life, and the whales find plenty to eat. As winter approaches, the whales head south. They have their young in the warm waters near Mexico and Korea, and remain for another two to three months before returning north. These whales travel more than 16,000 kilometres (10,000 miles) each year.

How do mammals protect themselves?

Some mammals actively protect themselves. They may hide, run, or fight. Others find safety in just being themselves. These animals depend on their natural size, colours, and habits for protection.

Killer whales and grizzly bears are enormous mammals. Few animals are likely to threaten them. But not all mammals have the advantage of size. Smaller mammals such as fennecs in the African desert rely on their colour to protect them. Fennecs are small sand-coloured foxes that blend in perfectly with their environment.

This badger, found in Minnesota, USA, protects itself in two ways. It is **nocturnal** and it hides in a burrow.

Mammals that create burrows have natural hiding places. Chipmunks build very complex burrows. They include tunnels and separate 'rooms' for sleeping, caring for babies, and storing food. The tunnels have well-hidden entrance holes and may run to 9 metres (30 feet) long, providing excellent hiding places.

Many mammals prefer to be active at night. These nocturnal animals escape not only the heat of the day, but also the daytime **predators**. Bats are the ultimate nocturnal animals. By having the ability to fly, by feeding only at night, and by retreating to caves and other sheltered places in the day, they escape many different threats.

Snowshoe hares live in Canada and the northern United States. In the winter, their coats are almost solid white. In the summer, new fur grows in that is brown and grey in colour. How do these winter and summer colours protect the animal from predators?

Great escapes

When many mammals feel threatened, they fight, run, roll up in a ball, or use other ways to protect themselves. Fighting mammals such as bears, wolves, and lions use their claws and teeth to deal with threats. Sometimes they even do battle with members of their own **species** to protect their young or defend their homes.

Herding animals usually just run from danger. However, this does not mean they are defenceless. Zebras can kick a predator senseless. And musk oxen can trample an enemy to death.

Skunks are gentle animals, but they do have one powerful weapon – their spray. When a skunk senses danger, it lowers its head, arches its back, and stamps its feet. If that doesn't scare an enemy away, the skunk lifts its tail and sprays a foul-smelling fluid.

Meerkats watch out for danger while other family members look for food. When they see danger, they make high-pitched sounds.

Certain small animals that live in colonies have ways of protecting the whole group. Some prairie dogs and meerkats station themselves as guards while the rest of the colony eats. When danger threatens, the guards bark out a warning and all of the members run for their burrows.

A few mammals defend themselves in very quiet ways. The Virginia opossum keels over and plays dead. Predators lose interest in the animal and leave it alone. The **pangolin** of Africa is covered in scales. When threatened, this toothless animal curls up into a tight ball and waits for the danger to pass.

Where do mammals live?

Mammals live in just about every place imaginable, from the equator to the Arctic. Small mammals live underground. Climbing and swinging mammals live in trees. Other mammals live in grasslands, forests, deserts, swamps, and caves.

Mammals such as walruses and seals that are built for icy cold regions have certain things in common. They have thick layers of fat for **insulation**. The mothers also produce very rich milk for their young. It helps them to gain weight quickly and add to their own insulation.

Those mammals that live in hot, dry areas are also **adapted** for their environments. The tiny, mouse-like elephant shrew of Africa has tan fur that blends with its surroundings. Although water is in short supply, the shrew gets all of the fluid it needs from eating ants, termites, and plants.

This four-toed elephant shrew lives in Kenya.

A deep-sea diver

The narwhal is a whale that lives in the frigid waters of the Arctic. It is known to dive as deep as 1,372 metres (4,500 feet) and to remain underwater for almost 30 minutes. The animal's rib cage is flexible and collapses slightly as the whale descends. During long stretches underwater, the narwhal shuts off its blood flow to certain organs. This is how it uses oxygen. By doing this, the whale does not have to return quickly to the surface to breathe.

A problem up high

Mammals that live high in the mountains face one big problem. There is not much oxygen available in the air. People who climb mountains often face this 'thin air'. They find themselves gasping for breath. But llamas can be found high in the mountains of South America, and deer mice can live up in the mountains of North America. Why aren't they gasping for air?

This llama is built for life in the mountains. It is sure-footed and can walk on rocky ground. Its coat protects it from the cold. And its blood cells easily take up oxygen.

The camel has several adaptations to protect it from wind and sand storms. The long eyelashes protect the eyes. The nostrils can clamp shut to keep out the blowing sand.

It's in their blood

The blood cells of llamas and deer mice are a bit different from those of other mammals. When mammals breathe in, oxygen enters their lungs. It next moves into the blood cells that are travelling in vessels through their lungs. The blood cells carry oxygen out to all of the body's tissues. In llamas and deer mice, the blood cells pick up oxygen much more easily than in other mammals. These animals do not gasp for oxygen. Their body tissues get plenty of it.

No matter where mammals live, they have adaptations that help them survive. Some mammals, such as the house mouse and the brown rat, have adapted to just about every environment. Today, they live almost everywhere on Earth.

How do mammals help us?

Mammals are important in nature and also helpful to humans. All mammals are **consumers**. This means they eat, or consume, plants and other animals. This helps to keep nature in balance. For example, little brown bats eat thousands of mosquitoes each night. Thanks to this bat, the mosquito population does not grow out of control.

Many mammals become food items for other mammals. Foxes eat mice, for instance, and polar bears eat seals. Those mammals that have no natural enemies are called the apex **predators**. They are large meat eaters that do not become **prey** for other animals.

This simple food web shows how mammals depend on plants and other animals for their food. The mouse eats grain and insects. Snakes, hawks, and foxes eat mice. Hawks eat snakes. Here, hawks and foxes are at the top of the web, as no other animals eat them.

hawk

fox

snake

mice

insect

grain

Humans often use cattle, deer, and many other mammals for their meat. People also drink goat, cow, and yak milk, or use it to make cream, cheese, and yoghurt. People use fur and leather made from animal skins for clothing. And many people rely on elephants and camels to carry loads, oxen to pull heavy wagons, and horses and donkeys for transportation.

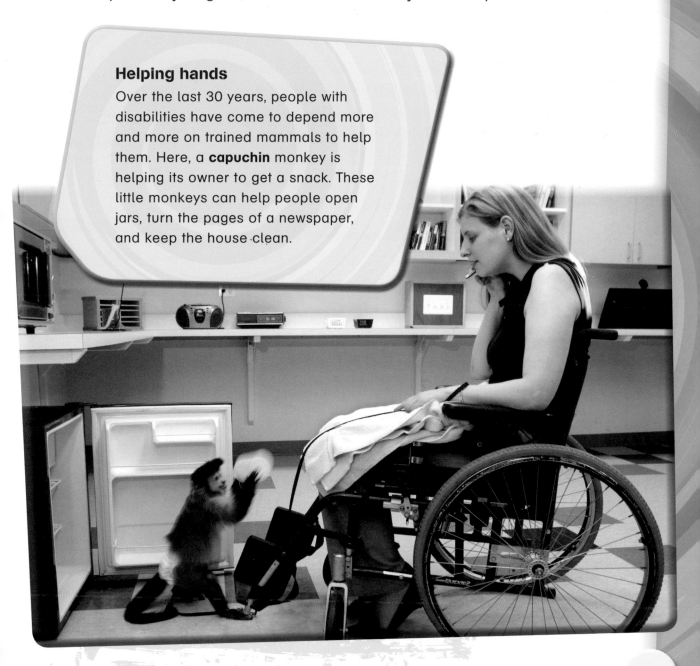

Helping hands

Over the last 30 years, people with disabilities have come to depend more and more on trained mammals to help them. Here, a **capuchin** monkey is helping its owner to get a snack. These little monkeys can help people open jars, turn the pages of a newspaper, and keep the house clean.

Problems from mammals

In some cases, mammals have caused problems. But this is not always their fault. When people move into new areas, they sometimes destroy mammal habitats. They fill in ponds and cut trees to make room for homes. They may not know they are destroying the mammals' food supply. But this may cause coyotes or mountain lions to come into town looking for prey. It may force wolves to attack sheep or cattle.

Mammals that are **invasive species** create immense problems. Invasive animals are those that are brought into new environments and begin to take over. They may have no natural enemies, so their numbers quickly increase. In Australia and New Zealand, the European wild rabbit is an invasive species. It was brought to these lands in the 1800s and spread quickly. The rabbit eats crop plants, grass, roots, seeds, leaves, and even bark. Experts are now trying different ways to remove these pests.

Some mammals can carry and spread disease. For instance, squirrels, prairie dogs, chipmunks, rats, and mice carry a germ that causes **plague**. The germ can spread to humans and cause fever, chills, and even death. Throughout history, the disease has wiped out millions of people. Fortunately, we now have ways to detect and treat the disease.

A foreign invader

The American mink is an invasive species in the British Isles. It was imported to be raised for its fur. However, some minks escaped, and their population grew in the wild. The American mink feeds on the water vole, a small rat-like mammal. Now, the vole's numbers have greatly decreased.

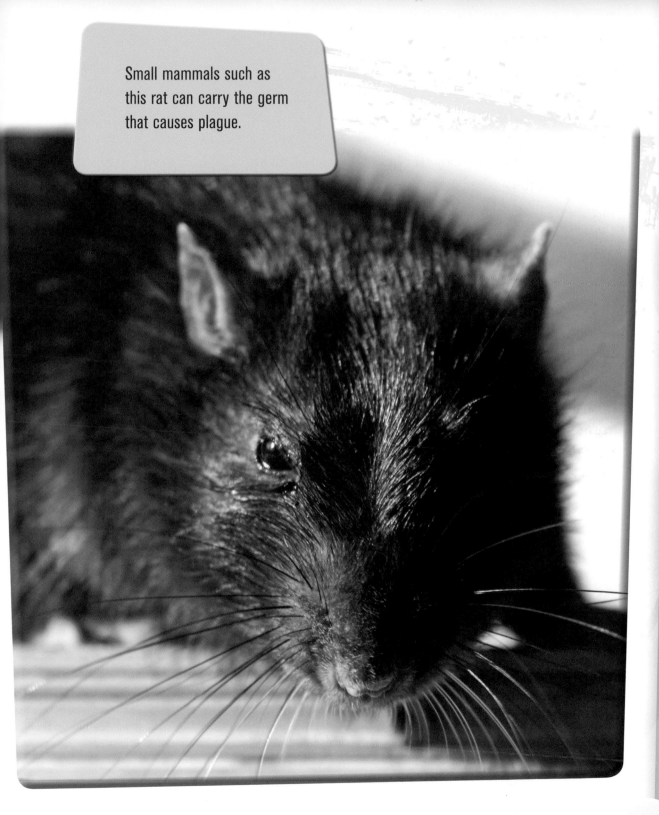

Small mammals such as
this rat can carry the germ
that causes plague.

How do mammals spend their time?

Mammals spend much of their time resting and sleeping. At rest, a mammal's breathing and heart rate slow down. Larger mammals such as elephants and hippopotamuses already have slow breathing and heart rates. An elephant's heart beats only about 30 times each minute. Very small mammals such as guinea pigs and gerbils have much faster rates. Either way, these processes speed up when the animals are active and slow down when they are not.

Tiny mammals such as this shrew live life in the fast lane. These animals eat constantly. They have a heart rate of about 15 beats per second, and they take more than 700 breaths each minute.

Some mammals really know how to slow things down – they hibernate. During hibernation, the body processes slow down to almost a dead stop. Bats, woodchucks, and ground squirrels are examples of hibernating animals. Before the cold weather comes, these animals eat constantly to build up their fat. They also find a den or burrow where they can hibernate. Once they slide into a hibernating state, they appear to be dead. Different **species** hibernate for different lengths of time, some for weeks and some for months. But when warm weather returns, they rouse themselves and become active again.

Hedgehogs in hibernation

Hedgehogs are animals that hibernate each winter. During hibernation, this animal's heart rate slows from 190 beats to 20 beats per minute. Its body temperature drops to almost freezing point.

Other things to do

When mammals aren't resting, they are usually busy looking for food, eating, or caring for their families. **Diurnal** mammals are animals that are active mainly during the day. They often have fur that blends in with their environment. This way, they can move about in the daytime and still be protected from their enemies.

Yum!

The giant anteater has arms, hands, and a head built for finding food. It uses its claws to make a hole in a termite mound or anthill. Next, it pokes its snout straight into the hole. Then the anteater flicks its long tongue back and forth, in and out, picking up the tiny insects and pulling them into its mouth. An adult anteater can slurp up more than 30,000 ants and termites a day!

Nocturnal mammals are busy at night. Some have unusually large eyes that help them see in the dark. But others, such as some bats, are different.

The insect-eating bats do not use their eyesight to find food in the dark. They use sound waves instead. As the bat flies about, it sends out sound waves. The waves hit other objects in the area and bounce back to the bat. The bat's brain interprets those returning waves, so the bat knows which objects are still and which ones are moving. The bat can even tell how fast insects are flying and their direction. This method of finding food is called **echolocation**.

This little tarsier is a nocturnal animal. Its huge eyes help it find food and spot **predators** in the dark.

How do mammals have babies?

Some mammals can have babies at any time of the year. They do not need to wait for a particular season that is best for bearing young. Humans are the perfect example of this. Other mammals, however, need to wait until food and water become plentiful. At that time, their young have the best chance of survival.

Before babies are born, the parents must choose each other as mates. In some mammals, chemicals help them make this choice. Many animals produce chemicals that are signals to other members of their **species**. In dogs, females produce these chemicals when they are ready to mate. Male dogs sense the chemicals, even from far away.

Courtship

Other mammals use courtship activities to attract mates. Male humpback whales seem to 'sing' to females, for up to 30 minutes, hoping to get their attention. Male Tasmanian devils are less delicate. During courtship, the males and females snarl and wrestle with each other before mating.

Sometimes males must see off their competition before attracting a female. The males of bighorn sheep butt heads to determine which ones will get to mate. Sometimes this goes on for hours. The more powerful sheep win the females. The weaker sheep might have to wait a whole year before they compete again, perhaps with better luck.

A nosy monkey

Proboscis monkeys live in trees on the large island of Borneo (located north of Australia). The male monkeys have huge noses that can reach a length of 18 centimetres (7 inches). Each time the male makes his *kee-honk* sound, the nose straightens out. Some scientists believe they might do this to attract females.

Time before birth

After mating, the young mammals grow or form within eggs in the bodies of their mothers. The length of time before birth is called the gestation period. It is different for different species. Babies of the Virginia opossum grow for only 12 days before they are born and crawl into their mother's pouch. Asian elephants have a much longer gestation period. It takes about 22 months before their babies are ready for birth.

Cycle of life

Once the babies are born, the life cycle begins again. The young grow up and learn to find food and shelter for themselves. Some die before they start families of their own. They cannot find food, are eaten by **predators**, or they become ill. If they survive, they find mates and have young of their own. Some mammals, such as field mice, lead busy, short lives. Other mammals, such as whales, may live into their forties and beyond. As long as the cycle continues, the species will survive.

Becoming parents

Large animals are usually much older than small ones when they are ready to have babies. Rats can give birth when they are only three months old. Hippopotamuses begin having babies when they are eight or nine years of age.

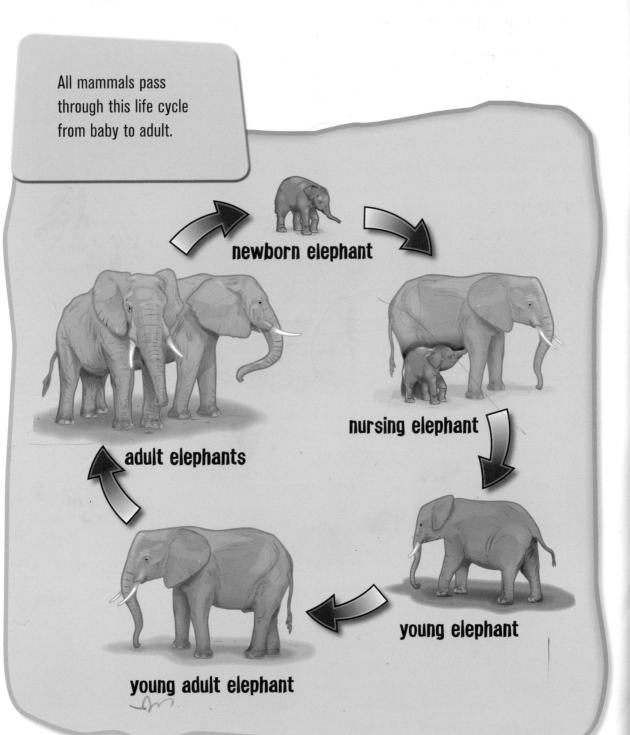

All mammals pass through this life cycle from baby to adult.

newborn elephant

nursing elephant

young elephant

young adult elephant

adult elephants

Mammal facts

What is the largest living mammal?

The African elephant is the largest land mammal. But at 30 metres (100 feet) in length, the blue whale is the largest of all living things. The whale's tongue alone weighs as much as an elephant!

What is the smallest living mammal?

The bumblebee bat of Thailand is the smallest mammal. It measures only 32 millimetres (1.3 inches) in length.

What is the fastest mammal?

The cheetah is the fastest land mammal. It can run at speeds of up to 113 kilometres per hour (70 miles per hour), but only for short bursts.

What is the loudest land mammal?

The howler monkey is the winner here. The cries of the male can reach other monkeys about 5 kilometres (3 miles) away!

Mammal classification

Scientists divide the 5,000 or so mammals into about 30 different orders. About 2,000 species are in the order of rats, mice, squirrels, and other **rodents**. Another 1,000 are included in the order of bats. All other orders are much smaller. They include the order of shrews and moles, and the order of **carnivores** such as jaguars, hyenas, and bears. The order of **primates** has about 300 **species** and includes humans, apes, and monkeys. The **platypus** and the aardvark each fit into an order of their own.

The aardvark is all alone in its order. This African mammal is **nocturnal** and eats termites. An adult weighs more than a large dog.

Glossary

adapt to adjust to new or different conditions

aquatic living in or near water, or dealing with water

canine belonging to the group of doglike animals

capuchin type of monkey

carnivore animal that eats other animals

Chordata phylum of animals that have a cord of nerve tissue down their backs at some time in their lives

consumer living thing that eats plants or animals

digestive having to do with digestion or breaking down food

diurnal active mainly during the daytime

echidna small, spiny monotreme of Australia

echolocation method of detecting things by bouncing sound waves off them

extinct having died out

fluke finlike part of a whale's tail

genus (pl. genera) classification level of the animal kingdom

herbivore animal that eats plants

insulation covering or layer for keeping something warm

invasive referring to something that intrudes or pushes its way in

kinkajou tree-living mammal with a long tail

lichen plantlike organism composed of a fungus and an alga living together

Mammalia class of animals that have hair and produce milk for their young

marsupial pouched mammal that gives birth to very small young, that then grow and develop in the pouch

migration trip made by animals, usually every year

monotreme mammal that lays eggs

nocturnal active mainly at night

omnivore animal that eats both plant and animal tissues

pangolin insect-eating mammal whose body is covered by scales

phylum one of the major groups within the animal kingdom

placental referring to mammals that do not have a pouch and that give birth to live young

platypus Australian mammal with a duck-like bill and that lays eggs

pods small group of animals traveling together

porpoise aquatic animal similar to the dolphin

prey animal that is eaten by other animals

primate mammal group consisting of humans, apes, and monkeys

proboscis unusually long snout

rodent animal with two large upper front teeth for gnawing.

solitary living or doing things alone

species particular kind of living thing

vertebrate animal with a backbone

Find out more

Books

Birth and Baby Animals: Compare the Way Reptiles, Mammals, Sharks, Birds and Insects are Born and How They are Reared (Wild Animal Planet), Michael Chinery (Southwater, 2008)

Classifying Mammals (Classifying Living Things), Louise Spilsbury and Richard Spilsbury (Heinemann Library, 2009)

Planet Animal: Mammals, Barbara Taylor (Carlton Books, 2009)

Small Mammals (Wildlife Watchers), Terry Jennings (QED Publishing, 2010)

Websites

http://www.ypte.org.uk/animal/kangaroo-grey-/136
This website has lots of interesting facts about kangaroos.

http://news.bbc.co.uk/cbbcnews/hi/newsid_7550000/
newsid_7552300/7552327.stm
This report suggests that eating kangaroo meat could save the planet!
Would you do it?

http://www.bbc.co.uk/cbbc/wild/helping/wildchild/hayley/photostory.shtml?1
Read this photo story about dolphin and whale watching off the east coast of Scotland.

http://www.wildlifewatch.org.uk/Activities/Outdoor/Make-a-bat-box
Help some small, furry mammals by building this home for bats.

Index

Contents

1 Introduction

This chapter shows how the spreadsheet, the electronic counterpart of the paper ledger, has evolved in Excel, taking advantage of the features of the different versions of Microsoft Office, and the Windows operating system.

The Spreadsheet Concept

Spreadsheets, in the guise of the accountant's ledger sheet, have been in use for many, many years. They consisted of paper forms with a two-dimensional grid of rows and columns, often on extra-large paper, forming two pages of a ledger book, for example (hence the term "spread sheet"). They were typically used by accountants to prepare budget or financial statements. Each row would represent a different item, with each column showing the value or amount for that item over a given time period. For example, a forecast for a 30% margin and 10% growth might show:

Don't forget

Ledger sheets pre-date computers and handheld calculators, and have been in use for literally hundreds of years.

Margin %	30					
Growth %	10					
				Profit Forecast		
		January	February	March	April	May
Cost of Goods		6,000	6,600	7,260	7,986	8,785
Sales		7,800	8,580	9,438	10,382	11,420
Profit		1,800	1,980	2,178	2,396	2,635
Total Profit		1,800	3,780	5,958	8,354	10,989

Any changes to the basic figures would mean that all the values would have to be recalculated and transcribed to another ledger sheet to show the effect, e.g. for a 20% margin and 60% growth:

Margin %	20					
Growth %	60					
				Profit Forecast		
		January	February	March	April	May
Cost of Goods		6,000	9,600	15,360	24,576	39,322
Sales		7,200	11,520	18,432	29,491	47,186
Profit		1,200	1,920	3,072	4,915	7,864
Total Profit		1,200	3,120	6,192	11,107	18,972

Don't forget

The first spreadsheet application was VisiCorp's VisiCalc (visible calculator). Numerous competitive programs appeared, but market leadership was taken first by Lotus 123, and now by Microsoft Excel.

To make another change, to show 10% margin and 200% growth, for example, would involve a completely new set of calculations. And, each time, there would be the possibility of a calculation or transcription error creeping in. With the advent of the personal computer, a new approach became possible. Applications were developed to simulate the operation of the financial ledger sheet, but the boxes (known as cells) that formed the rows and columns could store text, numbers, or a calculation formula based on the contents of other cells. The spreadsheet looked the same, since it was the results that were displayed, rather than the formulas themselves. However, when the contents of a cell were changed in the spreadsheet, all the cells whose values depended on that changed cell were automatically recalculated.

This new approach allowed a vast improvement in productivity for various activities, such as forecasting. In the second example shown on the previous page, you'd set up the initial spreadsheet using formulas, rather than calculating the individual cell values. A spreadsheet might contain these values and formulas, for example:

	A	B	C	D	E
1	Markup %	30			
2	Growth %	10			
3					
4			Jan	Feb	Mar
5	Cost of Goods	6000	=C5+C5*$B$2/100	=D5+D5*$B$2/100
6	Sales	=C5*(100+$B$1)/100	=D5*(100+$B$1)/100	=E5*(100+$B$1)/100
7	Profit	=C6-C5	=D6-D5	=E6-E5
8	Total Profit	=C7	=C8+D7	=D8+E7

Don't forget

The = sign signals to Excel that what follows is a formula and must be calculated.

However, what will be displayed in the cells are the actual values that the formulas compute, based on the contents of other cells:

	A	B	C	D	E	F	G	H	I
1	Markup %	30							
2	Growth %	10							
3									
4			Jan	Feb	Mar	Apr	May		
5	Cost of Goods		6000	6600	7260	7986	8785		
6	Sales		7800	8580	9438	10382	11420		
7	Profit		1800	1980	2178	2396	2635		
8	Total Profit		1800	3780	5958	8354	10989		

When you want to see the effect of changes, such as different values for margin and growth, for example, you change just those items and instantly see the effect, as the values calculated by the formulas are adjusted and redisplayed. The capabilities of the spreadsheet applications have evolved, and the use of spreadsheets has extended far beyond the original use for financial planning and reporting. They can now handle any activity that involves arrays of values interrelated by formulas, grading examination scores, interpreting experimental data, or keeping track of assets and inventories, for example. In fact, the newest spreadsheet applications seem to support just about any possible requirement.

Don't forget

Sets of predefined functions were added, plus support for writing small programs, or macros, to manipulate the data. Further developments incorporated graphs, images, and audio.

Microsoft Excel

VisiCalc and Lotus 123 were MS-DOS programs, subject to its command-line interface, but Microsoft Excel was developed for Windows. It was the first spreadsheet program to allow users to control the visual aspects of the spreadsheet (fonts, character attributes, and cell appearance). It introduced intelligent cell recomputation, where only cells dependent on the cell being modified are updated (previous spreadsheet programs recomputed everything all the time, or waited for a specific Recalc command). Later versions of Excel were shipped as part of the bundled Microsoft Office suite of applications, which included programs like Microsoft Word and Microsoft PowerPoint. Versions of Excel for Microsoft Windows and Office include:

There are also versions of Excel designed specifically for the Apple Macintosh ("Mac") computers – starting from Excel 1.0!

1987	Excel 2.0	Windows
1990	Excel 3.0	Windows
1992	Excel 4.0	Windows
1993	Excel 5.0	Windows
1995	Excel 95 (v7.0)	Office 95
1997	Excel 97 (v8.0)	Office 97
1999	Excel 2000 (v9.0)	Office 2000
2001	Excel 2002 (v10)	Office XP
2003	Excel 2003 (v11)	Office 2003
2007	Excel 2007 (v12)	Office 2007
2010	Excel 2010 (v14)	Office 2010
2013	Excel 2013 (v15)	Office 2013 / Office 365
2015	Excel 2016 (v16)	Office 2016 / Office 365

In this book, the New icon pictured above is used to highlight new or enhanced features in Excel 2016.

The newer versions of Excel provide many enhancements to the user interface, and incorporate connections with Microsoft Office and other applications. The basis of the program, however, remains the same. It still consists of a large array of cells, organized into rows and columns, containing data values or formulas with relative or absolute references to other cells. This means that many of the techniques included in this book will be applicable to whichever version of Excel you may be using, or even if you are using a spreadsheet from another family of products, though, of course, the specifics of the instructions may need to be adjusted.

Microsoft Office 2016

Microsoft Office 2016 is the latest version of Microsoft Office, and it is available in a variety of editions, including:

- **Office Home & Student 2016 (PC & Mac)**
- **Office Home & Business 2016 (PC & Mac)**
- **Office Professional 2016**

There are volume licensing versions for larger organizations:

- **Office Standard 2016 (PC & Mac)**
- **Office Professional Plus 2016**

There is also a subscription version of Microsoft Office known as Office 365, and this is also available in a number of editions:

- **Office 365 Home (PC & Mac)**
- **Office 365 Personal (PC & Mac)**
- **Office 365 University**
- **Office 365 Business**
- **Office 365 Enterprise**

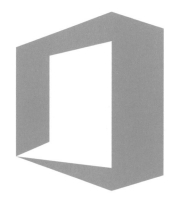

All of these editions include Microsoft Excel 2016. Whichever edition you obtain, your copy of Excel 2016 incorporates all the features and uses the Office result-oriented user interface, with the Ribbon, File tab, BackStage, Galleries, and Live Preview, etc.

Excel 2016 also uses the Microsoft Office file format, OpenXML, as the default file format. This is based on XML and uses ZIP compression, so the files will be up to 75% smaller than those in the older Microsoft Office file formats.

Other shared Office features include the Document Theme, which defines colors, fonts, and graphic effects for a spreadsheet or other Office document, and collaboration services for sharing spreadsheets and documents with other users.

Office Online Apps

Microsoft offers a free, web-based version of Office; this includes online versions of Word, Excel, PowerPoint, and OneNote. These online apps feature user interfaces similar to the full desktop products, and allow you to access Office documents, including Excel spreadsheets, via your browser. They also make it easier for you to share documents with users who may not have Office 2016 on their systems. However, the Office Online apps do not support the full feature set of the desktop products.

The Office Online apps work in conjunction with OneDrive, the online storage associated with your Microsoft account (or your Office 365 account, if you have a subscription).

System Requirements

To install and run Excel 2016, your computer should match or better the minimum hardware and operating system requirements for Office 2016. If you are upgrading to Office 2016, from Office 2010 or Office 2013, the hardware should already meet the requirements – though you may need to upgrade your operating system. For an upgrade from earlier versions of Office you will need to check that both hardware and operating system meet the minimum specifications for Office 2016. This includes:

Operating system	Windows 7, Windows RT, Windows 8/8.1, Windows 10 (32-bit or 64-bit) or Windows Server 2008/R2 or later (64-bit)
Processor	1GHz or higher (32-bit or 64-bit)
Memory	2GB (PC) or 4GB (Mac)
Hard disk	3GB (PC) or 6GB (Mac)
Monitor	1280 x 800 resolution or higher
Internet	Broadband connection recommended for download, product activation and OneDrive

These are minimum requirements. You may need other components (e.g. a sound card) for some Excel features.

Office 2016 (32-bit) runs on both 32-bit and 64-bit systems. Microsoft recommends this, rather than the 64-bit version, for add-in compatibility.

Your computer must also meet the hardware requirements for your chosen operating system. These may exceed the minimum specifications for Office 2016, especially with advanced systems, such as Windows 10 with Multitouch function.

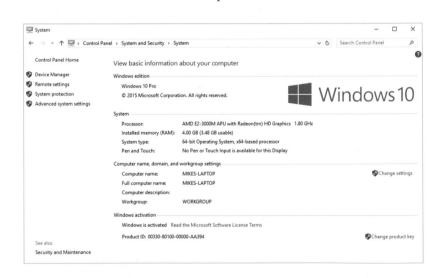

Additional Software Requirements

If you have another computer running an earlier version of Office, and you need to work with Excel files in the Office 2016 format, you can download the Microsoft Office Compatibility Pack, from **microsoft.com/downloads**. This will allow older versions of Excel to read the new file format.

Getting Office 2016

You can buy your preferred version of Microsoft Office 2016 in disk format from a retail source, or download it from Microsoft. Windows 10 provides a default "Get Office" item on the Start menu that launches your web browser at the Office download page **products.office.com**. Here, you can select one of the Office 365 subscription-based versions of Microsoft Office 2016. These provide fully installed Office apps that work across multiple devices and are continuously upgraded – so are always up to date. For example, you might choose the Office 365 Personal version, which lets you use Office on one PC, one tablet, and one phone. This also gives you a massive 1TB of storage for one user.

To compare the various versions of Office 365 visit **products. office.com/en-us/buy/ compare-microsoft- office-products**

1   Click the **Get Office** tile or Start menu item – to launch your web browser

2   Select your version then enter the purchase details – to begin installation

Get Office

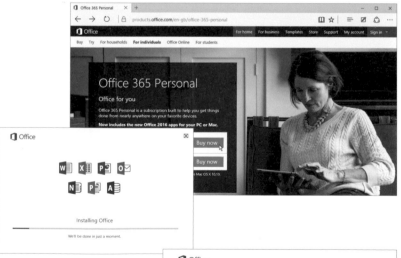

Installing Office

We'll be done in just a moment.

3   Take a break until the Office completion dialog appears

You're all set! Office is installed now
Click Start > All Apps.

Close

Microsoft is eager to encourage adoption of the subscription versions – Office 365 Personal edition also includes 60 minutes per month of Skype calls to cellphones and landlines.

Excel 2016 and Windows 10

With Microsoft Office 2016 installed under Windows 10, you have a number of ways to launch Excel 2016:

1 The installation of Office should have added colored icons for various Office apps on the Windows Desktop taskbar. Click the green icon 'X' to launch the Excel 2016 app

Don't forget

These options are available for the Windows 10 operating system.

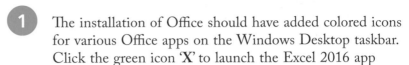

2 In either Desktop or Tablet mode, click or tap the Start button, then choose **All apps**

3 Now, scroll down the A-Z list to the **E** category heading

4 Choose the **Excel 2016** item to launch the Excel 2016 app

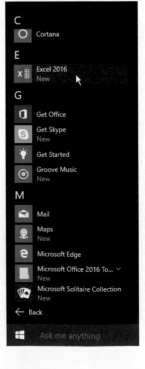

Hot tip

You can right-click the Excel 2016 item on the **All apps** list and select **Pin to taskbar** if the Excel icon isn't already visible on the taskbar.

5 In the taskbar Search box, type "excel" to search for the Excel app on your system

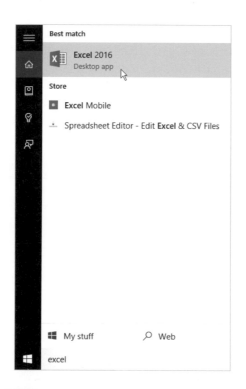

6 Now, click or tap the **Excel 2016** item from the search results to launch the Excel 2016 app

Hot tip

You can right-click the Excel 2016 item on the **All apps** list and select **Pin to Start** to add a tile to the Tablet mode Start screen and Desktop mode Start group.

15

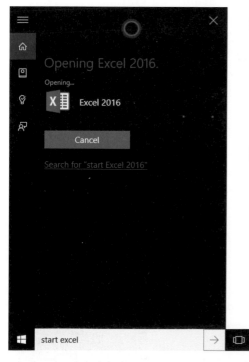

7 Say "Hey Cortana" into your system microphone to wake up your Personal Digital Assistant

Beware

8 Now, say "start Excel" into the microphone to launch the Excel 2016 app

Cortana is new in Windows 10 but performance may vary by region. If Cortana is not working or enabled in your country try setting your region to "United States" in **Settings > Time & language > Region & language**.

The Office 2016 Ribbon

The menus and toolbars used in earlier versions of Excel have been replaced by the Ribbon. With this, commands are organized in logical groups, under command tabs – **Home**, **Insert**, **Page Layout**, **Formulas**, **Data**, **Review** and **View** tabs – arranged in the order in which tasks are normally performed. When you click any of these tabs, the corresponding commands display in the Ribbon.

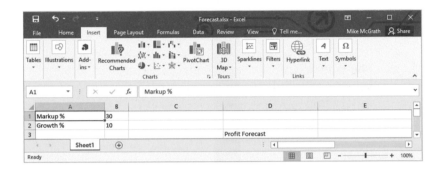

The Ribbon may also include contextual command tabs, which appear when you perform a specific task. For example, if you select some data and then click **Insert Column Chart** in the **Charts** group, chart tool tabs **Design**, **Layout**, and **Format** are displayed.

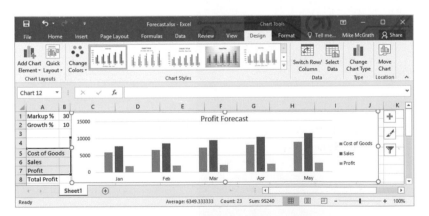

You can minimize the Ribbon, to make more room on the screen:

1   Click the **Ribbon Display Options** button and select **Show Tabs**

2   The tabs will still be displayed but the commands will be hidden

Other Office 2016 apps (Word, Access, Outlook, and PowerPoint) also have a Ribbon, which displays tabs appropriate to that particular app.

The **File** tab displays the BackStage view, which provides general document file functions, plus **Share**, **Export** and the **Excel Options**.

16

...cont'd

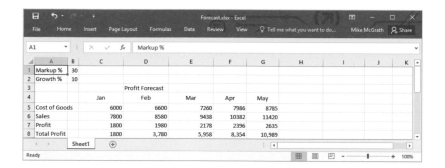

3 The Ribbon and the commands are redisplayed as a temporary overlay whenever you click a tab, or when you use the **Alt** key shortcuts (see page 118)

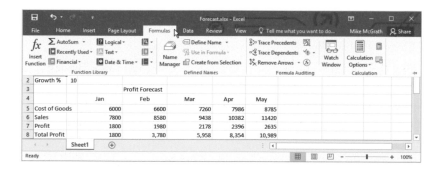

Touch/Mouse Mode
To enable Touch Mode:

1 Click the down arrow on the Quick Access Toolbar, then choose the **Touch** option

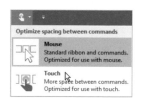

2 The Ribbon displays with extra spacing between buttons

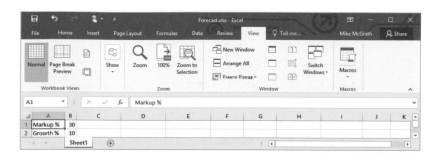

You can also choose **Auto-hide Ribbon**. Excel runs full-screen with no tabs or commands visible. Click the top of the application to display the Ribbon when it's hidden.

Office 2016 applications offer two interfaces – Mouse or Touch, where the latter is optimized for operation with touch-enabled devices. To add this option to the Quick Access Toolbar, click the down arrow and select **Touch/Mouse Mode**.

Exploring Excel 2016

If you are used to a previous version of Excel, you may not always know where to find the features you need. The following table lists some of the actions that you may want to carry out, and indicates the Ribbon tabs and groups where the associated commands for these actions may be found in Excel 2016:

Hot tip

Explore the Ribbon tabs and command groups in Excel 2016 to find the features that you need to carry out activities on your worksheets.

Action	Tab	Groups
Create, open, save, print, share, or export files, or change options	**File**	Backstage Commands – Info, New, Open, Save, Save As, Print, Share, Export, Close, Account, Options, and Feedback
Format, insert, delete, edit or find data in cells, columns, and rows	**Home**	Number, Styles, Cells, and Editing groups
Create tables, charts, sparklines, reports, slicers, and hyperlinks	**Insert**	Tables, Charts, Sparklines, Filters, and Links groups
Set page margins, page breaks, print areas, or sheet options	**Page Layout**	Page Setup, Scale to Fit, and Sheet Options groups
Find functions, define names, or troubleshoot formulas	**Formulas**	Function Library, Defined Names, and Formula Auditing groups
Import or connect to data, sort and filter data, validate data, flash fill values, or perform a what-if analysis	**Data**	Get External Data, Connections, Sort & Filter, and Data Tools groups
Check spelling, review and revise, and protect a sheet or workbook	**Review**	Proofing, Comments, and Changes groups
Change workbook views, arrange windows, freeze panes, and record macros	**View**	Workbook Views, Window, and Macros groups

There is a **Tell Me** text box on the Excel 2016 Ribbon where you can enter words and phrases, to quickly locate features or get help on what you want to do.

💡 Tell me what you want to do...

If you want to locate a particular command, you can search the list of all of the commands that are available in Excel 2016 (see next page).

...cont'd

To display the list of available commands:

1 Click the down arrow on the Quick Access Toolbar to display the **Customize** menu (see page 17) and select the option for **More Commands**

(see page 17)

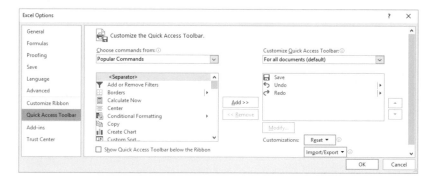

2 Click the box **Choose commands from**, and select **All Commands**

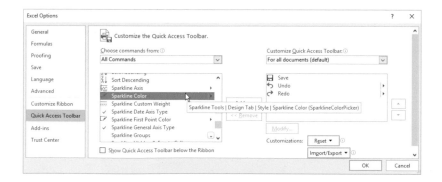

3 Scroll the list and move the Mouse pointer over a command name, and the Tool Tip will indicate the tab and group containing that command — for example:

Don't forget

You can also right-click the Ribbon and select **Customize the Ribbon** to display the list of commands and view the associated tool tips.

Hot tip

Some of the commands may not currently be included in any group and so are shown as **Commands not in the Ribbon**. You can use Customize to **Add** any of these commands to the Quick Access Toolbar or to the Ribbon.

19

Excel Online App

To use the Excel and other Office Online apps:

1 Launch your web browser and visit **office.com**, then sign into Office Online with your Microsoft Account

Hot tip

Office Online apps are touch-friendly web applications that let you create, edit and share your Excel, Word, PowerPoint and OneNote files from any browser. They can be used with your OneDrive storage.

2 Select the Office Online app you want to use, such as the Online Excel app

3 Open a blank workbook to begin working on a new spreadsheet

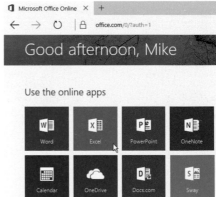

Beware

The functions provided in the Excel Online app are limited and you'll be offered a reduced set of tabs and commands.

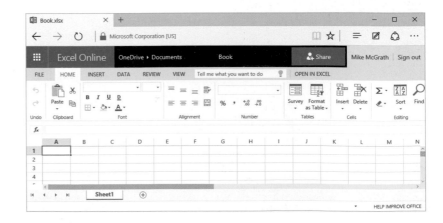

2 Begin with Excel

We start with a simple workbook, to show what's involved in entering, modifying, and formatting data, and in performing calculations. This includes ways in which Excel helps to minimize the effort. We cover printing, look at Excel Help, and discuss the various file formats associated with Excel.

The Excel Window

When you launch Excel, you usually start with the Excel window displaying a blank workbook called "Book1":

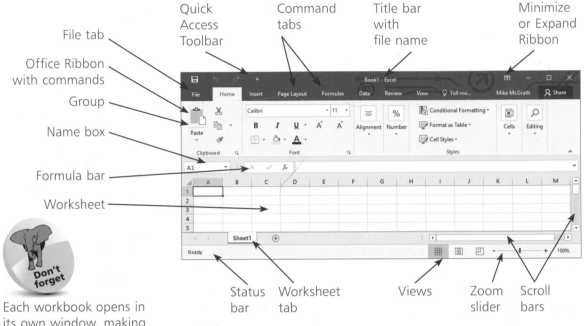

Quick Access Toolbar

Command tabs

Title bar with file name

Minimize or Expand Ribbon

File tab

Office Ribbon with commands

Group

Name box

Formula bar

Worksheet

Status bar

Worksheet tab

Views

Zoom slider

Scroll bars

Don't forget

Each workbook opens in its own window, making it easier to switch between workbooks when you have several open at the same time.

Hot tip

The **Home** tab contains all the commands for basic worksheet activities, in the **Clipboard**, **Font**, **Alignment**, **Number**, **Styles**, **Cells**, and **Editing** groups.

1 Move the mouse over a command icon in one of the groups (e.g. in **Alignment**, on the **Home** tab) to see the command description

2 Click the down-arrow next to a command (e.g. **Merge & Center**) to show the list of related commands

3 Click the arrow by the group name (e.g. **Alignment**) to see the associated dialog box

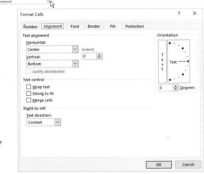

4 Select other tabs to view other cell formatting options

22

...cont'd

By default, Excel provides one array of data (called a worksheet) in the workbook. This is named "Sheet1". Click the + button to add "Sheet2", "Sheet3", etc.

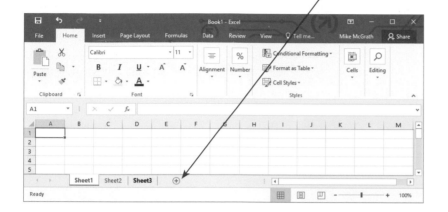

Beware

These are the theoretical limits for worksheets. For very large numbers of records, a database program may be a more suitable choice.

Each worksheet is the equivalent of a full spreadsheet and has the potential for up to 1,048,576 x 16,384 cells, arranged in rows and columns. The rows are numbered 1, 2, 3 and onwards, up to a maximum of 1,048,576. The columns are lettered A to Z, AA to ZZ, and then AAA to XFD. This gives a maximum of 16,384 columns. The combination gives a unique reference for each cell, from A1 right up to XFD1048576. Only a very few of these cells will be visible at any one time, but any part of the worksheet can be displayed on the screen, which acts as a rectangular "porthole" onto the whole worksheet.

Don't forget

The actual number of cells shown depends on screen resolution, cell size, and display mode (e.g. with Ribbon minimized or full-screen).

23

Use the scroll bars to reposition the screen view, or type a cell reference into the name box, e.g. ZN255.

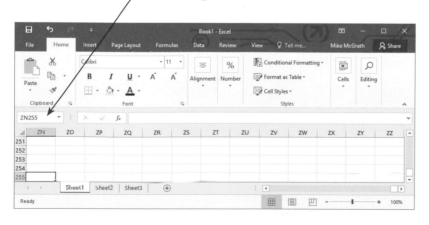

Hot tip

One worksheet is usually all you need to create a spreadsheet, but it can sometimes be convenient to organize the data into several worksheets. See page 44 for other ways to navigate through the worksheet using arrow keys, scroll functions, and split views.

Create a Workbook

We will start by creating a simple, personal budget workbook, to illustrate the processes involved in creating and updating your Excel spreadsheet.

1 When Excel opens, it offers a list of recent workbooks and allows you to open other workbooks, or you can select the blank workbook which is named "Book1" by default – this can be used as the starting point for your new workbook

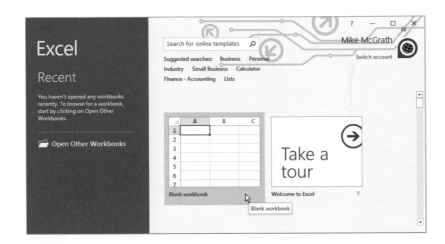

2 Type the spreadsheet title "My Personal Budget" in cell A1, and press the down-arrow, or the **Enter** key, to go to cell A2 (or just click cell A2 to select it)

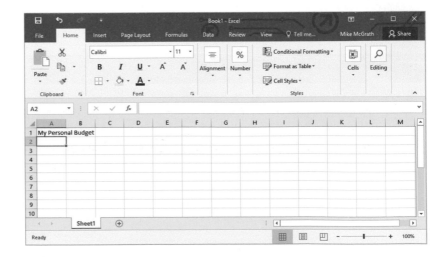

Add Data to the Worksheet

1 Continue to add text to the cells in column A, pressing the down-arrow or **Enter** to move down after each, to create labels in cells A2 to A13:

Income
Salary
Interest/dividend
Total income
Expenses
Mortgage/rent
Utilities
Groceries
Transport
Insurance
Total expenses
Savings/shortage

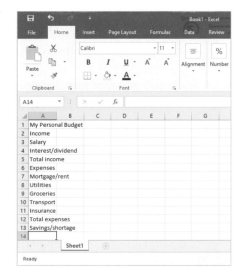

Hot tip

If the text is already available in another document, you can copy and paste the text, to save typing.

2 Click the **File** tab, and select **Save** (or press the **Ctrl + S** keyboard shortcut)

Beware

Save the workbook regularly while creating or updating spreadsheets, to avoid losing your work if a problem arises with the system.

Hot tip

Click **Add a tag** to classify the workbook, with Tag words, such as Title, or Subject. If you create numerous workbooks, these details can help you manage and locate your information.

3 Select a location (in OneDrive or on your computer, then type a file name, e.g. "My Personal Budget", and click **Save**, to add the workbook to the selected storage area

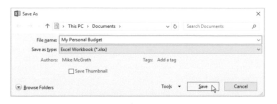

Build the Worksheet

We want to fill in the columns of data for each month of the year, but first, we need an extra row after the title, for the column headings. To add a row to the worksheet:

1 Select the row (click the row number) above where you want to insert another row, e.g. select row 2

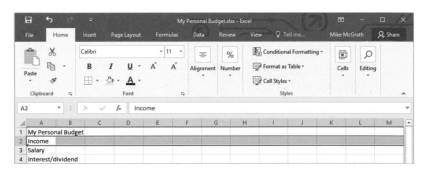

Hot tip

To insert multiple rows, select a block of as many rows as you need, and then click **Insert** – the new rows will be inserted above the selection. Use a similar procedure to insert one or more new columns.

2 Click the **Home** tab and then, in the **Cells** group, click the arrow below **Insert**, and click **Insert Sheet Rows**

3 Click cell B2 in the new row, and type "January", then press **Enter** twice, to move to B4

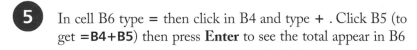

4 Type 3950 in cell B4, press **Enter**, type 775 in cell B5, and press **Enter** again

5 In cell B6 type = then click in B4 and type + . Click B5 (to get **=B4+B5**) then press **Enter** to see the total appear in B6

Don't forget

The = symbol signifies that what follows is a formula. This creates a formula in cell B6, to specify that Total income = Salary plus Interest/dividend. Excel automatically calculates the result and displays it in cell B6. Select the cell and look in the Formula Bar to see the formula.

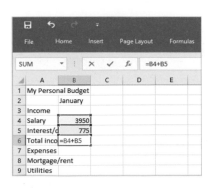

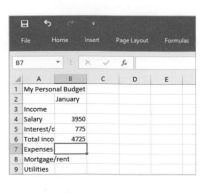

...cont'd

6 Click cell B8, and then type the values 2250, 425, 1150, 350, and 450 (pressing the down-arrow or **Enter** after each)

7 In cell B13, type **=SUM(** and then click B8, type a period, click B12, type **)** and press **Enter**, then click B13 to see the Formula Bar contents

Don't forget

You can click B13, then click the **Σ AutoSum** button in the **Editing** group on the **Home** tab. This automatically sums the adjacent cells, in this case the five cells above, giving **=SUM(B8:B12)**. See page 68 for more details of **AutoSum**.

Some of the labels in column A appear truncated. The full label is still recorded, but the part that overlapped column B cannot be displayed, if the adjacent cell is occupied.

To change the column width to fit the contents:

1 Select the column of labels (click the letter heading)

2 On the **Home** tab, in the **Cells** group, select **Format**

3 Under **Cell Size**, select **AutoFit Column Width**

4 Alternatively, move the mouse pointer over the column boundary, and drag to manually widen or double-click to **AutoFit** to contents

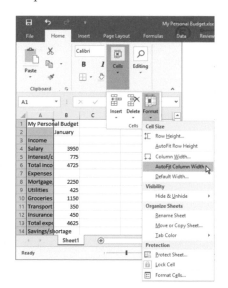

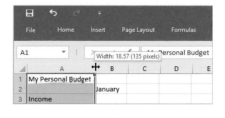

Don't forget

Column width is measured in characters (assuming a standard font). The default is 8.43, but you can set any value from 0 to 255.

Hot tip

To change a group of columns, select the first, hold down **Shift** and select the last. For non-adjacent columns, select the first, hold down **Ctrl** and click other columns.

Fill Cells

We've typed "January", but the rest of the monthly headings can be automatically completed, using the Fill Handle:

1 Select the B2 cell with a "January" heading

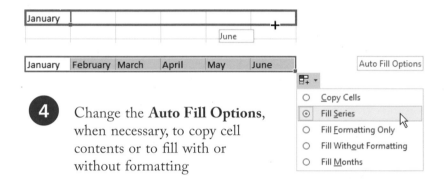

2 Move the mouse to the bottom right corner of the cell to see the + Fill Handle appear

3 Click the Fill Handle and drag adjacent cells to select them, then release the mouse button to fill those cells

4 Change the **Auto Fill Options**, when necessary, to copy cell contents or to fill with or without formatting

Excel recognizes various entry types. If you start with "Jan", rather than "January", adjacent cells fill with "Feb", "Mar", "Apr", etc.

5 Select cell B4, and fill cells C4:G4 with a copy of B4. Repeat for B6 to C6:G6, and for B13 to C13:G13. Select the block of cells B8:B9, and fill cells C8:G9

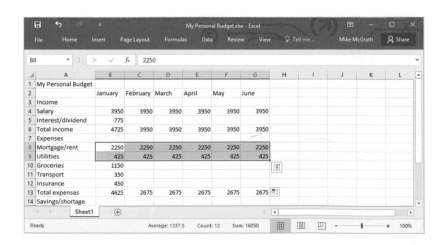

Hot tip

You can also use the right-click menu to edit (cut/copy/delete) a selection of cells and to insert copied cells at another location. Just select the cell(s) with the mouse and right-click to see the options available.

28

Hot tip

Flash Fill detects what you want to do, then enters the rest of your data, following the pattern it recognizes in your data so far.

Don't forget

Formulas are adjusted to show the column change, e.g. **=B4+B5** will become **=C4+C5**, **=D4+D5**, etc. See page 61 for more details on this effect, which is called relative addressing.

Complete the Worksheet

1 Select cell H2, and type "Period" as the heading

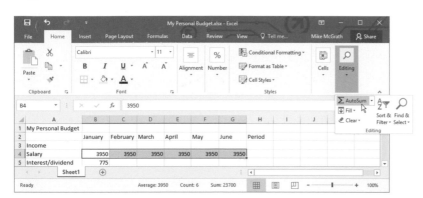

It is sometimes more efficient to fill a whole range of cells, then clear the ones that are not necessary.

2 Select cells B4 to G4, click **AutoSum** in **Editing**, on the **Home** tab, and see that the total gets entered in cell H4

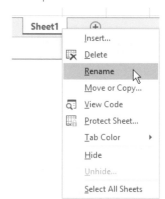

3 Select cell H4, and fill cells H5 to H14, then select cell H7 and press **Delete** (no values to total)

You can right-click the tab for Sheet1 and select **Rename**, calling it "My Personal Budget", for example.

4 Select cell B14, type **=B6-B13**, then press **Enter** (type the whole formula, or select the cells to add their addresses)

5 Select cell B14, then drag and fill to copy the formula, for Total Income-Total Expenses, to the cells C14:G14

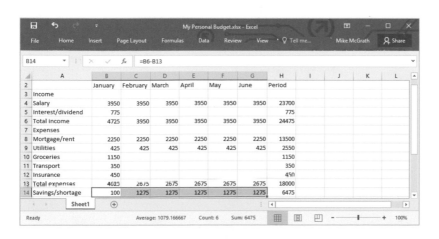

Format the Text

Although not essential for the actual functioning, formatting the text can make it easier to view the workbook, and make prints more readable.

There are numerous changes that you could make, but at this stage we will just make some changes to font size and styles, and to the text placement:

1 Click cell A3, press and hold **Ctrl**, and click cells A6, A7, A13 and A14, then click the arrow next to **Font Size** (in the **Home** tab **Font** group) and select size 14, then click the **Bold** font button

2 Click column label cell B2, press **Shift** and click cell H2, and then select font size 14, **Bold** for cells B2:H2, and select **Align Right** in the **Alignment** group from the **Home** tab

3 Select cell range A1 to H1, then, on the **Home** tab, select **Merge & Center** in the **Home**, **Alignment** group, and select font size 20, **Bold** for the workbook title

30

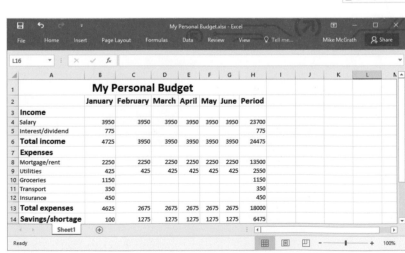

	A	B	C	D	E	F	G	H
1	**My Personal Budget**							
2		January	February	March	April	May	June	Period
3	**Income**							
4	Salary	3950	3950	3950	3950	3950	3950	23700
5	Interest/dividend	775						775
6	**Total income**	4725	3950	3950	3950	3950	3950	24475
7	**Expenses**							
8	Mortgage/rent	2250	2250	2250	2250	2250	2250	13500
9	Utilities	425	425	425	425	425	425	2550
10	Groceries	1150						1150
11	Transport	350						350
12	Insurance	450						450
13	**Total expenses**	4625	2675	2675	2675	2675	2675	18000
14	**Savings/shortage**	100	1275	1275	1275	1275	1275	6475

Format the Numbers

To apply a specific format to numbers in your worksheet:

1 Select the cells that you wish to reformat, and click the down-arrow in the **Number** format box

See page 58 for details of the various types of formats available for numbers in cells.

2 Select **More Number Formats** then choose, for example, **Number**, 2 **Decimal places**, and red for **Negative numbers**

3 Click **OK**, to apply the format

4 Change the width of the columns to display all data (see page 27)

5 Click **Save** from time to time

The **General** format isn't consistent. Decimal places vary, and Excel may apply rounding, to fit numbers in if the column is too narrow.

February	Febru	Febr
3950	3950	3950
567.75	567.8	568
4517.75	4518	4518
2250	2250	2250
425.04	425	425
1124.9	1125	1125
437.5	437.5	438
450	450	450
4687.44	4687	4687
-169.69	-169.7	-170

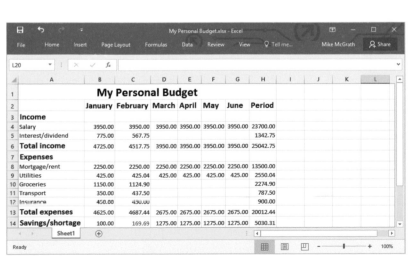

31

Print the Worksheet

If you want to print only part of the data in the worksheet, select the range of cells before selecting **Print**. See page 33.

Beware

If you ever scroll past the end of the data, and accidentally click a key or the spacebar, Excel will think this is part of the worksheet data.

Don't forget

Press the **Zoom to Page** button to toggle between close-up and full-page view. Click the **Show Margins** button to toggle margin indicators.

1 Select the worksheet you want to print (if there's more than one) and click the **File** tab, then click **Print**

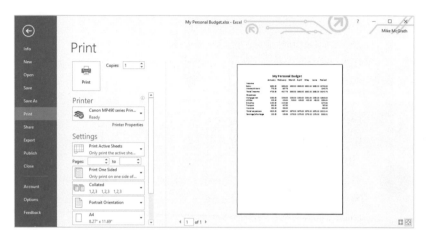

2 You'll see the print options, plus the print preview for your current worksheet

3 Check to see exactly what data will be printed, especially if there are more pages than you were expecting

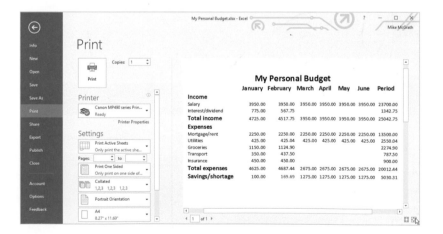

Excel will select a print area that will include all the cells that appear to have data in them (including blanks), and as a result could select a larger print area than you might have anticipated.

...cont'd

4 Click the **Printer** button to change the printer if desired

5 Click the **Settings** button to choose between the active sheet, the entire workbook, or just the current selection

6 Other **Print** settings let you choose the pages to print and to specify duplex, orientation, and paper size

7 Specify the number of copies, then click the **Print** button to send the document to the printer

For printing part of the worksheet, you can preset the print area:

1 Select the range of cells that you normally want printed

2 Select the **Page Layout** tab, click the **Print Area** button in the **Page Setup** group, and select **Set Print Area**

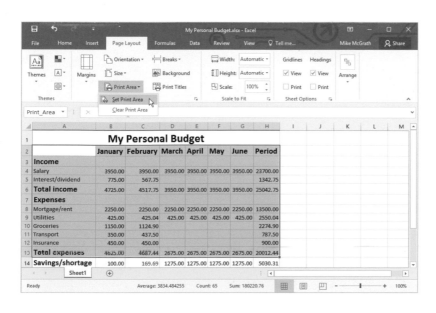

Don't forget

If there is a print area defined, Excel will only print that part of the worksheet. If you don't want to limit the print this time, select **Ignore Print Area**.

Hot tip

If you are sure that the default print settings are what you require, you can add the **Quick Print** button to the Quick Access Toolbar (see page 119) and use this to print immediately.

Insert, Copy and Paste

You can rearrange the contents of the worksheet, or add new data, by inserting rows or columns and copying cells. For example, to add an additional six months of information:

1 Click in column H, press **Shift**, and click in column M

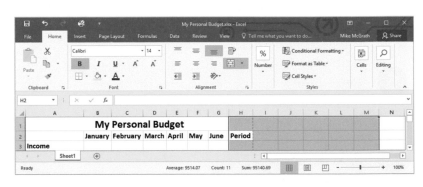

Don't forget

Select ✂ **Cut**, click the new location, and then select 📋 **Paste**, to move the contents of the highlighted cells.

2 Select the **Home** tab, then, in the **Cells** group, click the arrow next to **Insert** and choose **Insert Sheet Columns**

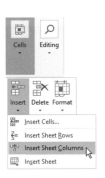

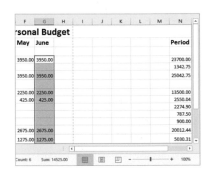

Hot tip

Select the existing month headers and use the Fill Handle (see page 28) to extend the headers through to "December".

3 Select the range G4:G14, click the 📋 **Copy** button, select the range H4:M14, and click the 📋 **Paste** button

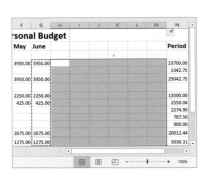

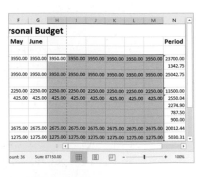

Hot tip

After copying the data range, change the formula in N4 from **=SUM(B4:G4)** to **=SUM(B4:M4)**, and copy the formula into cells N5:N6 and N8:N14.

34

Excel Help

There are two ways to get help when using the Excel app – you can seek help using the **Tell Me** box on the Excel tab bar, or call upon the online **Help** facility for more comprehensive assistance:

1 Click the **Tell Me** box on the tab bar, then type in the topic you want help with. For example, type "fill cells" into the box

2 Choose one of the top five options for local help

3 Alternatively, press the **F1** key on your keyboard to call up online help – a browser-style dialog window appears at the Excel 2016 Help page, listing **Top categories** such as **Getting started** and **Worksheet Basics**

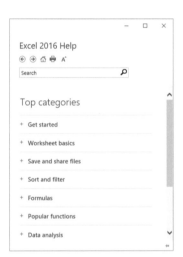

4 Click the + button beside any category to expand that topic and reveal more detailed help

5 To get online help, type "fill cells" into the Search box in the dialog then click the search button

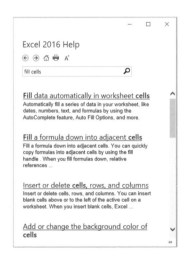

6 Or, click the **Get Help on "fill cells"** item on the **Tell Me** menu to see the same link results list

7 Now, choose a link from the list for specific help

The **Tell Me** box is a great new feature in Excel 2016. It can provide help and also perform a **Smart Lookup**, returning information on any term you enter.

Don't forget

You can use the Back and Forward arrows on the toolbar alongside the Search box to scroll through the results.

Contextual Help

You do not always need to search for help – you can get specific information on a particular command or operation via tooltips:

1 Open a command tab, then move the mouse pointer over a command in one of the groups to reveal the tooltip

Don't forget

Some tooltips have just a brief description, plus a keyboard shortcut, where appropriate. Other tooltips are more expansive.

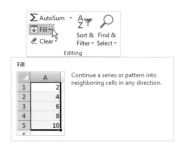

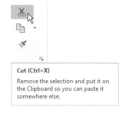

2 If you see the **Help** icon at the foot of the tooltip, click that entry or press **F1** (with the tooltip still visible) to see the relevant article

3 Click a link from a listed item to scroll to the detailed entry

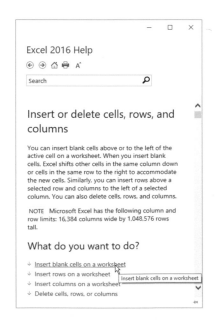

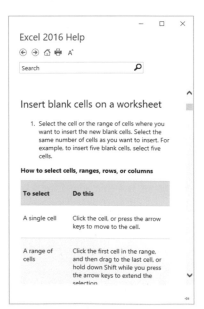

Hot tip

You can still use the Search box to locate additional articles on the topic of interest.

Excel File Formats

When you save a workbook in Excel 2016 (see page 25, Step 2) it uses the default file type **.xlsx**. To save your workbook in the format for previous versions of Excel:

1 Click the **File** tab and select **Save As**, then select the location, e.g. **Documents**

2 Click the box for **Save as type**, and select the **Excel 97–2003 Workbook (*.xls)** file type

3 Change the file name, if desired, and click the **Save** button

4 If you keep the same file name, you will see two documents with different file types

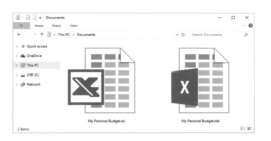

A workbook created in an earlier version of Excel will remain as file type **.xls** if modified – unless you choose to save it in Excel 2016 file format.

You can save and open files in the **Strict Open XML Spreadsheet (*.xlsx)** file format, which allows you to read and write ISO8601 dates to resolve a leap year issue for the year 1900 (see page 59).

The file icons indicate the specific file type, but to see the file extensions, select the **View** tab in File Explorer and click **File name extensions** in the **Show/hide** group.

...cont'd

You can save your workbooks in a variety of other file formats, which will make it easier to share information with others, who may not have the same applications software.

1 Click the **File** tab, select **Save As** and choose the format you want to use, for example, **CSV (Comma delimited)**

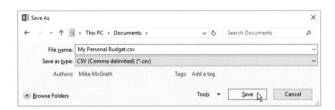

Hot tip

You can also display the **Save As** dialog by pressing the **F12** key.

2 You may be warned of potential conflicts. For example, you should use negative signs or brackets in numbers rather than the red code, since colors are removed

3 Text and number formatting will be removed, and only the current worksheet is saved

Don't forget

Text (Tab delimited) or **CSV (Comma delimited)** formats are often used to exchange information, since most applications will support these formats.

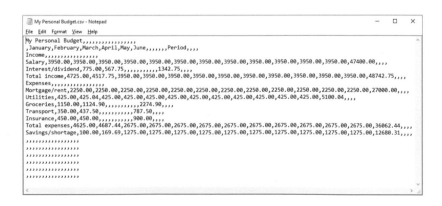

If there's more than one worksheet in your workbook, you'll need to save each one to a separate file.

3 Manage Data

This chapter introduces navigation tools, commands, and facilities, to enable you to find your way around and work with large spreadsheets. It shows how existing data can be imported into Excel, to avoid having to retype information.

Use Existing Data

To identify the file types that can be opened directly in Excel:

1 Within a blank workbook/worksheet, select the **File** tab and click **Open** (or press **Ctrl + O**) and select the file location, e.g. **Documents**

2 Click the file type box, alongside the **File name** box

3 Identify a file type supported by the other application (e.g. **Text** or **CSV**) and then click **Cancel** for the moment

4 Extract data from the other application, as that file type

For example, you might have a number of MP3 tracks created by transferring your CD collection to the hard drive.

Each file stores particulars of the music it contains, including title, album, artist, composer, recording date, quality (the bit rate used for conversion), genre, etc. This information is stored in the music file in the form of MP3 tags.

Don't forget

If the information you want to add to a workbook already exists in another application, you may be able to import it into Excel and use it without having to retype the data, as long as you can prepare it in a suitable file format.

Hot tip

Excel uses features of File Explorer in Windows 10. If you select the box **File name extensions** on the **View** tab in File Explorer (see page 37), you'll see the extended details for the supported file types.

Applications such as **Mp3tag** (**mp3tag.de/en/download.html**) can scan the MP3 files and extract the tags, allowing you to make changes or corrections to the details that are saved.

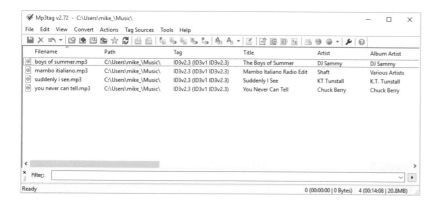

Details of the music are downloaded from the internet when you transfer the tracks to the hard disk, using an application like Windows Media Player. It also records the settings used for the conversion to MP3.

You can scan the music files and then **Export** the tags as a tab-delimited text file, comma-separated **CSV** file, or **HTML** file, with data fields and paragraph marks between the individual lines.

The first line gives field names for data items, and each subsequent line relates to one MP3 file with values for each data field.

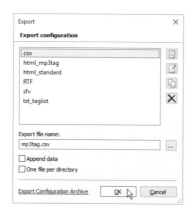

This is just an illustration of how you might extract data from an existing application. Whatever the contents, most applications provide a method for exporting data, usually to a text file format.

mp3tag.csv - Notepad

File Edit Format View Help

Title;Artist;Album;Track;Year;Length;Size;Last Modified;Path;Filename;
The Boys of Summer;DJ Sammy;Heaven;4;2002;314;5.98 MB;1/8/2013;C:\Users\mike_\Music\;boys of summer.mp3;
Mambo Italiano Radio Edit;Shaft;Latino Summer;10/42;2011;170;6.58 MB;1/8/2013;C:\Users\mike_\Music\;mambo italiano.mp3;
Suddenly I See;KT Tunstall;Eye to the Telescope;4;2004;202;4.62 MB;1/8/2013;C:\Users\mike_\Music\;suddenly i see.mp3;
You Never Can Tell;Chuck Berry;St. Louis to Liverpool;6;1964;162;3.71 MB;2/3/2009;C:\Users\mike_\Music\;you never can tell.

Mp3tag - File Overview

file:///C:/Users/mike_/Music/mp3tag.html

Mp3tag - File Overview

11/5/2015

Title	Artist	Album	Track	Year	Genre	Filename
The Boys of Summer	DJ Sammy	Heaven	4	2002	Dance	boys of summer.mp3
Mambo Italiano Radio Edit	Shaft	Latino Summer	10/42	2011	Pop	mambo italiano.mp3
Suddenly I See	KT Tunstall	Eye to the Telescope	4	2004	Pop	suddenly i see.mp3
You Never Can Tell	Chuck Berry	St. Louis to Liverpool	6	1964	Other	you never can tell.mp3

Import Data

1 Within Excel, select **Open** on the **File** tab, then **Browse** to select the data file you exported and click **Open**

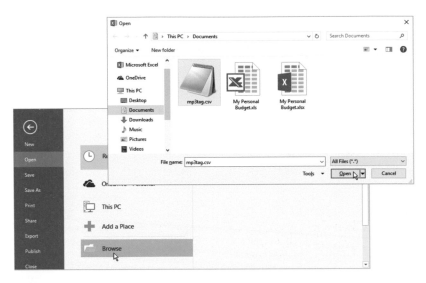

Select the file type you used to export data from the application, and follow the prompts. This example shows the process for text files.

2 This launches the **Text Import Wizard**, which assesses your file and chooses the appropriate settings

Check the settings applied by the import wizard, and make any changes that are required for your particular files.

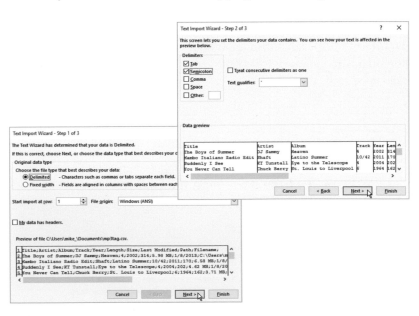

3 Adjust the delimiters and the text qualifier for your file, if any changes are needed, and preview the effect

4 Review each column, decide whether you want to skip that data item, change the format, or accept the suggestion

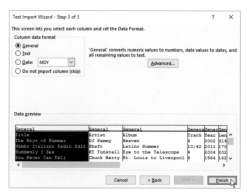

5 Click the **Finish** button to load the data into your Excel worksheet, with lines as rows and data items as columns

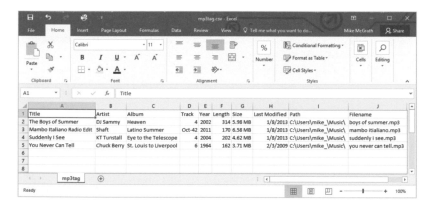

6 Select **Save As**, from the **File** tab, change the file type to "Excel Workbook" and press the **Save** button

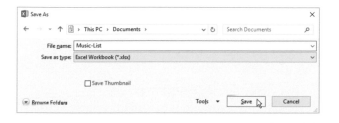

Navigate the Worksheet

If you've transferred information from an existing application and then find yourself with some rather large worksheets, you'll welcome the variety of ways Excel provides to move around the worksheet.

Arrow keys

1 Press an arrow key to move the point of focus (the active cell) one cell per tap, in the direction of that arrow

2 Hold down the **Ctrl** key and press the arrow key, to move to the start or end of a range of data (an adjacent set of occupied cells)

3 To select cells while scrolling to the start or end of a range, hold down the **Ctrl** and **Shift** keys and press the arrow key

4 Press **Ctrl + Shift + (arrow)** again to extend the selection

Scroll Lock

If you press **Scroll Lock** to turn on scroll locking, this changes the actions performed by the arrow keys.

1 The arrow key now moves the window view up or down one row, or sideways one column, depending which arrow key you use (the active cell is not changed)

2 Press **Ctrl + (arrow)** key to shift the view vertically, by the depth of the window, or horizontally, by the width of the window, depending on the arrow key you choose

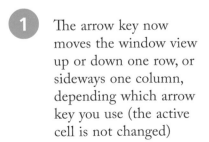

Scroll Bars

1 Click the vertical scroll arrows, to move one row up or down

2 Click on the vertical scroll bar to move the window view up or down

3 Click the horizontal scroll arrows, to move one column to the left or right

4 Click on the horizontal scroll bar to move the window view left or right

5 Click one of the scroll boxes. Excel displays the row number or column letter as you drag the box

Split View

You can split the window, so you can scroll separate parts of the worksheet in two or four panes, independently.

1 Select the cell where you want to apply the split then select the **View** tab and click **Split** in the **Window** group

2 The worksheet now has four panes with separate scroll bars

Don't forget

A scroll box is the thumb button that slides along a scroll bar.

Don't forget

The sizes of the scroll boxes are based on the ratios of visible data to total data, and their positions are the relative vertical and horizontal locations of the visible area within the worksheet.

Hot tip

To reposition either the horizontal or vertical split divider, move the mouse pointer over the bar and drag using the doubled-headed arrow. To remove just double-click the bar.

45

Scroll with the Wheel Mouse

1 Rotate the wheel forward or back, to scroll a few lines at a time

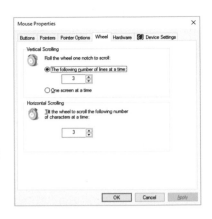

2 To change the amount scrolled, open the Control Panel and select **Mouse**, then click the **Wheel** tab and change the number of lines, or select **One screen at a time**

The **Wheel**, **Mouse Properties** in Windows also allows horizontal scrolling, if the wheel can be tilted left or right.

Continuous Scroll

1 Hold down the wheel button, then drag the pointer away from the origin mark, in the direction you want to scroll

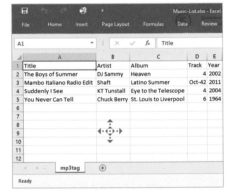

2 Release the wheel when you reach the required position

Hands-Free Scroll

Move the pointer away from the origin mark to speed up scrolling. Move the pointer closer to the origin mark to slow down scrolling.

1 To scroll automatically, click and release the wheel button, then move the mouse in the required direction

2 The further away from the origin mark you place the mouse pointer, the faster the scrolling

3 To slow down scrolling, move the mouse pointer back, closer to the origin mark

4 To stop automatic scrolling, click any mouse button

Keystrokes and Touch

The use of the arrow keys for navigation is covered on page 44. Here are some additional keyboard shortcuts:

End Key

With **Scroll Lock** off, press **End**, then press one of the arrow keys, to move to the edge of the data region

With **Scroll Lock** on, press **End** to move to the cell in the lower-right corner of the window

Ctrl + End moves to the last used cell (end of lowest used row)

Ctrl + Shift + End extends the selection to the last used cell

Home Key

With **Scroll Lock** off, press **Home** to move to the beginning of the current row

With **Scroll Lock** on, press **Home** to move to the cell in the upper-left corner of the window

Ctrl + Home moves to the beginning of the worksheet

Ctrl + Shift + Home extends the selection to the beginning

Page Down Key

Page Down moves one screen down in the worksheet

Alt + Page Down moves one screen to the right

Ctrl + Page Down moves to the next sheet in the workbook

Ctrl + Shift + Page Down selects the current and next sheet

Page Up Key

Page Up moves one screen up in the worksheet

Alt + Page Up moves one screen to the left

Ctrl + Page Up moves to the previous sheet in the workbook

Ctrl + Shift + Page Up selects the current and previous sheet

Tab Key

Tab moves one cell to the right in the worksheet

Shift + Tab moves to the previous cell in the worksheet

If you have a tablet PC or a touch-enabled monitor, you can easily scroll through the worksheet by dragging the screen horizontally or vertically.

Swipe the screen to move across the worksheet by a larger amount.

You can also use touch gestures to select ranges and autofill cells.

Display Excel **Help** (see page 35) for more information about using touch gestures in Excel.

Sort Rows

If you are looking for particular information, and don't know exactly where it appears in the worksheet, you can use Excel commands to help locate the items.

1 Click the column that contains the information and select **Sort & Filter** from the **Home** tab's **Editing** group

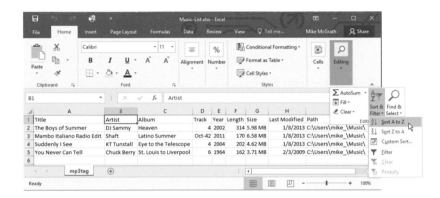

2 Choose **Sort A to Z** (or **Sort Z to A**, if the required information would be towards the end of the list)

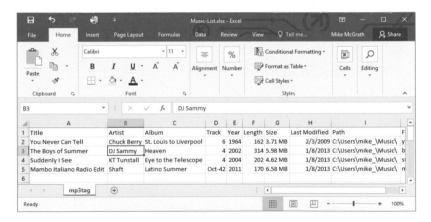

3 Scroll through the list (using the navigation techniques described on pages 44-45) to locate the relevant entries

4 Click **Don't Save** when you close the workbook, to keep the original order

Custom Sort (see page 82) allows you to sort the worksheet by several fields – "Artists" and "Albums", for example.

Excel will sort the rows of data, using the column selected, so all the related data will stay together.

Excel provides a more structured way of handling a range of data like this, with the Excel Table – see page 72.

48

Find Entries

If you'd rather not change the sequence of the rows, you can use the **Find** command to locate appropriate entries.

1 Click the column with the information, choose **Find & Select** from the **Editing** group on the **Home** tab, then click **Find** (or press **Ctrl + F**)

2 Click the **Options** button, if necessary (Excel remembers the last setting)

3 Specify a word or phrase, and select the options. For example, within the **Sheet**, search **By Columns**, look in **Values**, then click **Find Next**

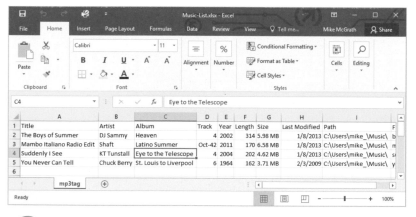

4 Repeat **Find Next**, to locate subsequent matching entries

5 You can click **Find All** to get a list of the cell addresses for matching entries

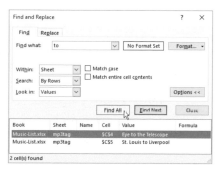

49

Don't forget

Select all the cells in the column – the search will be restricted to that part of the worksheet.

Hot tip

You can include case in the check, and you can require a full match with the entire cell contents.

Filter Information

The **Filter** part of the **Sort & Filter** command can be very helpful in assessing the information you have imported, because it allows you to concentrate on particular sections of the data.

1 Select all the data (for example, click in the data region, press **Ctrl + End**, then press **Shift + Ctrl + Home**)

If there's only one block of data, you can press **Ctrl + A** to select all the cells in the worksheet.

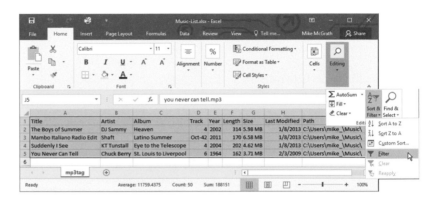

2 Select **Sort & Filter** from the **Home** tab, **Editing** group, and then click the **Filter** command

Arrow boxes will now appear in each column heading

3 Click the arrow box in any column heading, to see a list of unique column values

If you want just a few entries, clear the **(Select All)** box, which clears all the boxes, then just reselect the ones you want.

4 Clear the boxes for unwanted values, to leave those you want to view, e.g. your favorite artists

5 Click **OK** to display only those selected entries

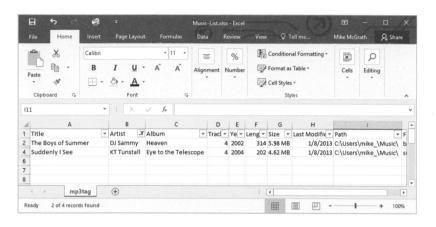

6 Make the changes that are required (e.g. select the "Artist" cells and click the red **Font** button to change the color)

7 Click the arrow button in the column heading again, to see the list of unique values once more

8 Select the **Clear Filter From** option, then click **OK** to see the complete worksheet with the filtered changes

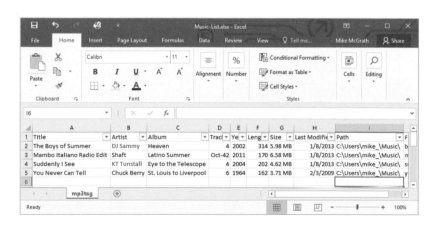

Remove Duplicate Entries

A duplicate entry is where all values in the row are an exact match for all the values in another row.

To find and remove duplicate values:

1 Select the range of cells

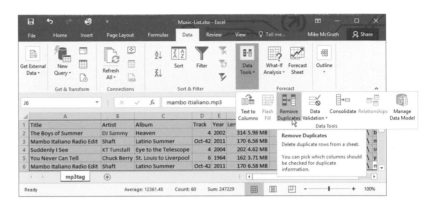

Sorting (see page 48) may help you spot repeated entries when data gets imported twice – but Excel offers a more systematic method.

Duplicate values are based on the displayed value, not on the stored value, so differences in format will make the entry appear unique.

If you want to keep the original worksheet with the duplicates, save the revised version under a new name.

2 Select the **Data** tab, then, from the **Data Tools** group, click **Remove Duplicates**

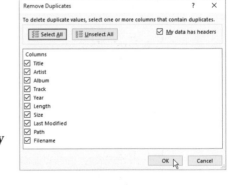

3 Click **Select All**, to ensure all columns are checked

4 Clear the box for **My data has headers**, if you suspect these may be repeated

5 Click **OK** to detect and delete the duplicates

A message is displayed, indicating how many duplicate values were removed and how many unique values remain.

6 Click **OK**. There's no Undo for this operation – it's permanent

Check Spelling

A spelling check is sometimes a useful way to assess the contents of some sections of your worksheet.

1 Select the relevant parts: for example, click one column, press and hold **Ctrl**, then click more columns in turn

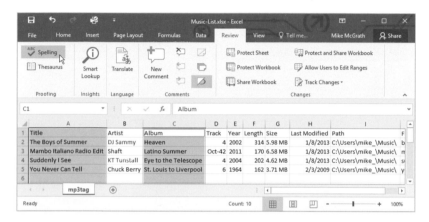

Select columns of data that contain text values that need spell-checking.

2 Select the **Review** tab, then click the **Spelling** command in the **Proofing** group (or press **F7**)

3 Click **Change All**, if the word being corrected is likely to appear more than once

4 Click **Ignore All**, if there are spelling warnings for valid terms or foreign words

You can add foreign language dictionaries if they are required to spell check text in your worksheets.

5 Click **OK** when the check is completed

Freeze Headers and Labels

When you navigate a worksheet, column headings and row labels will move off screen, making it more difficult to identify the data elements. To keep these visible, start by clicking on the worksheet:

There are predefined options for a single heading row, or a single label column.

1 Click the cell below the headings and to the right of the labels (e.g. with one row and one column, choose cell B2)

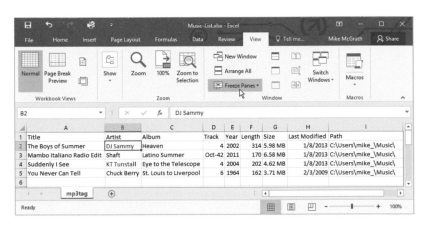

54

You can now scroll down and the headings stay visible. Similarly, if you scroll across, the row labels now stay visible.

2 Select the **View** tab and click the **Freeze Panes** command, from the **Window** group – then click an option from the list

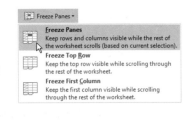

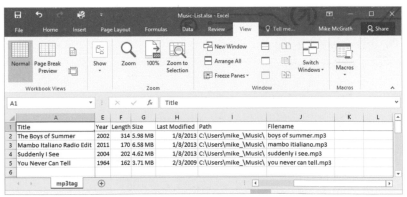

You cannot freeze rows and columns when you share your workbooks for collaborative changes.

3 The first entry in **Freeze Panes** now changes to the undo option, **Unfreeze Panes**

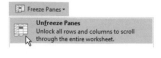

Hide Columns or Rows

To make it easier to view particular portions of the worksheet, you can tell Excel not to display certain columns or rows:

1 Select the columns or rows that you want to hide. For example, to select non-adjacent columns, select the first column, hold down **Ctrl**, then select subsequent columns

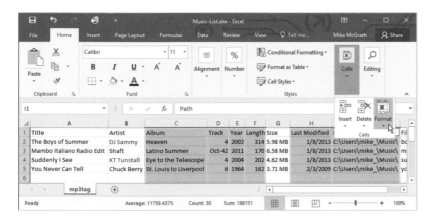

2 Select the **Home** tab, then click the **Format** command from the **Cells** group

3 Select **Hide & Unhide**, then click **Hide Columns** or **Hide Rows**, as required

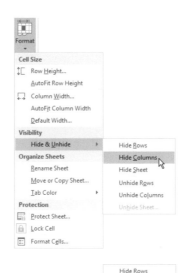

To redisplay the hidden columns or hidden rows:

1 Select both columns either side of hidden columns, or select the rows above and below hidden rows

2 Open the **Hide & Unhide** menu and select **Unhide Columns** or **Unhide Rows**

Hot tip

You can also right-click a selected group of rows or columns, and then click **Hide** or **Unhide** from the context menu that appears.

Hot tip

You cannot cancel the selection of a cell, or range of cells in a non-adjacent selection, without canceling the entire selection.

Don't forget

A column or row also becomes hidden if you change its column width or row height to zero. The **Unhide** command will reveal columns and rows hidden in this way.

Protect a Worksheet

56

1 Select any column (e.g. "Track") that you might want to update

2 On the **Home** tab, select **Format** from the **Cells** group, then click **Format Cells**

3 Select the **Protection** tab, then uncheck the **Locked** box, and **Lock Text** box if also displayed

4 To protect the remaining part of the worksheet, select the **Review** tab and click **Protect Sheet** in the **Changes** group

5 Ensure that all users are allowed to select locked and unlocked cells, then click **OK**

6 You can edit cells in the chosen columns, but you get an error message if you edit other cells

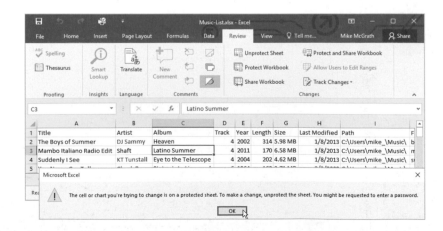

4 Formulas and Functions

Various formats for numbers are explained, and options for referencing cell locations are reviewed. These provide the basis for an introduction to functions and formulas, beginning with operators and calculation sequence, including formula errors and cell comments.

Number Formats

The cells in the worksheet contain values, in the form of numbers or text characters. The associated cell formats control how the contents are displayed.

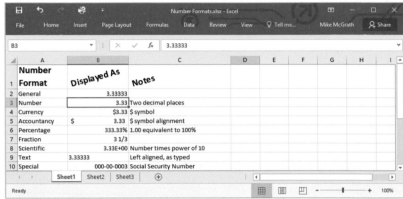

The default format is **General**, which is based on the cell contents. Use **Number** when you need decimal places, and **Currency** or **Accounting** for monetary values. The **Special** format is for structured numbers, e.g. zip or postal codes.

Cells B2 to B10 above, all contain the same value (3.33333) but each cell has a different format, which changes the way the number appears on the worksheet. To set the number format:

1 Select the cell or cells, then click the **Home** tab and choose a format from the drop-down menu on the **Number** group

2 For greater control of how numbers appear, such as negative numbers, select **More Number Formats** from the drop-down menu and choose in the **Format Cells** dialog

The values can be typed directly into the cells, imported from another application (see page 42), or created by a formula.

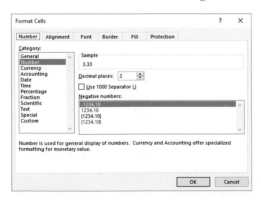

...cont'd

Date and **Time** are also number formats, but in this case the number is taken as the days since a base point in time.

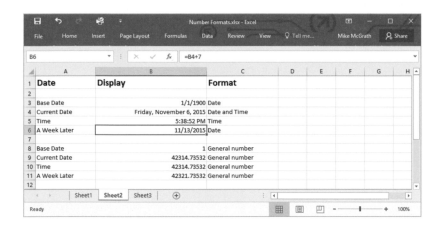

Cells B3 to B6 are formatted as **Date** or **Time**. The same numbers are shown in cells B8 to B11, formatted as **General**. This shows that day 1 is January 1st 1900, day 42314 is November 6th 2015, while day 42321 is a week later. Decimals indicate part days.

To set or change the date or time format:

1 Open **Format Cells**, select the **Number** tab, and click **Date** or **Time** to see the list of format options

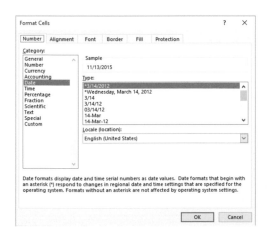

2 Choose a format option and click **OK**, or click **Custom** to see other time and date formatting options

Because dates and times are stored as numbers, you can use them in formulas and calculations.

Some of the formats depend on the specific country and locations defined in the Windows regional options, found in the Control Panel.

When dates are based on 1/1/1900, day 60 is incorrectly treated as February 29th 1900. In Excel 2016 this can be resolved using the **Strict Open XML** file format (see page 37).

Text Formats

Excel recognizes cells containing text, such as header and label cells, and gives them the **General** format, with default text format settings (left-aligned, and using the standard font). You can view or change the format for such cells:

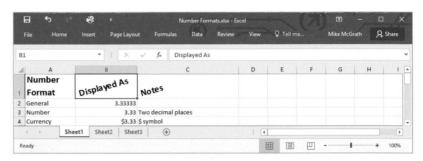

1 Select a cell or range of cells, then click the bottom right-hand corner button on the **Font** group to open **Format Cells**

2 Select the **Font** tab to adjust the font, style, size, or color

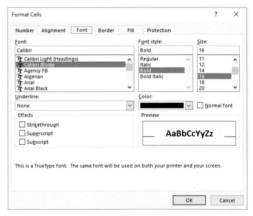

3 Select the **Alignment** tab and change the text controls, alignment, or orientation settings

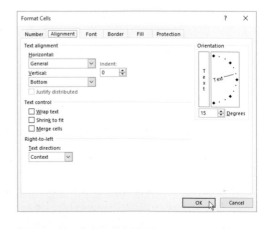

Relative References

A cell could contain a formula, rather than an actual value. Excel performs the calculation the formula represents, and displays the result as the value for that cell. For example:

In this worksheet, cell D3 shows the amount spent on DVDs (price times quantity), calculated as **=B3*C3**.

The formulas for D4 and D5 are created by copying and pasting D3. The cell references in the formula are relative to the position of the cell containing them, and are automatically updated for the new location.

A cell reference in this form is known as a "relative reference", and this is the normal type of reference used in worksheets.

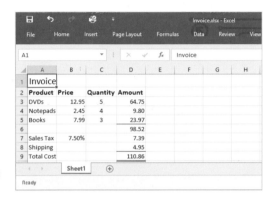

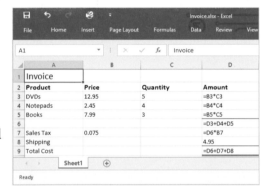

Hot tip

The cells hold formulas as stored values, but it is the results that normally get displayed. To switch between results and formulas, press **Ctrl+`**

 (grave accent key), or select the **Formulas** tab and click **Show Formulas**.

61

The results of formulas can be used in other formulas, so the total in cell D6 is calculated as **=D3+D4+D5**.

The sales tax in cell D7 is calculated as **=D6*B7**. Note that B7 is displayed as a value of 7.5%, the cell format being **Percentage**. The actual value stored in the cell is 0.075.

The worksheet could have used a constant value instead, such as **=D6*7.5/100** or **=D6*7.5%**. However, having the value stored in a cell makes it easier to adapt the worksheet when rates change. It also helps when the value is used more than once.

The shipping cost in cell D8 is a stored constant.

The final calculation in the worksheet is the total cost in cell D9, which is calculated as **=D6+D7+D8**.

Don't forget

The value B7 is a relative cell reference, like the others, but this may not be the best option. See page 62 for the alternative, the absolute cell reference.

Absolute References

Assume that calculation of the sales tax per line item is required. The value in cell E3 for the DVDs product would be **=D3*B7**.

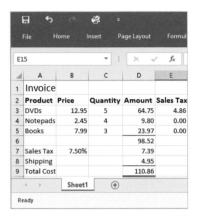

C	D	E
Quantity	Amount	Sales Tax
5	=B3*C3	=D3*B7
4	=B4*C4	=D4*B8
3	=B5*C5	=D5*B9
	=D3+D4+D5	
	=D6*B7	
	4.95	
	=D6+D7+D8	

To fix the column, place $ before the column letter. Likewise, to fix the row, put $ before the row number. The other part of the reference will change when the formula is copied.

You might be tempted to copy this formula down into cells E4 and E5, but, as you see above, the results would be incorrect, giving zero values, because the relative reference B7 would be incremented to B8 and then B9, both of which are empty cells. The answer is to fix the reference to B7, so that it doesn't change when the formula is copied. To indicate this, you edit the formula, to place a $ symbol in front of the row and column addresses.

Select a cell reference in a formula, and press F4 to cycle between relative, absolute, and mixed cell references.

C	D	E
Quantity	Amount	Sales Tax
5	=B3*C3	=D3*$B$7
4	=B4*C4	=D4*$B$7
3	=B5*C5	=D5*$B$7
	=D3+D4+D5	
	=D6*B7	
	4.95	
	=D6+D7+D8	

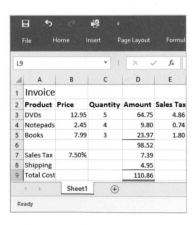

Copy this formula down into cells E4 and E5, the reference **$B$7** doesn't change, so the results are correct. This form of cell reference is known as an "absolute reference". A cell reference with only part of the address fixed, such as **$D3** or **D$3**, would be known as a "mixed reference".

Name References

Names provide a different way of referring to cells in formulas. To create a name for a cell or cell range:

1 Select the cell, or the group of cells you want to name

2 Click the Name box, on the left of the Formula Bar

3 Type the name that you'll be using to refer to the selection, then press **Enter**

4 Click the **Formulas** tab and select the **Name Manager**, in the **Defined Names** group, to view names in the workbook

Names create absolute references to cells or ranges in the current worksheet. They can be used in formulas, and when these are copied, the references will not be incremented.

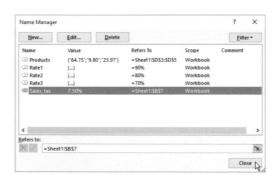

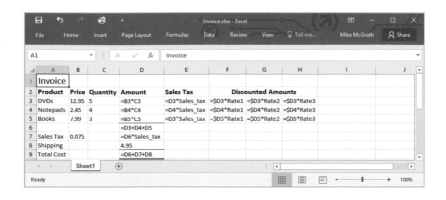

Names must start with a letter, underscore, or backslash. They can contain letters, numbers, periods, and underscores, but not spaces, and case is ignored. Their maximum length is 255 characters.

Hot tip

Names can be defined for a cell, for a range or group of cells, or for constants and functions.

Beware

You cannot use certain names, such as "R1", "R2", "R3", since these are actual cell references. You must specify non-ambiguous names, such as "Rate1", "Rate2", "Rate3", etc.

Operators

The formulas shown so far have used several operators (+, *, %), but there are many other operators you might use, in a number of categories, including the following:

Operator	Meaning	Examples
Arithmetic		
+ (plus sign)	Addition	**A7+B5**
- (minus sign)	Subtraction Negation	**C6-20** **-C3**
* (asterisk)	Multiplication	**C5*C6**
/ (forward slash)	Division	**C6/D3**
% (percent sign)	Percent	**20%**
^ (caret)	Exponentiation or Power	**D3^2**
Comparison		
= (equal)	Equal to	**A1=B1**
> (greater than)	Greater than	**A1>B1**
< (less than)	Less than	**A1<B1**
>= (greater than with equal)	Greater than or equal	**A1>=B1**
<= (less than with equal)	Less than or equal	**A1<=B1**
<> (not equal)	Not equal	**A1<>B1**
Text		
& (ampersand)	Connect/join	**"ABCDE"&"FGHI"**
Reference		
: (colon)	Range	**B5:B15**
, (comma)	Union	**SUM(B5:B15,D5:D15)**
(space)	Intersection	**B2:D6 C4:F8**

Don't forget

Operators can be applied to constants, cell references, or functions.

Don't forget

The results of any of these comparisons will be a logical value – either True or False.

Hot tip

The Intersection of two ranges is a reference to all the cells that are common between the two ranges.

Calculation Sequence

The order in which a calculation is performed may affect the result. As an example, the calculation **6+4*2** could be interpreted in two different ways. If the addition is performed first, this would give **10*2**, which equals 20. However, if the multiplication is performed first, the calculation becomes **6+8**, which equals 14.

To avoid any ambiguity in calculations, Excel evaluates formulas by applying the operators in a specific order. This is known as "operator precedence". The sequence is as follows:

1	: ▯ ,	Colon Space Comma
2	-	Negation
3	%	Percentage
4	^	Exponential
5	* /	Multiplication Division
6	+ -	Addition Subtraction
7	&	Concatenation
8	= < > <= >= <>	Comparison

When the formula has several operators with the same precedence, multiplication and division for example, Excel evaluates the operators from left to right.

These are some example formulas that illustrate the effect of operator precedence on the calculation result:

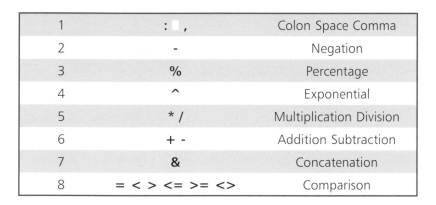

You use parentheses to change the order of evaluation, since the expressions within parentheses are evaluated first. If there are parentheses within parentheses, Excel evaluates the expression in the innermost pair of parentheses first, then works outwards.

Operator precedence is a mathematical concept used by all programming languages and applications, such as spreadsheet programs that include computation.

Operator precedence in Excel is not always the same as mathematical precedence. For example, take the expression **-3²**. This is entered as **-3^2** which Excel evaluates as **(-3)^2** which is +9. However, mathematically you'd expect **-(3^2)** which is -9.

	A	B
1	9	=-3^2
2	9	=(-3)^2
3	-9	=-(3^2)

Functions

Functions are predefined formulas that perform calculations based on specific values, called arguments, provided in the required sequence. The function begins with the function name, followed by an opening parenthesis, the arguments for the function separated by commas, and a closing parenthesis. They are used for many types of calculation, ranging from simple to highly complex.

If you are unsure which function is appropriate for the task, Excel will help you search for the most appropriate. To select a function in the example Invoice worksheet:

Hot tip

Arguments can be numbers, text, cell references, or logical values (True or False).

Don't forget

Several functions in Excel 2016 can be found in the various categories offered on page 88.

Hot tip

To select or change the arguments, click the **Collapse Dialog** button, select the cells on the worksheet, then press the **Expand Dialog** button.

1 Click the cell where you want to use a function as the formula, the total amount cell D6, for example

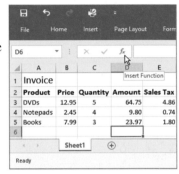

2 Click **Insert Function**, on the Formula Bar

3 Enter the phrase "Add numbers" in the **Search for a function** box, and click **Go** to list related functions

4 Select the most appropriate function, in this case **SUM**, and click **OK**

5 Review the arguments suggested, in this case range D3:D5, see the answer this gives, adjust if needed then click **OK** to **Insert Function**

...cont'd

AutoComplete

Even when you know the function needed, Excel will help you set it up, to help avoid possible syntax and typing errors:

1 Click the worksheet cell, and begin typing the function. For example, click the total cost cell D9 and type **=s**

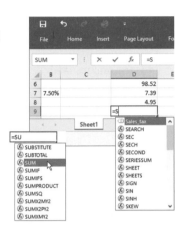

2 Excel lists functions that match so far, so you can select a function and see its description, scroll down to see more names, or continue typing, for example **=su**, to narrow the list

Hot tip

Click on the function name in the prompt, to display help for that function.

3 When you find the function that you require, double-click the name, then enter the arguments that are shown

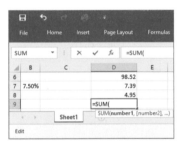

4 For example, click D6, press period, and click D8

5 Type the closing parenthesis, and then press **Enter**

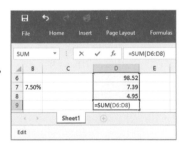

Don't forget

Type the range name, if you have already defined the required cells (see page 63).

6 The formula with the function is stored in the cell, and the result of the operation will be displayed

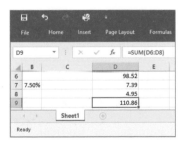

As always, you should save the spreadsheet from time to time, to preserve your changes.

AutoSum

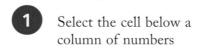

1 Select the cell below a column of numbers

2 Click **AutoSum**, in the **Editing** group on the **Home** tab

3 Press **Enter**, or click on the tick in the Formula Bar, to add the function

4 Similarly, select the cell to the right of a row of numbers and click **AutoSum** to total them

When the selected cell could be associated with a row or a column, **AutoSum** will usually favor the column. However, you can adjust the direction or extent of the range in the formula before you apply it to the worksheet.

The **AutoSum** function is also provided in the **Function Library** group, on the **Formulas** tab, along with **Insert Function**, **Recently Used**, and various sets of functions such as **Financial** and **Logical**.

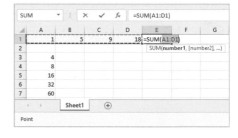
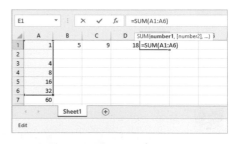

Formula Errors

Excel helps you to avoid some of the more common errors when you are entering a formula:

1 When you type a name, Excel outlines the associated cell or range, so you can confirm that it is the correct selection

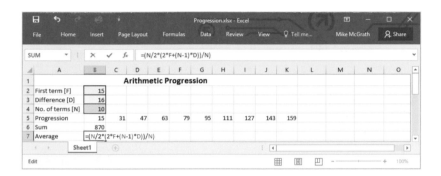

2 With nested functions, Excel colors the parentheses, to help you ensure that they are in matching open/close pairs

3 If you do make an error, such as the extra parenthesis shown above, it is often detected and corrected

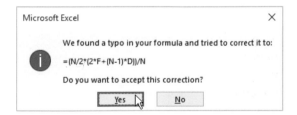

4 If the result overflows the available space, Excel displays **#** hash signs

5 There's a similar display for other errors, but, in addition, a green flash shows in the top left-hand corner of the cell

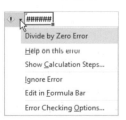

6 Select the cell, then click the information icon for more details

This totals and averages the terms in a number series, with formulas that have several levels of parentheses. Here, the final parenthesis needs to be deleted, as Excel will detect.

In this example, F, D, and N are defined names.

Other common errors displayed this way include **#REF!** (invalid reference) and **#NAME?** (name not recognized).

Add Comments

You can add notes to a cell, perhaps to explain the way in which a particular formula operates:

1 Click the cell where the comment is meant to appear

2 Select the **Review** tab, and click **New Comment**, in the **Comments** group

3 Your username is shown, but you can delete this, then add your comments

> **Mike McGrath:**
> 31 This formula displays the next number in the series, until the required N terms have been displayed, then it displays a blank. It is copied into the cells to the right.

4 Format the text, if desired, and then click outside the comment box to finish

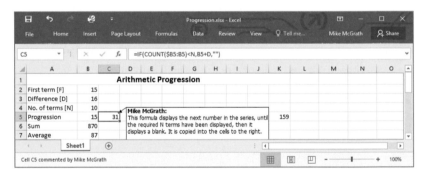

5 The presence of a comment is indicated by the red flash at the top right corner of the cell, and the comment box appears when you move the mouse over the cell

6 The **Edit Comment** command replaces the **New Comment** command, when the selected cell contains an existing comment

5 Excel Tables

The Excel table structure helps you to keep sets of data separate, so that you don't accidentally change other data when you are inserting or deleting rows and columns. There are other benefits also, such as structured cell references, automatic filters, sorts, and subtotals.

Create an Excel Table

To make it easier to manage and analyze a group of related data, you can turn a range of cells into an Excel Table. The range should contain no empty rows or empty columns.

To illustrate this feature, a table is used to interpret the genre (music classification) codes contained in the MP3 tags for music files (see page 40). This field often appears as a genre code such as (2) for Country music, or (4) for Disco. Search on the internet for "ID3 genre code table", and select a suitable web page. For example, we found a useful table online at **gnu.org.ua/software/idest/manual/html_section/Genre-Codes.html**

Hot tip

In an "Excel Table", the rows and columns are managed independently from the data in other rows and columns on the worksheet. In earlier releases of Excel, this feature was called an "Excel List".

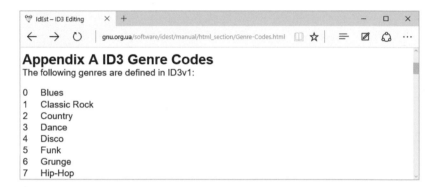

1 Select the table in your web browser, then press **Ctrl + C**

2 Open the "Music-List" worksheet, and type headers "GenreID#" and "Genre" in two empty columns

Beware

The Genre code is contained in brackets, and the value will therefore be treated as a negative number when the data is imported to an Excel worksheet.

3 Select the second cell in the first of those columns then press **Ctrl + V** to copy the code table into the worksheet

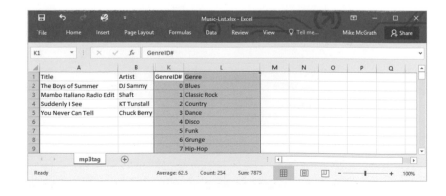

...cont'd

4 With the data and headers selected, click the **Insert** tab, then click **Table** in the **Tables** group

5 Check that the appropriate range of data is selected

6 If the first row has headers, select **My table has headers**, otherwise you'd let Excel generate default headers

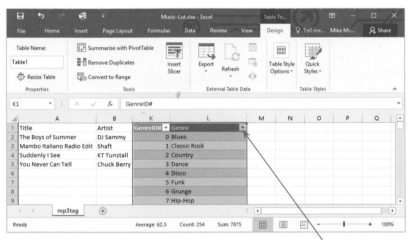

The table is given the default banding style, and **Filter** buttons are automatically added in the header row of each column, allowing you to sort or filter the contents. The table will be given a default name, such as "Table1". To change this name:

1 Click in the table, and click the **Design** tab

2 Click the **Table Name** box in the **Properties** group, to highlight the name

3 Type a new name for the table, e.g. "Code", and press **Enter** to apply the change (and update all references to the old table name)

It may be best to remove worksheet protection and unfreeze panes, before you insert the new data.

If you click in the table, the context-sensitive **Table Tools** and **Design** tabs are displayed, so that you can customize or edit the table.

You can also change the names of tables, using the **Name Manager** on the **Formulas** tab (see page 63).

Edit Tables

You can insert more than one table in the same worksheet, and work with each of them independently. Inserting or deleting rows or columns in one table will not affect other tables.

Click adjacent cells to delete more than one column or row in the table at a time.

Don't click the **Delete** button itself, or you will delete the cells rather than display the menu. If you do delete cells, press the **↩ Undo** button on the Quick Access Toolbar.

1 Select the music data and click **Table** on the **Insert** tab, to create another table, and change its name to "Music"

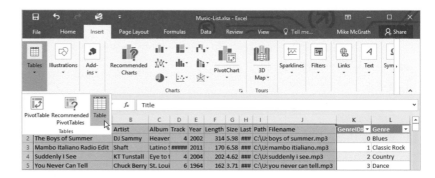

2 Click any unrequired columns in the new "Music" table, then select **Home**, click the arrow next to **Delete** in the **Cells** group, and choose **Delete Table Columns**

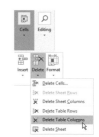

3 Click in the last cell of the "Code" table, and press **Tab** – to add a row

4 Type an entry, such as "126", "New", then add another row with "127", "New" and another with "255", "Other"

5 Select the cells with values 126 and 127, then select the **Home** tab, and choose **Cells**, **Delete**, **Delete Table Rows**

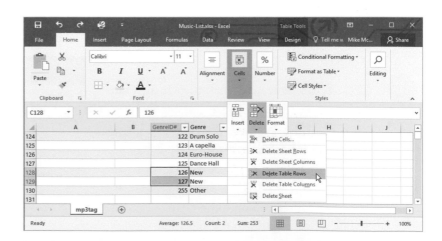

Table Styles

The **Design** tab provides options to change the formatting of the rows and columns in the table.

1 Specify if there's a header row, and turn banding on or off, using settings in the **Table Style Options** group

Styles are grouped into light, medium, and dark sets, with additional effects for end columns, and for banding.

2 Click the **Quick Styles** button, in the **Table Styles** group, to view the full list of styles

3 The Styles Selection bar is displayed, if there's room on the ribbon, and you can scroll the styles, or press the **More** button to show the full list

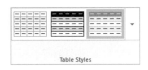

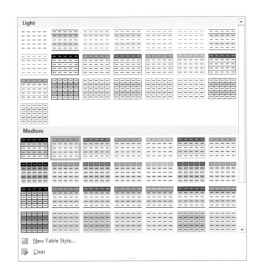

4 Make changes to the **Table Style Options**, and the new effects are incorporated into the **Styles Selection** panel

Move the mouse pointer over any one of the style options, and the table will immediately illustrate the effects that would be applied, if you selected that option.

Table Totals

You can add a Total Row at the end of the table, and display the totals for columns (or use another function appropriate to the type of information stored in the column). To do this:

1 Click in the table, select the **Design** tab, and click the **Total Row** box in the **Table Style Options** group

2 The Total Row is added as the last row of the table, and the last column is given a total value – 8 (Filename) here

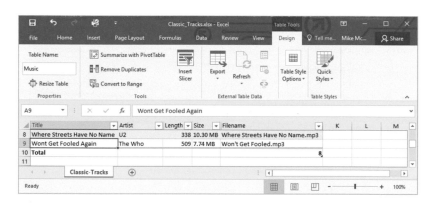

3 Select the Total cell, and click the arrow to see the function applied (in this case the function is **COUNT**)

4 You can apply a Total to any column. For Title you could use **COUNT** again, but for Length you might prefer **SUM**

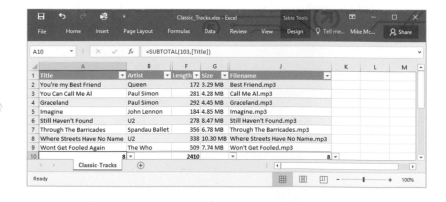

The **Subtotal** function is inserted, with a number to indicate the operation:

101	AVERAGE
102	COUNT
103	COUNTA
104	MAX
105	MIN
106	PRODUCT
107	STDEV
108	STDEVP
109	SUM
110	VAR
111	VARP

Subtotal uses structured references for the table (see page 78).

The **More Functions...** drop-down menu option allows any Excel function to be used to compute the total for that column.

Count Unique Entries

For the Artist column, you can count all unique entries, to give the numbers of individual artists stored in the table:

1 Click in the Total cell for the Artist column, and begin typing the function **=sum(1/countif(**

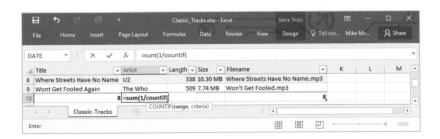

2 Click the Artist header, to extend the formula

3 Type a comma, click the Artist header again, and then type two closing parentheses

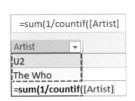

4 This is an array formula, so press **Shift + Ctrl + Enter** (rather than just **Enter**), and the count will be displayed

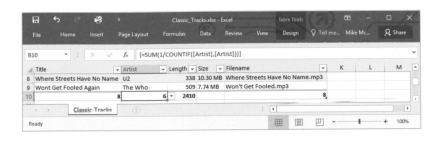

Hot tip

This calculates the frequency for each entry, inverts these counts, and sums up the resulting fractions. For example, if an entry appears three times, you get 1/3 + 1/3 + 1/3 for that entry, giving a count of 1. Each unique entry adds another 1.

77

Beware

This method of counting the number of duplicate entries assumes there are no empty cells in the range being checked.

Structured References

The formulas shown for the totals illustrate the use of structured references. These allow you to refer to the contents of a table, using meaningful names, without having to be concerned about the specific row numbers and column letters, or changes that are caused when rows and columns are added or deleted. The structured references use the table name and column specifiers:

=Music	All data in a table named "Music"
=Music[Length]	All data in a Music table's column named "Length"

You can add a special item specifier, to refer to particular parts:

=Music[#All]	The entire Music table, including headers, data and totals
=Music[#Data]	All data in a Music table
=Music[#Headers]	The header row of a Music table
=Music[#Totals]	The totals row of a Music table
=[@Length]	The intersection of the "Length" column with the active row (n)

Formulas within the table, such as subtotals on the Totals Row, can leave off the table name. This forms an unqualified structured reference, e.g. **[Filename]**. However, outside the table, you need the fully qualified structured reference, e.g. **Music[Filename]**.

The use of structured references in formulas is more efficient than using full column references (e.g. **$F:$F**), dynamic ranges, or arrays.

Earlier versions of Excel referenced this intersection as **Music [[#This Row],[Length]]**, but it's simplified in Excel 2016 to **[@Length]**.

You should avoid the use of special characters, such as space, tab, line feed, comma, colon, period, bracket, quote mark, or ampersand in your table and column names.

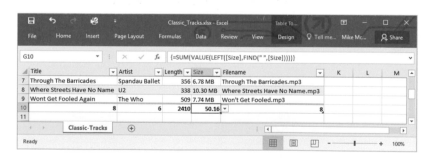

The formula in cell G10 on the total row above includes two unqualified structured references to the Size column. It separates the numeric values from the "MB" text by finding the single space within each cell to display the total file size of all tracks.

Calculated Columns

You can add a calculated column to an Excel table. This uses a single formula that adjusts for each row, automatically expanding to include additional rows.

Start by inserting a new column in the table:

1 Click the far right column of a table, then select the **Home** tab, and click the arrow next to **Insert** – which is found in the **Cells** group

2 Click **Insert Table Columns to the Right**, and then rename the new column as "Style" (i.e. style of music)

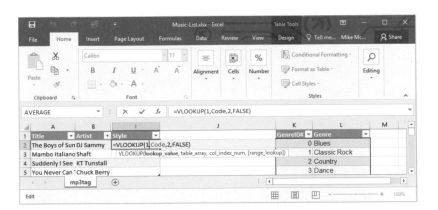

3 Click anywhere in the Style column and type a formula e.g. **=VLOOKUP(1,Code,2,FALSE)** then press **Enter** – to see it automatically filled into all cells of the column

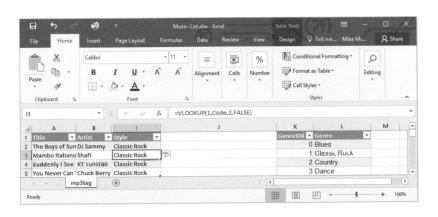

You need to enter the formula only once, and you won't need to use the **Fill** or **Copy** command when the table grows.

The **VLOOKUP** formula in this example is a vertical table lookup. It matches the value 1, in the first column of the Code table (the GenreID#). It then copies the associated value on that row in the second column of the code table (the Genre) into the Styles column. See page 90 for an example of an **HLOOKUP** (a horizontal lookup).

Insert Rows

1 Scroll to the last cell in the table, press **Tab** to add a new row and you'll see that the new formula is replicated

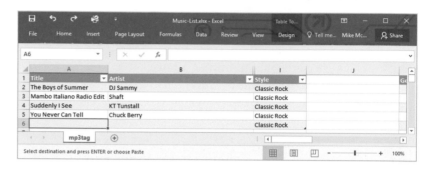

Beware

Adding empty rows may cause temporary errors in formulas that need data in all cells, as illustrated here. The problems will be resolved as soon as the data gets added.

2 To add data from a text file (see page 42), click a cell in an empty part of the worksheet and select **From Text** (on the **Data** tab in the **Get External Data** group)

3 Locate and double-click the data file, then use the **Text Import Wizard** to specify the structure of the data file

Hot tip

You cannot import data directly from an external source into the table, so you must use another part of the worksheet as an interim.

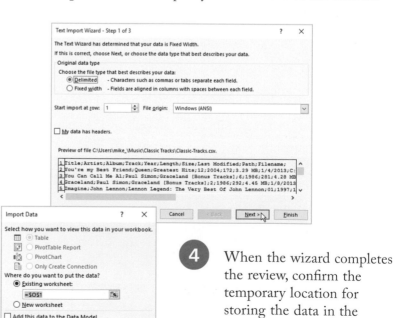

4 When the wizard completes the review, confirm the temporary location for storing the data in the worksheet

5 Highlight the new data (excluding the header row), select the **Home** tab, and click **Copy** from the **Clipboard** group

Hot tip

You can type new rows directly into the table, pressing **Tab** at the end of each row, ready to enter the next row.

6 Select the first cell in the new row added to the table then click **Paste**, from the **Clipboard** group

7 Additional rows are inserted into the table as necessary, to hold the new data records

Don't forget

When the rows have been inserted, you can delete the temporary data stored in the worksheet.

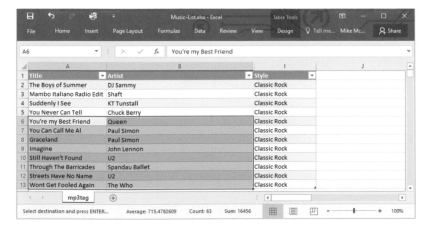

8 The data rows are copied into the extended table

9 You'll see that Style, the calculated column, is extended and updated to display values for the new data rows

Beware

Adding new rows or columns to the table causes worksheet data outside the table to be shifted. You should check for potential problems in data that is not in a defined table.

Custom Sort

When new rows are inserted, it may be appropriate to sort the table, to position the new rows where they belong. To do this:

The sorting criteria used for each table will be saved when the workbook is saved, so it is easy to re-sort in the same way, after future updates and modifications. The **Filter** box icon for relevant columns is modified to show sorting is in effect.

1 Click in the table, select the **Home** tab, click **Sort & Filter** in the **Editing** group, and select **Custom Sort**

Or

Click in the table, select the **Data** tab, and click **Sort**, in the **Sort & Filter** group

2 The first time, there are no criteria defined, so click the arrow in **Sort by** to add a header, e.g. Artist

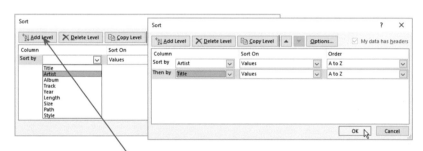

By default, columns with text values are sorted A to Z, while columns with number values are sorted smallest to largest.

3 Click the **Add Level** button, choose a second header (e.g. Title), and then click **OK**

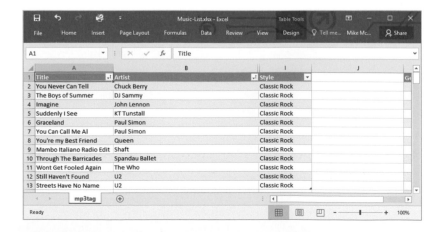

Print a Table

You can print a table without having to select the print area explicitly (see page 32):

1 Select any cell in the table to activate that cell

2 Use **Filters** to restrict the area to print, for example, a specific Artist

3 Press the **File** tab, then select **Print** (or press **Ctrl + P**)

4 For **Settings**, choose **Print Selected Table**, then adjust the paper size and scaling, if needed

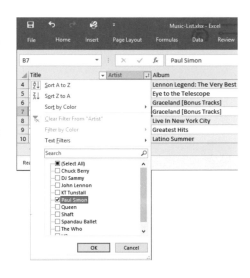

5 Specify the number of copies required, then click the **Print** button to complete the process

Hot tip

You may wish to change to a different table style; one more suitable for printing (or select **None** for a plain effect).

Table Styles

Beware

Some formulas on a Total Row, if present, may continue to reference the whole of the table contents.

Don't forget

You can print the active worksheet, the entire workbook, the selected data, or the active table.

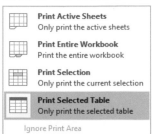

83

Summarize a Table

You can summarize the data, using the **PivotTable** feature. See page 165 for another example.

Select **Insert** and click **Recommended PivotTables** to see the suggestions that Excel 2016 makes for the data in your worksheets.

1 Click in the table, select the **Insert** tab, and then click the **PivotTable** button, in the **Tables** group

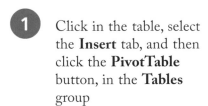

2 Choose the location for the **PivotTable** report, either a new worksheet or an empty portion of the current worksheet, e.g. A100, and then click **OK**

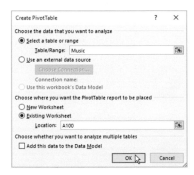

Click the **Collapse Dialog** box, select the first cell of the location, then click the **Expand Dialog** box to add the report to the worksheet.

3 An empty **PivotTable** report is added there

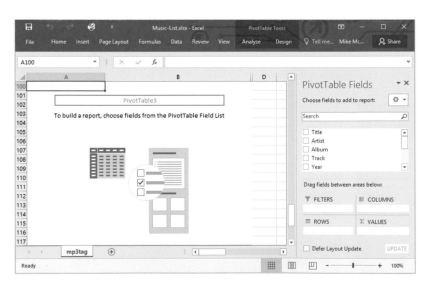

By default, text fields are added to the **Row Labels** area, and fields containing numbers are added to the **Values** area.

4 Check the boxes to select fields from the list (for example, Title, Artist, and Length)

5 Selected fields will appear in the **ROWS** area by default, but they can be moved to other areas

6 Rearrange the fields by dragging between areas, or right-click a name and select the area where it should appear. For example, move the Length field to **VALUES**

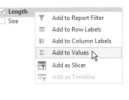

7 Click any field's arrow button to move it, or to change its **Field Settings**, for example any **Value**

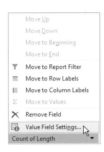

8 Choose how to summarize the values (e.g. Sum, Count, Average)

9 Choose a **Custom Name** for the field if you like, then click **OK** to see the Pivot Table report – **Analyze** and **Design** tabs now get added to the Ribbon

When you click a field name that has text values, and then select **Field Settings**, it will display appropriate text options for that field.

Excel 2016 provides automatic relationship detection among the tables used for your workbook's data model.

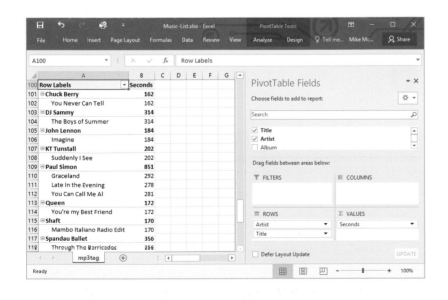

On the **Analyze** tab click **Show**, then **Field List** to hide or reveal the **Pivot Table Fields** list. From there, you can also collapse or expand the report details.

Convert to a Range

You can turn an Excel Table back into a range of data:

1 Click in the table, then select the **Design** tab and click **Convert to Range** in the **Tools** group

If you have just created a table from a range of data (see page 72), you can switch back to the range form by clicking **Undo** on the Quick Access Toolbar.

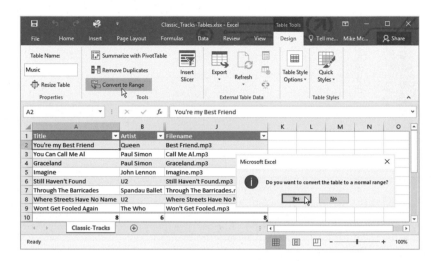

2 Click **Yes** to confirm that you do want to convert the table to a data range – the cell styles will be preserved, but the filter boxes will be removed from the headers

3 The Total Row will still appear, but all references will now be standard **$A$1**-style absolute cell references

4 To convert the range back into the table, you will need to recreate formulas for the totals row and calculated columns

To remove the table style from the cells, select all the data, click the **Home** tab, click the down-arrow next to **Cell Styles** in the **Styles** group, and choose the **Normal** style.

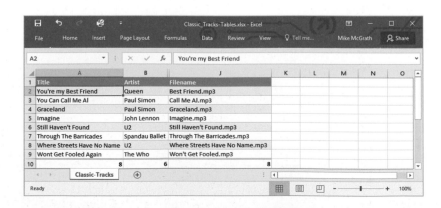

6 Advanced Functions

There is a large library of Excel functions available. To help locate the ones you want, related functions are grouped by category, and there's a Recently Used list. More functions are provided via Excel Add-ins. With nested functions in your formulas, use the Evaluate command to see how they work.

Function Library

1 Select the **Formulas** tab to see the **Function Library** group, with a Ribbon style that depends on your current window size

This starts with the **Insert Function** command, which allows you to enter keywords to search for a function (see page 66). It provides the syntax and a brief description for any function that you select, plus a link to more detailed help. Alternatively, you can select from one of the categories.

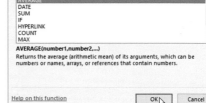

2 Click any category command for an alphabetical list of the names of the functions that it includes. The categories, and the number of functions included in each, are:

AutoSum	5	**Text**	27
Recently Used	10	**Logical**	9
Financial	55	**Information**	20
Date & Time	24	**Engineering**	54
Math & Trig	74	**Cube**	7
Statistical	108	**Compatibility**	41
Lookup & Reference	19	**Web**	3

AutoSum
AutoSum (introduced on page 68) provides quick access to functions (**SUM, AVERAGE, COUNT, MIN** and **MAX**) that are likely to be the most often used functions in many workbooks.

Recently Used
Recently Used remembers the functions you last used, allowing you to make repeated use of functions with the minimum of fuss, and without having to remember their particular categories.

Logical Functions

Sometimes the value for one cell depends on the value in another cell. For example, test scores could be used to set grade levels.

1 The formula in C2 is **=B2>=50** and gives the result True or False, depending on the value in B2

2 To display the more meaningful Pass or Fail, use an **IF** formula, such as in D2, with **=IF(B2>=50,"Pass","Fail")**

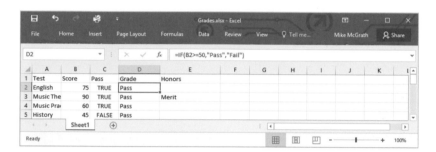

3 Sometimes you need to check two conditions, e.g. in the E3 formula **=IF(AND(B3>=50,B4>=50),"Merit","n/a")**

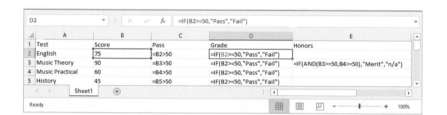

The **IF** functions can be nested, with the False value being replaced by another **IF** function, to make a further test. For example, this formula gives the country code, if the name matches, or goes on to test for the next country name in the list.

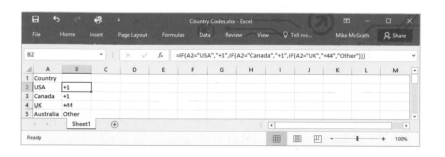

Comparisons (e.g. using the <, =, or > operators) that are either True or False are the basis of logical functions.

The **AND** function includes a set of logical tests, all of which must be True, to give a True result.

You could use an **OR** function for the first two countries here, since a match for either would give the same code.

Lookup/Reference Functions

If you have a number of items to check against, set up a list.
To do this:

1 This example uses a list of country names (in alphabetical order), with their country codes stored in rows D1:HU2

You can have up to 64
levels of nesting, but
long **IF** formulas can be
awkward to type in. A
better alternative may be
a **lookup** function.

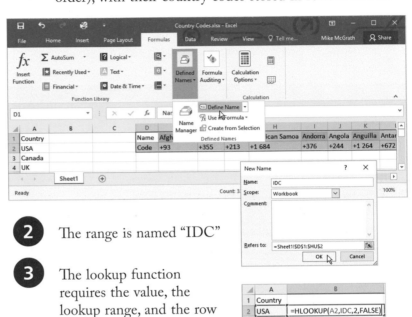

2 The range is named "IDC"

3 The lookup function
requires the value, the
lookup range, and the row
number for the result (in
this case row 2)

4 Copy the formula downwards, to look up the codes for
the other countries – a mistype of "Andorra" results in
#N/A, indicating that no match could be found

For the "range_lookup"
argument, you specify
a logical value of **TRUE**,
to get close matches, or
FALSE, to allow exact
matches only.

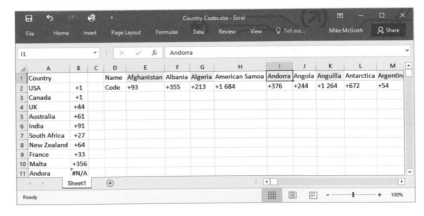

...cont'd

To reverse the process, and replace a number with a text value, you could use the **CHOOSE** function. For example:

1 To convert the value in cell B2 into a rank, enter
=CHOOSE(B2,"First","Second","Third","Fourth","Fifth")
– then copy the formula across to rank cells B3 to F3

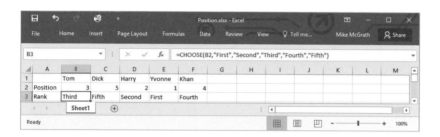

The contents of B2 are used as an index, to select from the list of 5 values provided. A maximum of 254 values could be used.

2 To apply a suffix to the position value, use the formula
=B2&CHOOSE(B2,"st","nd","rd","th","th") – then copy the formula across to rank cells B4 to F4

Here, the suffix chosen from the list is appended to the index number.

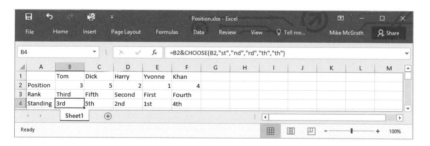

3 You could store the values in a range of cells, but you must list the relevant cells individually in the formula. You should use absolute cell references for the values, so you can copy the formula without changing the references

Index values outside the range provided (in these examples, 1-5) will cause a **#VALUE!** error.

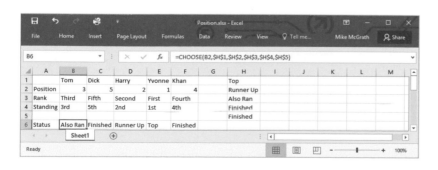

91

Financial Functions

Excel includes specialized functions for dealing with investments, securities, loans, and other financial transactions. For example, to calculate the monthly payments required for a mortgage, you'd use the **PMT** function. To illustrate, assume a purchase price of $250,000, interest at 6% per annum, and a 30-year period:

1 Enter the initial information into a worksheet, then, for the payment, begin typing the function **=PMT(**

2 Click the **Insert Function** button, to display the input form for the function arguments

3 For **Rate**, enter **B2/D2** (6%/12). In the **Nper** term box, enter **C2*D2** (30*12), and in the **PV** value box, enter A2 ($250,000). Click **OK** to see the monthly payment

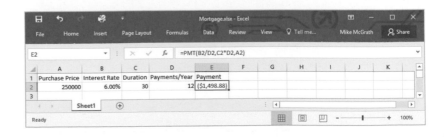

...cont'd

Perhaps you'd like to know what would happen if you paid the mortgage off over a shorter period:

1 Select the existing values and calculation, then drag down, using the Fill Handle, to replicate into three more rows

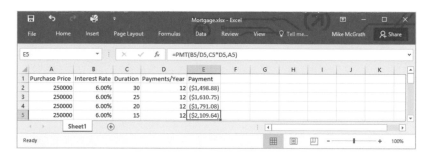

Don't forget

You could type a new value into the Duration cell and see the new payment. However, copying the rows makes it easier to compare the different options.

2 Change the duration to 25, 20 and 15 years, on successive rows, and observe the revised monthly payments required

3 Add a column for total interest paid, then enter the cumulative interest function **=CUMIPMT(** and click the **Insert Function** button once more

The **CUMIPMT** function arguments are similar to those for **PMT**, with "Type" now mandatory (set it to 0, for payment at end of month). Copy the formula down, to see the cumulative interest for all loan durations.

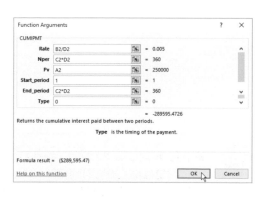

Hot tip

You can calculate the interest over any part of the loan, but putting the first and last payments gives the total interest over the whole period of the loan.

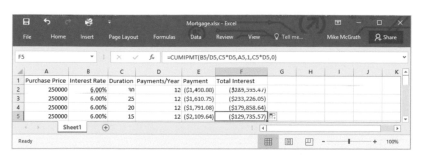

Date & Time Functions

Date and time values (see page 59) are stored as numbers, and count the days since the starting point (usually January 1st, 1900). However, they can be displayed in various date or time formats.

 The whole-number portion of the value converts into month, day, and year (with account taken for leap years)

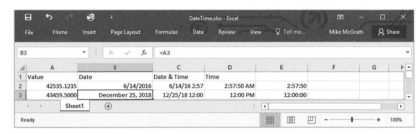

see page 59

Hot tip

Excel also supports the 1904 date system, the default for Apple Mac computers, where a date value of 1 is taken as January 2nd, 1904.

Beware

You can use date and time values in formulas, but, because of the calendar effects, the results may not always be what you'd expect.

 The decimal portion indicates the time of day, so .123 is 2:57, and .767 is 6:24PM (or 18:24 on the 24-hour clock)

Date and Time Calculations

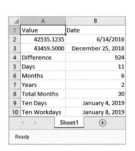

	A	B
1	Value	Date
2	42535.1235	6/14/2016
3	43459.5000	December 25, 2018
4	Difference	924
5	Days	11
6	Months	6
7	Years	2
8	Total Months	30
9	Ten Days	January 4, 2019
10	Ten Workdays	January 8, 2019

	A	B
1	Value	Date
2	42535.1235	=A2
3	43459.5000	=A3
4	Difference	=A3-A2
5	Days	=DAY(A3)-DAY(A2)
6	Months	=MONTH(A3)-MONTH(A2)
7	Years	=YEAR(A3)-YEAR(A2)
8	Total Months	=(YEAR(A3)-YEAR(A2))*12+MONTH(A3)-MONTH(A2)
9	Ten Days	=A3+10
10	Ten Workdays	=WORKDAY(A3,10)

Don't forget

In the example, the value of the date is displayed to illustrate the options. You type the date, e.g. as 6/14/2016, and Excel automatically converts it into a number value, and then stores it in the cell. The cell format controls what's displayed.

B4	Difference in days
B5	Subtracts calendar day numbers (may be minus)
B6	Subtracts calendar months (may be minus)
B7	Difference in years (ignores the part year)
B8	Twelve months for every year +/- the difference in months
B9	Adding ten days to A3 gives Jan 4, 2014
B10	Adding ten work days (to allow for weekends and holidays) gives the later date Jan 8, 2014

There's a worksheet function named **DATEDIF** that's not listed in the **Date & Time** category, or in Excel **Help**. The syntax is:

=DATEDIF(StartDate, EndDate, Interval)

The interval code controls the result the function produces:

Interval value	Calculates the number between the dates of
"y"	Whole years
"m"	Whole months
"d"	Days in total
"ym"	Whole months, ignoring the years
"yd"	Days, ignoring the years
"md"	Days, ignoring the months and years

Hot tip

Excel's Visual Basic for Applications (VBA) has a similar function called **DateDiff**, but without the **"ym"**, **"yd"**, and **"md"** interval parameters.

When entering the interval code into **DATEDIF** as a constant, you enclose it in quotes. However, if your interval code is stored in a worksheet cell, it should not be enclosed in quotes in the cell.

1 Use the **DATEDIF** function with each of these codes in turn, to calculate the difference between the dates that are stored in cells B2 and B3

	A	B	C
	B4	fx	=DATEDIF($B$2,$B$3,"y")
1	DateDiff		
2		7/4/2015	
3		10/23/2020	
4	Y	5	
5	M	63	
6	DateDiff	1938	
7	YM	3	
8	YD	111	
9	MD	19	

Sheet1 | Sheet2 |

Ready

2 This function becomes useful when you need to calculate someone's exact age, in years, months, and days. For example, **DATEDIF** applied to the date of birth and the current date gives the following result:

Hot tip

DATEDIF is applied three times, to obtain the years, months, and days, and the results are joined together into a single statement.

DateTime.xlsx - Excel

File | Home | Insert | Page Layout | Formulas | Data | Review | View | Tell me what you want to do...

B3 | fx | =DATEDIF(B1,B2,"y")&" Years "&DATEDIF(B1,B2,"ym")&" Months"&DATEDIF(B1,B2,"md")&" Days"

	A	B	C
1	Date of Birth	Saturday, August 25, 1990	
2	Current Date	Tuesday, November 10, 2015	
3	Age	25 Years 2 Months16 Days	

The **&** operators concatenate the results of the calculations, with literal text values for years, months and days.

Text Functions

Values can be presented in many different ways, even though they remain stored as numbers. Sometimes, however, you actually want to convert the values into text (enclosed in quotes), perhaps to include them in a specific format, in a report or message. This uses the **TEXT** function. Its syntax is **=TEXT(value, format)**.

The **DOLLAR** function will display the value in the default currency format for your system, for example, using the Pound Sterling symbol (£) for UK systems.

96

1 Format a number as text, with a fixed number of decimal places, and with a comma as the thousands separator, if desired

2 Display a number in money format, using any currency symbol

3 Display a number using the default currency for your system

4 Show the day of the week, for a date value, using the long or short form of the day name

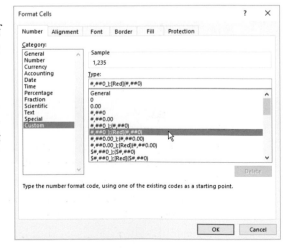

	A	B
1	Value	1234.5678
2		
3	"=TEXT(B1,"0.00")	1234.57
4	"=TEXT(B1,"#,##0.00")	1,234.57
5		
6	"=TEXT(B1,"€0.00")	€1234.57
7		
8	"=DOLLAR(B1)	$1,234.57
9		
10	"=TEXT(DATE(2016,7,4),"dddd")	Monday
11	"=TEXT(DATE(2016,12,25),"dddd")	Sunday

5 For examples of the number formats, choose the **Custom** category in the **Format Cells** dialog, and scroll the list

You can use any of the number formats shown in the **Format Cells** dialog (see page 58), other than **General** format.

Format Cells ? ×

Number | Alignment | Font | Border | Fill | Protection

Category:
General
Number
Currency
Accounting
Date
Time
Percentage
Fraction
Scientific
Text
Special
Custom

Sample
1,235

Type:
#,##0_);[Red](#,##0)

General
0
0.00
#,##0
#,##0.00
#,##0_);(#,##0)
#,##0_);[Red](#,##0)
#,##0.00_);(#,##0.00)
#,##0.00_);[Red](#,##0.00)
$#,##0_);($#,##0)
$#,##0_);[Red]($#,##0)

Delete

Type the number format code, using one of the existing codes as a starting point.

OK | Cancel

...cont'd

There are several functions provided to help you manipulate a piece of text, to make it more suitable for presentation:

1 Remove all extraneous blanks, leaving a single space between words

2 Convert all the characters in the text into lower-case format

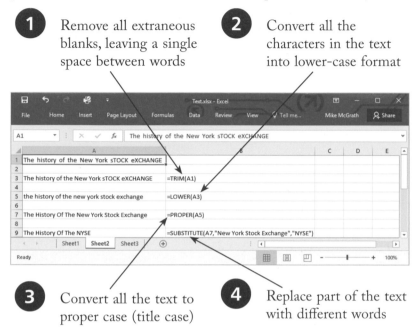

3 Convert all the text to proper case (title case)

4 Replace part of the text with different words

Excel does not have a Word Count function, but the text functions can be used in combination, to find the number of words in a cell.

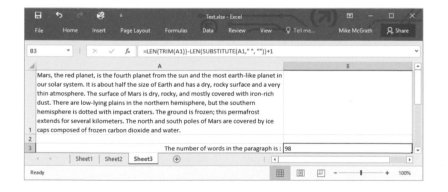

The **TRIM** function removes multiple spaces from the text, then the first **LEN** function counts all the characters, including spaces. The **SUBSTITUTE** function removes all spaces from the text, then the second **LEN** function counts the remaining characters. The difference between the two lengths is the number of spaces between words. Add one to find the number of words in the cell.

Hot tip

These functions don't change the text in cell A1. Only the working copies used during the calculation are modified.

Don't forget

The **SUBSTITUTE** function replaces every instance of the text specified, unless you indicate the specific occurrence that you want to change.

Hot tip

The text functions can help you tidy up text data you import from an external source – especially if you repeat the import on a regular basis to update the data.

Math & Trig Functions

These functions allow you to carry out calculations using cell contents, computed values, and constants. For example:

1 The **PRODUCT** function multiplies price times (1 - discount) quantity to get the cost of the item

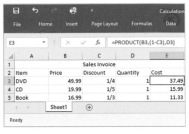

2 Copy the formula, to calculate the costs for the other items

3 The total cost is the sum of the individual item costs

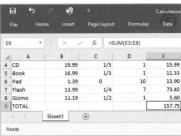

You may sometimes want to make calculations without showing all of the intermediate values. For example:

1 The total cost (before discount) is the sum of the products of the item prices and item quantities, i.e. **B3*D3 + B4*D4 + ...**

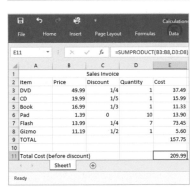

2 This value is calculated with the **SUMPRODUCT** function, which multiplies the sets of cells and totals the results

3 Rather than using the **SUMPRODUCT** function to calculate the total discount, you can simply subtract actual cost from total cost. This avoids problems with rounding errors, which can show up in even straightforward functions, such as **SUM**

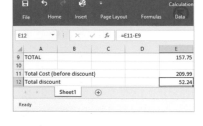

Don't forget

With 74 functions, this is the largest of the main categories in the **Function Library**.

Beware

Since this is a single function, the detailed workings won't be revealed, even when you use the **Evaluate** command (see page 104) to perform the calculations in single steps.

To illustrate the type of problem that can arise, imagine placing an order for goods where there's a special gift offered for spending $140 or more.

1 A quick check seems to indicate that the total is just over the amount required

2 But the total that Excel calculates appears to be just under that amount

	A	B	C	D	E	F
			Sales Invoice			
2	Item	Price	Discount	Quantity	Cost	
3	DVD	49.99	1/3	1	33.33	
4	CD	19.99	1/3	1	13.33	
5	Book	16.99	1/3	1	11.33	
6	Pad	1.39	1/3	10	9.27	
7	Flash	13.99	1/3	7	65.29	
8	Gizmo	11.19	1/3	1	7.46	
9	TOTAL				139.99	? 140.01
10			Spend $140 to get that Special Gift			
11	Total Cost (before discount)				209.99	
12	Total discount				70.00	

E9 · fx =SUM(E3:E8)

Calculations.xlsx - Excel

Excel hasn't got its sums wrong – the stored numbers that it totals aren't quite the same as those on display.

33.326667
13.326667
11.326667
9.266667
65.286667
7.460000
139.993333

3 Change the cell format, to show more decimal places, and you'll see the actual values are slightly lower than those shown

4 Click cell E3, and add the **ROUND** function – to round item cost to 2 places

E3 · fx =ROUND(PRODUCT(B3,(1-C3),D3),2)

	A	B	C	D	E	F
			Sales Invoice			
2	Item	Price	Discount	Quantity	Cost	
3	DVD	49.99	1/3	1	33.33	
4	CD	19.99	1/3	1	13.33	
5	Book	16.99	1/3	1	11.33	
6	Pad	1.39	1/3	10	9.27	
7	Flash	13.99	1/3	7	65.29	
8	Gizmo	11.19	1/3	1	7.46	
9	TOTAL				140.01	
10			Special Gift Enclosed			
11	Total Cost (before discount)				209.99	
12	Total discount				69.98	

5 Copy the new formula into cells E4:E8 to see the expected amount

The **ROUND** function rounds up or down. So 1.234 becomes 1.23, while 1.236 becomes 1.24 (rounded to two decimal places). You can specify a negative number of places, to round the values to the nearest multiple of ten (-1 places) or of one hundred (-2 places), etc.

33.330000
13.330000
11.330000
9.270000
65.290000
7.460000
140.010000

Random Numbers

It is sometimes useful to produce sets of random numbers. This could be for sample data, when creating or testing worksheets. Another use might be to select a variety of tracks from your music library, to generate a playlist.

RAND generates a number from 0 to 1. **=RAND()*99+101** would give numbers between 101 and 200. Unlike those produced by the **RANDBETWEEN** function, these aren't whole numbers.

1 Click A1 and enter the function **=RAND()**, then copy A1 down through A2:A5 – to generate random numbers from 0 to 1 in each cell

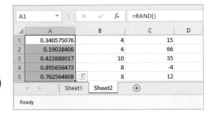

2 Click B1 and enter **=RANDBETWEEN(1,+10)** then copy B1 down through B2:B5 – to generate random whole numbers less than or equal to 10 in each cell

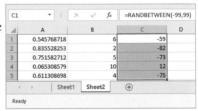

3 You can generate negative random numbers. For example, C1:C5 has values from -99 to +99

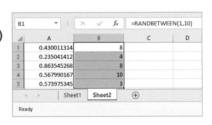

4 Select the **Formulas** tab, then click **Calculate Now** in the **Calculation** group and the numbers will be regenerated

To generate a random number that doesn't change each time the worksheet is recalculated, type **=RAND()** on the formula bar, and then press **F9**. The generated number is placed into the cell as a literal value.

Other Functions: Statistical

There's a large number of statistical functions, but the most likely one to be used is the **AVERAGE** function.

1 Create a block A1:E5 of random numbers between 101 and 200, to use as data for the functions

Sample	▾	:	×	✓	fx	=RANDBETWEEN(101,200)

⊿	A	B	C	D	E	F	G
1	141	167	178	102	113		
2	124	165	198	178	128		
3	115	122	173	178	121		
4	116	163	143	145	188		
5	149	116	181	118	152		

Sheet1 ⊕

Hot tip

Use **Copy**, **Paste Special**, **Paste Values**, to replace the formulas, so that the set of random numbers generated won't later be affected by recalculation of the worksheet.

2 Define a name "Sample" for the range **$A$1:$A$5**

3 Select and copy A1:E5, then select the **Home** tab, click the arrow on the **Paste** command, and select **Paste Values** (to replace the formula with the literal value, in each cell)

Calculate some typical statistics:

1 The arithmetic mean is **=AVERAGE(Sample)**

2 The number in the middle of the sample is **=MEDIAN(Sample)**

E7	▾	:	×	✓	fx	=AVERAGE(Sample)

⊿	A	B	C	D	E	F	G
1	121	186	146	184	119		
2	106	161	123	130	144		
3	151	154	129	147	171		
4	194	198	165	175	149		
5	147	159	105	191	174		
6							
7		=AVERAGE(Sample)			153.16		
8		=MEDIAN(Sample)			151		
9		=MODE(Sample)			147		
10		=COUNT(Sample)			25		
11		=COUNTIF(Sample,">=150")			13		
12		=MAX(Sample)			198		
13		=MIN(Sample)			105		

Sheet1 ⊕

3 The most frequently occurring value is **=MODE(Sample)**

Don't forget

There are a number of different ways to interpret the term "average". Make sure that you use the function that's appropriate for your requirements.

4 The number of values in the sample is **=COUNT(Sample)**

5 The number of values in the sample that are greater than or equal to 150 is **=COUNTIF(Sample,">=150")**

6 The maximum value in the sample is **=MAX(Sample)**

7 The minimum value in the sample is **=MIN(Sample)**

Other Functions: Engineering

There are some rather esoteric functions in the **Engineering** category, but some are quite generally applicable, for example:

 Convert from one measurement system to another, using the function **=CONVERT(value, from_unit, to_unit)**

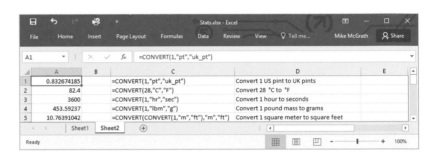

This function deals with units of weight and mass, distance, time, pressure, force, energy, power, magnetism, temperature, and liquids. There are functions to convert between any two pairs of number systems, including binary, decimal, hexadecimal, and octal.

2 Convert decimal values to their binary, octal, and hexadecimal equivalents

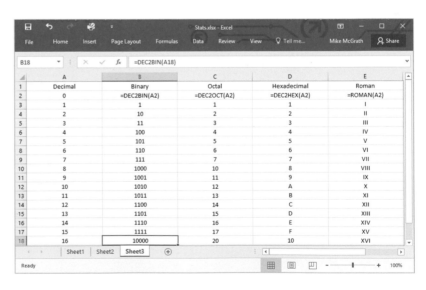

=ROMAN(1499,0)	MCDXCIX
=ROMAN(1499,1)	MLDVLIV
=ROMAN(1499,2)	MXDIX
=ROMAN(1499,3)	MVDIV
=ROMAN(1499,4)	MID

There's also a Roman numeral conversion, but it's just a one-way conversion between Arabic numerals and Roman numerals (and it comes from the **Math & Trig** category, rather than **Engineering**).

Excel Add-ins

There are **Add-ins** included with Excel, but they must be loaded before they can be used:

1 Click the **File** tab, and then click the **Options** button

2 Click the **Add-Ins** category, and, in the **Manage** box, click **Excel Add-ins** and then click **Go**

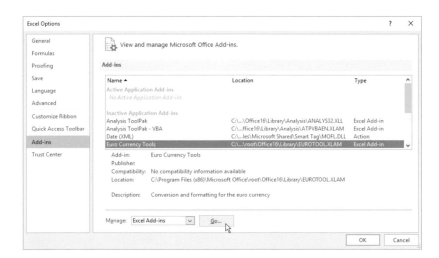

Hot tip

If you are still looking for the functions you need, you may find them in an **Excel Add-in**, such as the **Analysis ToolPak** or the **Solver Add-in**.

3 To load the Excel **Add-in**, select the associated check-box, and then click **OK**

4 You may be prompted to install some of the add-in programs that you select

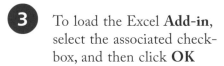

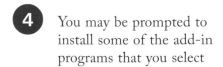

Don't forget

To unload an Excel **Add-in**, clear the associated check-box, and then click **OK**. This does not delete the **Add-in** from your computer.

5 The new functions can be found on the **Formulas** tab **Solutions** group, or on the **Data** tab **Analysis** group

Evaluate Formula

If you are not sure exactly how a formula works, especially when there are nested functions, use the **Evaluate** command to run the formula one step at a time. To use this:

1 Select the cell with the formula you wish to investigate

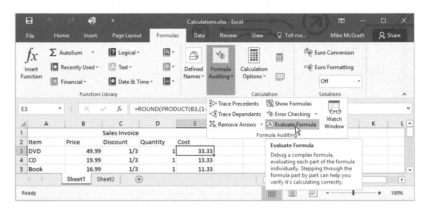

2 Select the **Formulas** tab, click the **Formula Auditing** button, and then select the **Evaluate Formula** command

3 Press the **Evaluate** button, to move the calculation on, step-by-step

4 The expressions in the formula are calculated in turn

Evaluation:
= ROUND(PRODUCT($B$3,(1-0.333333333333333),D3),2)

Evaluation:
= ROUND(PRODUCT($B$3,(0.666666666666667),D3),2)

5 The intermediate values are displayed

Evaluation:
= ROUND(PRODUCT($B$3,0.666666666666667,D3),2)

Evaluation:
= ROUND(33.3266666666667,2)

Evaluation:
= 33.33

This is the formula for rounding the item costs, as shown in step 4 on page 99.

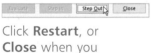

Press the **Step In** button, to check details like the value of a constant, or to see the expansion of range or table names.

Click **Step Out** to carry on with the evaluation.

Click **Restart**, or **Close** when you reach the end.

104

7 Control Excel

To keep control of your worksheets, audit the formulas, and check for errors. Make backup copies, and use the automatic save and recover capabilities. You can also control Excel through startup switches, shortcuts, KeyTips for the Ribbon commands, the Quick Access and Mini toolbars.

Audit Formulas

When you are reviewing a worksheet and the formulas it contains, use the tools in the **Formula Auditing** group.

1 Click the **Formulas** tab, to see the **Formula Auditing** group

2 If the commands are grayed, click the **File** tab, select **Excel Options**, then click **Advanced**

3 In the **Display options for this workbook** section, make sure that the **All** option is selected

Precedents are those cells that are referred to by the formula in the selected cell.

4 Select a cell, and click the **Trace Precedents** button in the **Formula Auditing** group

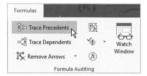

5 With cells where there is no formula, such as B3, you receive a message

The cell you select must contain a formula for the **Trace Precedents** button to operate.

6 With cells that contain a formula, such as E9, the arrow and box show the cells that are directly referred to by that formula

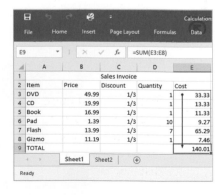

7 Click **Trace Precedents**, to see the next level of cells (if the first level of precedent cells refer to more cells)

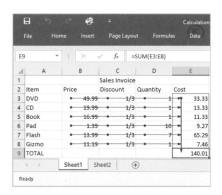

8 Click the **Trace Dependents** button, to show the cells that rely on the value in the selected cell

9 Click the **Remove Arrows** button, in **Formula Auditing**

Dependents are those cells that contain formulas that refer to the selected cell.

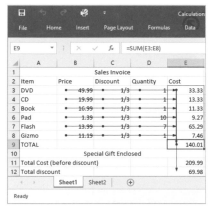

You can analyze the role of cells that contain only literal values:

1 Click a cell, e.g. B2, that contains no formula, and click **Trace Dependents**

2 If there are no cell references, you receive a warning message

Pressing **Trace Dependents** multiple times shows you the direct and indirect references to the value in the selected cell.

3 Select B3, and click **Trace Dependents** three times to see the references to that cell

Protect Formulas

1 Click **Show Formulas** on the **Formulas** tab, to display the formulas in the worksheet

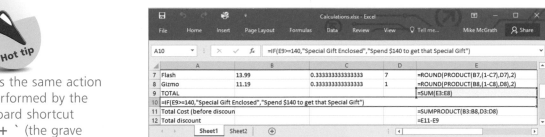

Hot tip

This is the same action as performed by the keyboard shortcut **Ctrl + `** (the grave accent key).

2 To hide a formula, select the cell, then click the **Home** tab, **Format**, and **Format Cells**

3 Click in the box labeled **Hidden**, and then click **OK**

Don't forget

You can select ranges of cells, to protect multiple formulas at once.

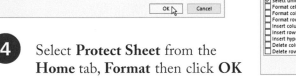

4 Select **Protect Sheet** from the **Home** tab, **Format** then click **OK**

5 The cell's formula is no longer shown on the Formula Bar, and is hidden when you choose **Show Formulas**

Hot tip

When you print the worksheet with the formulas revealed, ensure you include the column and row headings. Select the **Page Layout** tab, and click **Print Headings** in the **Sheet Options** group.

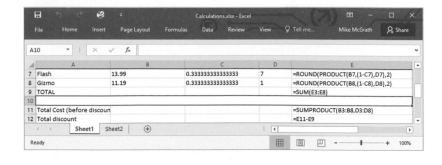

Check for Errors

Excel applies rules to check for potential errors in formulas:

1 Click the **File** tab, select **Options**, then click **Formulas**

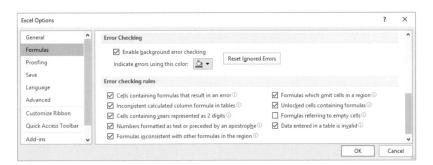

Hot tip

Some errors will just be warnings, and some may be due to information not yet recorded.

2 Select or clear the check-boxes, to change the errors that Excel will detect

3 Select **Formulas,** and click the arrow on **Error Checking,** in the **Formula Auditing** group

4 Click **Error Checking,** to review errors one by one, making corrections on the Formula Bar

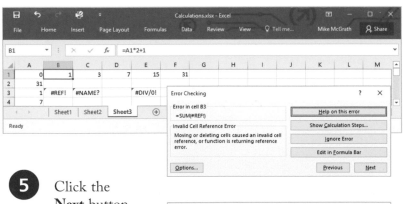

Beware

If the worksheet has previously been checked, any **Ignored** errors will not appear until you press the **Reset Ignored Errors** button, in **Excel Options**.

5 Click the **Next** button, to review subsequent errors

...cont'd

You can also review individual errors on the worksheet:

1 Click an error, and then select **Trace Error**, from the **Error Checking** menu in **Formula Auditing**

The **Error Checking** options become very useful when you have large worksheets, where errors and warnings are off screen and out of view.

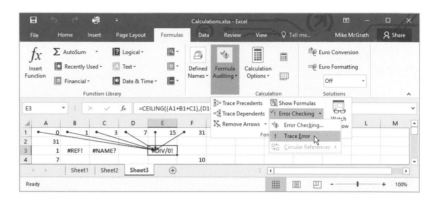

2 You can select **Circular References**, to see the cells that refer to their own contents, directly or indirectly

3 Click a cell from the list, to navigate to that location

4 Press **F9** to recalculate the worksheet, and the cells involved in circular references will be identified

Click **Trace Empty Cell**, to identify the empty cells referred to, directly or indirectly, by the selected formula.

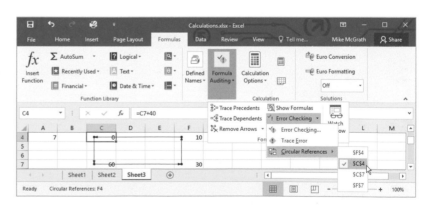

5 Click the **Information** button on an individual error, to see more options, which are tailored to the particular type of error being reviewed

Backup

1 To make a copy of your workbook, click the **File** tab and select **Open** (or press the **Ctrl + O** shortcut key)

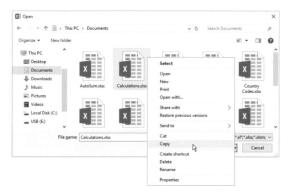

You can keep extra copies of your workbooks in your OneDrive (see page 180).

2 Right-click the file for the workbook, and then select **Copy** from the menu

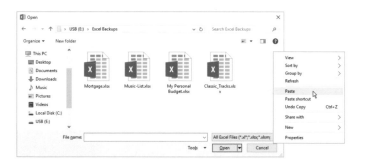

If there's already a copy, Windows compares the two versions and lets you choose to replace the file, or skip copying the workbook.

3 Switch to the backup folder, right-click an empty area, and then select **Paste**

4 The file is copied to the folder, unless there's an existing copy in the backup folder

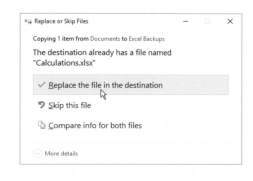

5 Compare file info to confirm which version you want

When you are working on a large worksheet it is often helpful to make a copy before you apply significant changes, so that you can undo them, if necessary.

AutoSave and AutoRecover

To review and adjust the **AutoRecover** and **AutoSave** settings:

1 Click the **File** tab, then click **Options**, and select **Save**

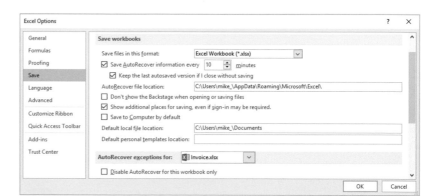

Hot tip

Excel will automatically save your worksheet periodically, and can recover the file if your system shuts down in the middle of an update.

Hot tip

The **Document Recovery** task pane displays up to three versions of your file, with the most recent at the top.

2 Check the **Save AutoRecover information** box, review the frequency, then click **OK** to save any changes

If your system shuts down without saving the current changes, the next time you start up Windows and Excel, you'll be given the opportunity to recover your changes, as recorded up to the last **AutoSave**.

1 Select an entry, click the arrow and choose **Open**, **Save As** or **Delete** as appropriate

Don't forget

Excel will keep the last **AutoSave** version, even when you deliberately close without saving, so you can still recover your latest changes.

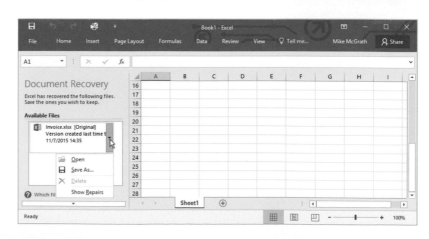

Startup Switches

When you start Excel in the usual way, the Excel splash screen is displayed, and the Excel Start screen then opens where you can select a new blank workbook, a recent workbook or a template.

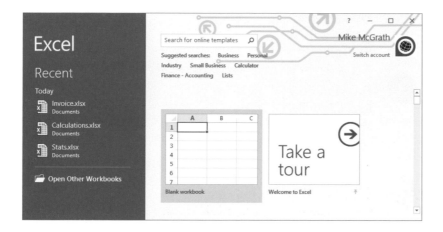

Hot tip

Excel 2016 normally opens at the Excel Start screen, but you can bypass this if you wish.

To start Excel without these items displaying:

1 Press the **Windows key + R**, type **excel.exe /e**, and then press **Enter**

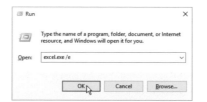

Hot tip

You can create a shortcut to Excel, with your required parameters, and place this on the Desktop or the Taskbar.

2 Select the **File** tab to create or open a workbook

Don't forget

Use this method to start Excel in safe mode by typing **excel.exe /safe**. This can be useful if you are having problems opening a particular workbook.

Create a Shortcut

To create a shortcut to Excel:

1 Locate the **Excel.exe** file on your hard drive, typically at **C:\Program Files (x86)\Microsoft Office\root\Office16\Excel.exe**

2 Right-click the Desktop, and then select **New**, **Shortcut**

Hot tip

If necessary, use Windows Search to locate the **Excel.exe** program, and then note the location.

3 Browse to the **Excel.exe** file and select it, then add the required switch (e.g. **/e** or **/safe**) outside the quote marks

Beware

Make sure that you enter a space between the final quote mark and the command-line switch.

4 Name the shortcut and click **Finish** to create a shortcut icon on the Desktop

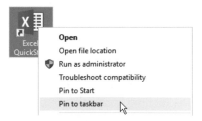

5 Right-click the shortcut icon on the Desktop, and then select **Pin to taskbar** (or **Pin to Start**)

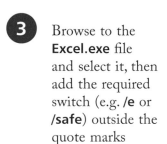

Open
Open file location
Run as administrator
Troubleshoot compatibility
Pin to Start
Pin to taskbar

6 Select the entry to launch the program, or right-click the entry to unpin it

Excel QuickStart
Unpin this program from taskbar

Ribbon Key Tips

Although the Ribbon is designed for mouse and touch selection, it is still possible to carry out any task available on the Ribbon without moving your hands from the keyboard.

1 Press and release the **Alt** key (or press the **F10** key) to show Key Tips (the keyboard shortcuts for the Ribbon)

2 Press the letter for the command tab that you want to display. For example, press **W** for **View**

3 Press the letter(s) for the command or group that you want. For example, press **ZS** for **Show/Hide**

Hot tip

If you hold down the **Alt** key for a couple of seconds, the Key Tips will display. Click **F10** to hide them, temporarily.

Don't forget

The Key Tips change when you select a tab, and further Key Tips display when you select specific commands.

Hot tip

It doesn't matter if **Alt** is pressed or not – the shortcut keys in the Key Tips will still operate. You can also use uppercase or lowercase.

Using Key Tips

1 To go to a specific cell, C7 for example, press these keys:

Hot tip

You can go to a cell, using keystrokes only.

Alt

H

FD

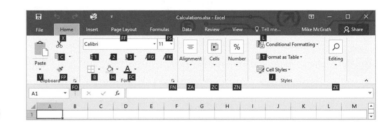

Beware

The action associated with a particular letter may change, as you switch to another command tab or command group. For example, **N** can be the **Insert** tab, or **New window** in **View**.

G

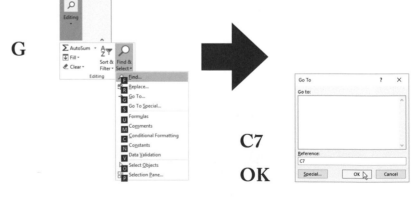

C7

OK

2 The active cell changes to C7, the cell address required

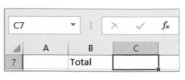

3 With C7 selected, to insert **AutoSum**, press these keys:

Hot tip

You can insert the **AutoSum** function into the active cell using keystrokes only.

Alt

H

ZE

U

Hot tip

ZE expands the **Editing** group, but you can bypass this and go straight to **U** (**AutoSum**) if you don't need the visual prompt.

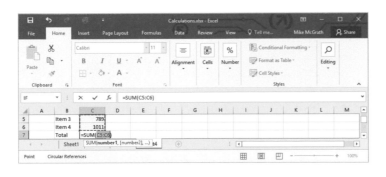

S

Don't forget

For tasks that you perform often, the Key Tips option can become the quickest way to operate, as you become familiar with the keystrokes needed.

Enter

Up arrow

Collapse the Ribbon

Hot tip

You can also double-click the current tab, or press keys **Ctrl + F1**, to collapse the Ribbon.

Don't forget

To redisplay the Ribbon, double-click the current tab, or press keys **Ctrl + F1**, or select **Show Tabs and Commands**.

Hot tip

When you close down Excel with the Ribbon collapsed, it will still be collapsed when Excel restarts. When the Ribbon is fully displayed at close down, it will be displayed on restart.

1 Right-click the Ribbon, Tab Bar, or Quick Access Toolbar and select **Collapse the Ribbon**, or click **Ribbon Display Options** and select **Show Tabs**

2 With the Ribbon minimized, single-click a tab to display the Ribbon temporarily, to select commands from that tab

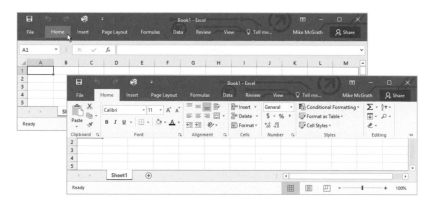

3 The **Alt** key and the Key Tips still operate, even when you have the Ribbon minimized

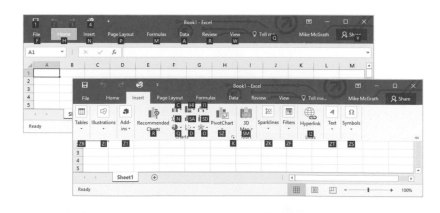

Quick Access Toolbar

The Quick Access Toolbar contains a set of commands that are independent of the particular Command tab being displayed. Initially there are three commands (**Save**, **Undo**, and **Redo**) plus a **Customize** button, but you can add other commands. By default, the Quick Access Toolbar is located above the **File** tab, but you can move it below the Ribbon.

1 Right-click the Command tab bar, and select **Show Quick Access Toolbar Below the Ribbon**

2 To restore the default, right-click the Command tab bar, and select **Show Quick Access Toolbar Above the Ribbon**

3 To add a command, click **Customize Quick Access Toolbar**

4 Choose a command from the list, or select **More Commands**

5 Choose a command category, select a command, click **Add** then click **OK** to place that command on the toolbar

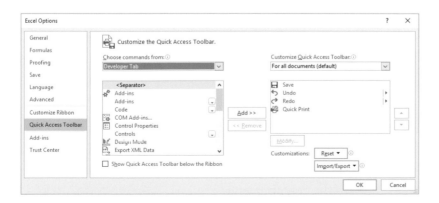

The instruction on the menu is modified to show the reverse process.

119

You can also right-click any command on the Ribbon, then select **Add to Quick Access Toolbar**, from the menu.

Mini Toolbar

The Mini Toolbar appears when you select text, or when editing the contents of a cell (and also when working with charts and text boxes). It offers quick access to the tools you need for text editing, such as font, size, style, alignment, color, and bullets. To see the Mini Toolbar:

1 Choose a cell with text content, enter edit mode by pressing **F2**, and then select (highlight) part of the text

2 The Mini Toolbar appears above the cell

3 Move the mouse pointer away from the cell, and the Mini Toolbar fades out and may disappear completely

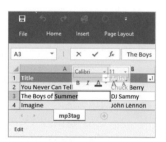

This is a rather transient feature in Excel, but it may be more evident in the mainly text-oriented Word and PowerPoint applications.

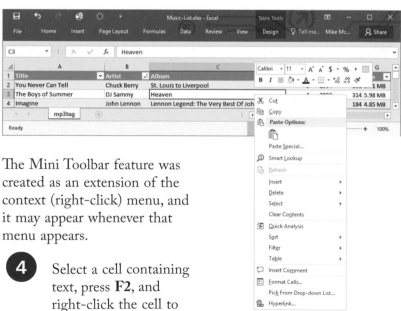

The Mini Toolbar feature was created as an extension of the context (right-click) menu, and it may appear whenever that menu appears.

4 Select a cell containing text, press **F2**, and right-click the cell to see the Mini Toolbar above the context menu

Print Worksheets

To preview printing for multiple worksheets:

1 Open the workbook, and click the tab for the first sheet

2 To select adjacent sheets, hold down the **Shift** key, and click the tab for the last sheet in the group

3 To add other, non-adjacent sheets, hold down the **Ctrl** key and click the tabs for all of the other sheets required

If you change any cell while multiple sheets are selected, the change is automatically applied to all selected sheets.

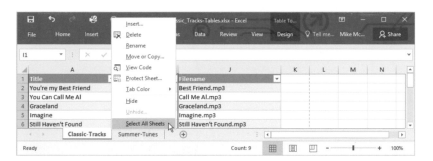

4 To select all the sheets, right-click any tab, then click **Select All Sheets**

5 Click the **File** tab, and select **Print**, for the **Print Preview** and the settings

6 Alternatively, press the keyboard shortcut **Ctrl + F2**

7 If you prefer to use Key Tips shortcuts, press **Alt F P V**

When multiple sheets are selected, the term **[Group]** appears on the Excel Title Bar.

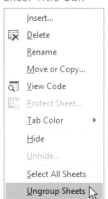

To cancel the selection, click any unselected tab, or right-click any tab and click **Ungroup Sheets**.

The **Preview** pane shows print previews for selected sheets.

...cont'd

Review the print preview before sending it to the printer:

1 Click the **Next Page** arrow to go forward, or the **Previous Page** arrow to go back

Click the **Page Setup** link to make detailed changes to the print settings. Click the **Printer Properties** link to control the printer.

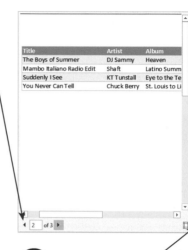

2 Click the **Show Margins** button, to display margins, and click and drag the margins to adjust their positions

3 Click the **Zoom to Page** button to switch between close-up and full page views

4 Click the **Settings** options to adjust items such as paper size, orientation, scaling, and collation

If the settings are already correct, you can use the **Quick Print** button (see page 33) to start the **Print**, without previewing.

5 Click the **Printer** button to select a different printer

6 Click the **Print** button to start the printing

8 Charts

Excel makes it easy to turn your worksheet data into a chart. You can apply formatting, change the type, reselect the data, and add effects, such as 3-D display. Special chart types allow you to display data for stocks and shares. You can print the completed charts on their own, or as part of the worksheet.

Create a Chart

The following information about share purchases and prices will be used for the purpose of illustrating the Excel charting features:

- Total value of shares in portfolio at start of each year (to be charted)

- The individual prices of the shares on those dates (for calculations)

- The total number of shares held (constants, for simplicity)

To create a chart you can modify and format later, start by entering the data on a worksheet. Then select the data and choose the chart type.

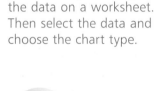
If you let Excel choose the data, ensure there is a blank row and column between the data you want to plot, and other data on the worksheet.

If the cells you want are not in a continuous range, you can select non-adjacent cells, or ranges, as long as the final selection forms a rectangle. You can also hide rows or columns that you don't need.

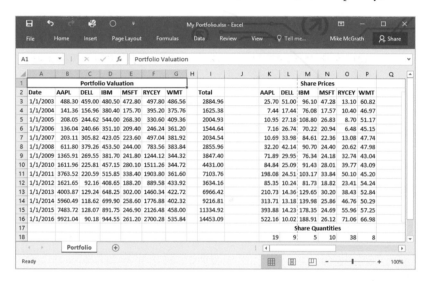

Select the Data

Some chart types, such as pie and bubble charts, require a specific data arrangement. For most chart types, however, including line, column, and bar charts, you can use the data as arranged in the rows or columns of the worksheet.

 Select the cells that contain the data that you want to use for the chart (or click a cell and let Excel select the data)

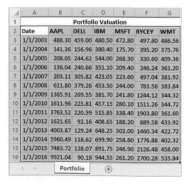

2 Click the **Insert** tab, and then select a chart type (**Column** for example) from the **Charts** group

3 Choose the chart subtype, e.g. **2-D Stacked Column** (to show how each share contributes to the total value)

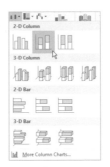

4 The chart is superimposed over the data on the worksheet, and **Chart Tools** (**Design, Layout,** and **Format** tabs) are added to the Ribbon

Hot tip

When you move the mouse pointer over any of the chart subtypes, you get a description and an indication of when that chart subtype might prove useful.

Stacked Column

Use this chart type to:
• Compare parts of a whole.
• Show how parts of a whole change over time.

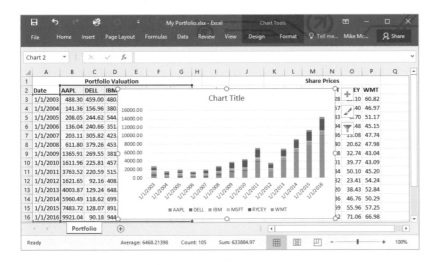

5 Click **Move Chart,** in the **Location** group on the **Design** tab, to choose where you want the chart to be placed. For example, choose **New sheet** to create a separate chart sheet with a default name of "Chart1"

Don't forget

You can also move the chart on the worksheet, by clicking on the border and dragging it to another part of the worksheet.

125

Default Chart Type

Excel will recommend chart types for your selected data:

1 Click the **Recommended Charts** button (or click the arrow on the corner of the **Charts** group)

The **Recommended Charts** button lets you pick from a variety of charts that are right for your data.

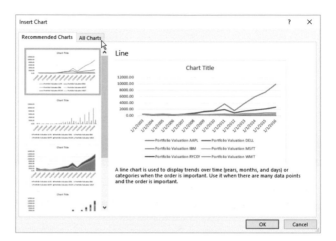

The usual default chart type is a **2-D Clustered Column**, which compares values across categories, using vertical rectangles.

2 Click the **All Charts** tab to see the range of charts

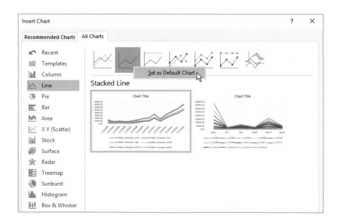

The **2-D Stacked Line** chart selected as the new default shows the trend in the contribution, from each of the categories.

3 Right-click any chart type and select **Set as Default Chart** from the context menu

4 With a data range selected, press **F11** and the default chart type is displayed on a chart sheet, using the next free name ("Chart1" in this case)

Change Chart Layout

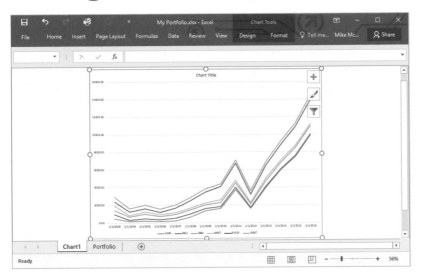

Select **Quick Layout** from **Chart Layouts** to quickly try out some predefined chart layouts.

1 Select the **Design** tab **Chart Layouts** group and click **Add Chart Element**

2 Select **Chart Title** and choose the position, e.g. **Above Chart**

3 Right-click the sample words "Chart Title", then select **Edit Text**, to amend the wording, and **Font** to amend its style

In the same way, you can add **Axis Titles** and adjust the **Gridlines**.

127

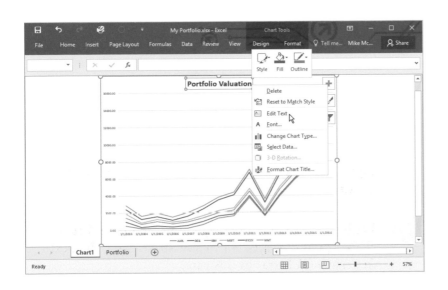

Instead of typing the titles directly, link to a cell on the worksheet. Click in the title, type = on the Formula Bar, select the cell with the text, then press **Enter**.

Legend and Data Table

1 Select **Design**, **Add Chart Element**, **Legend** and choose its position (and alignment) on the chart, e.g. **Right**

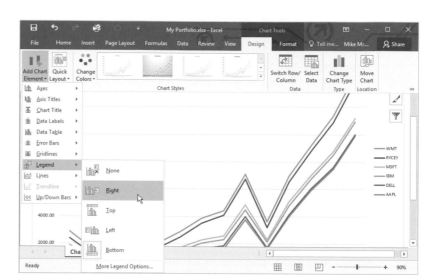

Hot tip

The **Legend** provides the key to the entries on the chart. In this case, the stock symbols for all of the shares.

Hot tip

You can also display data labels, to show the data values at each point on the lines.

2 To show the full details, click **Data Table**, and choose where to position the table, and whether to display keys

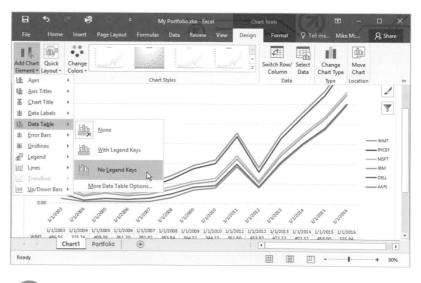

Don't forget

If you show the data for the chart in a table and include **Legend** keys, you can then select **None** to turn off the display of the **Legend** itself.

3 Again, you can adjust the text size and style for the entries in the **Legend** and the **Data Table**

Change Chart Type

1 Select the **Design** tab, and click **Change Chart Type** from the **Type** group

2 In the **Change Chart Type** dialog, select the chart type and subtype (for example, chart type **Area** and subtype **Stacked Area**), then click **OK**

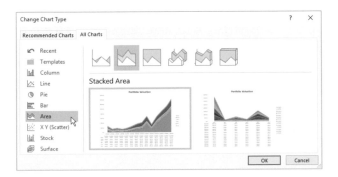

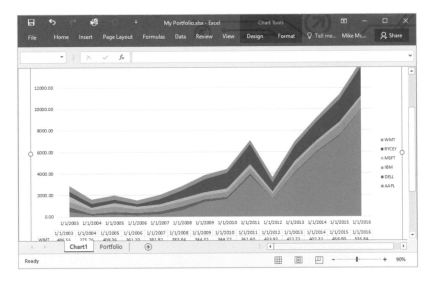

3 The **Design, Chart Styles** group allows you to change the colors and the overall visual style for your chart

Chart Styles

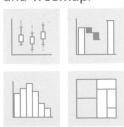

Pie Chart

A **Pie Chart** compares contributions of individual items to the total. This is intended for a single set of data, such as a year's share values.

Excel 2016 will first load a placeholder for large charts and then load text right away – so you can start editing without delay.

1 Select the data labels and one set of data in an adjacent row (or hold down **Ctrl** to select non-adjacent cells)

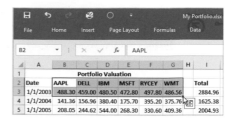

	A	B	C	D	E	F	G	H	I
1				Portfolio Valuation					
2	Date	AAPL	DELL	IBM	MSFT	RYCEY	WMT		Total
3	1/1/2003	488.30	459.00	480.50	472.80	497.80	486.56		2884.96
4	1/1/2004	141.36	156.96	380.40	175.70	395.20	375.76		1625.38
5	1/1/2005	208.05	244.62	544.00	268.30	330.60	409.36		2004.93

2 Click the **Insert** tab, select Pie from the **Charts** group, and choose the chart type – the standard **2-D Pie Chart**, for example

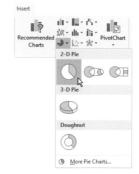

3 Click the **Design** tab, and select **Move Chart**, to create a chart sheet – "Chart2", for example

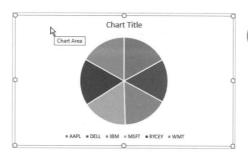

4 Select **Quick Layout**, in the **Chart Layouts** group, and choose a predefined layout to handle data labels, legend and titles

This layout shows the data labels, and the relative percentage contributions to the total value, shown on the pie chart segments, rather than using a separate legend box.

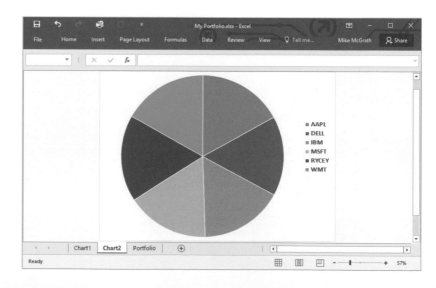

...cont'd

You can also change the data series selected for the chart:

1 Select the **Chart Tools Design** tab, and then click **Select Data**, in the **Data** group

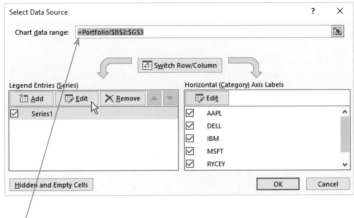

You can also right-click the chart and choose **Select Data**, to modify the data source settings.

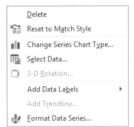

2 Here, the data range is for 2003. Click the data selection (usually "Series1"), and then click the **Edit** button

3 Edit the values to select a new data range, such as the 2012 values, then click **OK** to update the pie chart

Note how Excel decides where to put the data label, moving it outside the segment if the text won't fit into the space available.

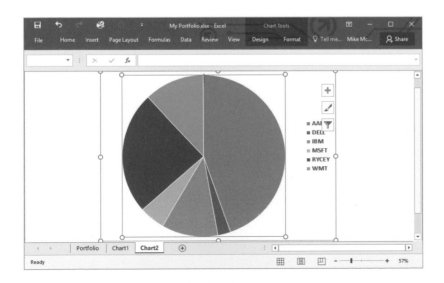

131

3-D Pie Chart

One of the subtypes for the pie chart offers a 3-D view.

1 Select the **Chart Tools Design** tab, click **Change Chart Type**, select **Pie**, **3-D Pie**, and then click **OK**

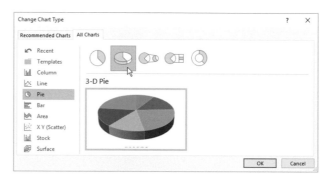

Don't forget

In a 3-D pie chart, it is the chart segments that are displayed in 3-D format, rather than the data itself (hence the grayed Z component).

132

2 Right-click the chart, select **3-D Rotation**, then set rotation values (e.g. X: 270°, Y: 30°, Perspective: 15°), then click **Close**

3 The information is presented in 3-D display form. You can select **Chart Tools, Format** to adjust the appearance, e.g. to add a background color

Hot tip

Experiment with the rotation and format options, to find the most effective presentation form for your data.

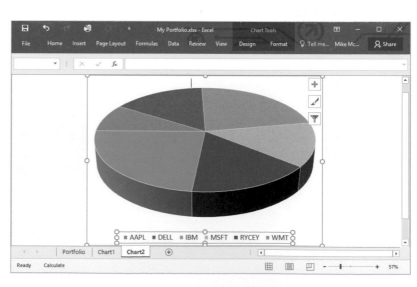

3-D Column Chart

A true 3-D chart has three sets of values to plot, giving three axes.
In the example data, these are "Shares", "Values", and "Dates".

1 Select the data, click **Insert**, **Charts**, **Column**, and select
the **3-D Column** chart type

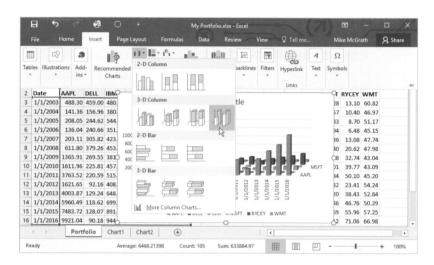

Hot tip

The **3-D Area** chart also
presents data using three
axes, to give a true 3-D
representation.

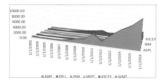

2 Select **Chart Tools**, **Design**, and **Format**, to make the
desired adjustments to the appearance. Right-click and
select **3-D Rotation** to change orientation and perspective

3 Right-click the chart and choose **Move Chart**, then select
New sheet as say, "Chart 3"

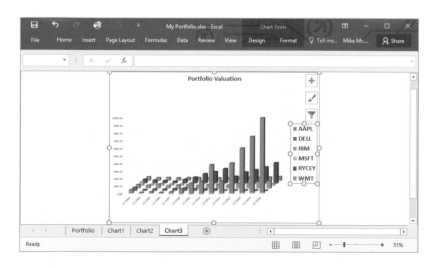

Don't forget

Click **Chart Tools**,
Design, **Select Data**,
and click the **Switch
Row/Column** button
to exchange the
horizontal and depth
axes, to give a different
view of the data.

Share Price Data

The share prices in a portfolio worksheet could be taken from price history tables downloaded from the Yahoo Finance website.

1 Go to **finance.yahoo.com**, search for the stock code, **MSFT** for example, then click the **Historical Prices** link

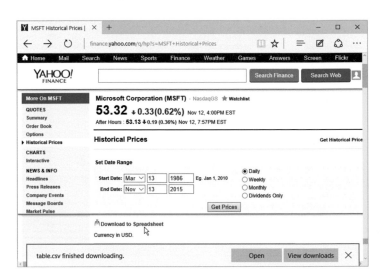

Don't forget

The price history table from **Yahoo! Finance** provides information in reverse date sequence, on a daily, weekly, or monthly basis. Use the **Adjusted Close** values to ensure that the prices are comparable over time.

2 Scroll down to the end of the list, and click **Download to Spreadsheet**

This provides a comma-separated file of dates, prices, and volumes for the selected share. The data can be sorted and converted into an Excel lookup table.

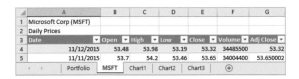

Hot tip

See page 72 for details on converting a range into an Excel table. See page 90 for an example of using the **HLOOKUP** function.

The lookup table for each share is used to find the price of the share on particular dates.

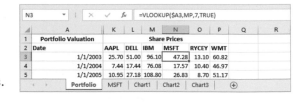

Line Chart

The charts, so far, have used just a few dates from the tables. The complete tables, however, provide a continuous view of the data.

1 The **Historical** worksheet contains the date column and adjusted closing price column for each of the shares

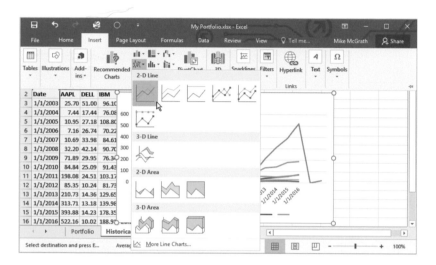

135

Hot tip

You can choose line, stacked line, or 100% stacked line (with or without markers). There's also a **3-D Line**, but this is just a perspective view, not three axes of data.

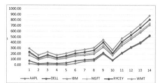

2 Select the data, click **Insert**, **Chart and Line**, then choose the **2-D Line** chart subtype, to get a plot for each share

3 Right-click the chart and choose **Move Chart**, then select **New sheet** as say, "Chart 4"

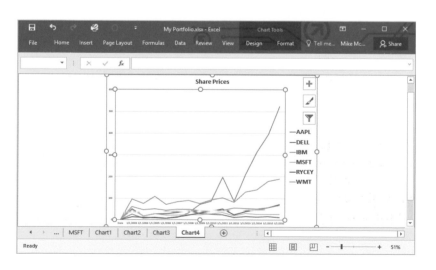

Don't forget

As with all the charts, you can move this chart to a separate chart sheet and adjust position and styles for the titles and the legend.

Stock Chart

The downloaded share data can also be used for a special type of chart, known as the **Stock** chart.

1 From the shares table, filter the data (e.g. for 2014), and then select the columns for Date, Open, High, Low, and Close

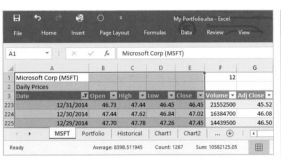

2 Open the **Insert Chart** dialog (see page 126), select the **Stock** charts, select type **Open-High-Low-Close**, and then click **OK**

3 The prices are plotted, with lines for high/low, hollow boxes for increases, and solid boxes for decreases

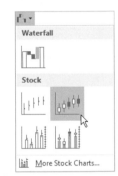

Beware

This chart type requires data in a specific layout for the chart subtype, e.g. **High-Low-Close** or **Open-High-Low-Close** (and the date values can be used as data labels).

Hot tip

Move the chart to a separate chart sheet, add titles, and format the titles and the legend. Right-click the axis, and select **Format Axis** to change the minimum and maximum, to emphasize the price spreads.

Mixed Types

You can have more than one type of chart displayed at the same time, as in the **Volume** subtypes of the **Stock** chart.

1 Insert a table column after the Date column, and move the Volume column to that position

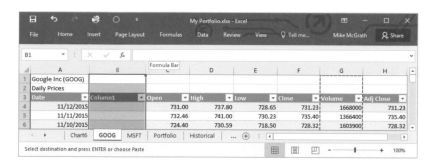

2 Select the data, including headings, and **Insert** the **Stock** chart, choosing type **Volume-Open-High-Low-Close**

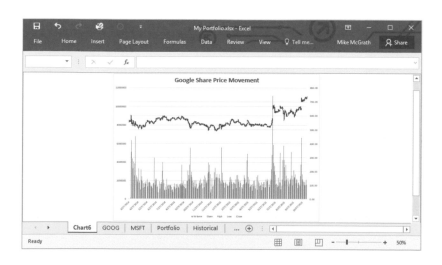

3 The chart uses two vertical axes, to show volume and price values

Print Charts

When you have an embedded chart in your worksheet, it prints as positioned, along with the data, when you select **Print** from the **File** tab and click the **Print** button. To print the chart on its own:

1 Select the chart, then select the **File** tab and click **Print**

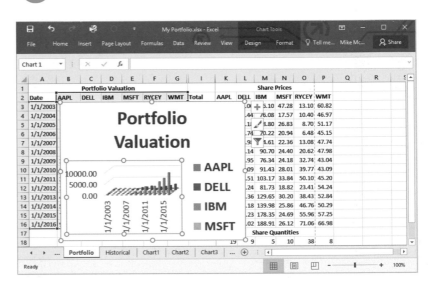

2 An extra "Print what" option (**Selected Chart**) appears, and the other options are grayed, so only the chart will print

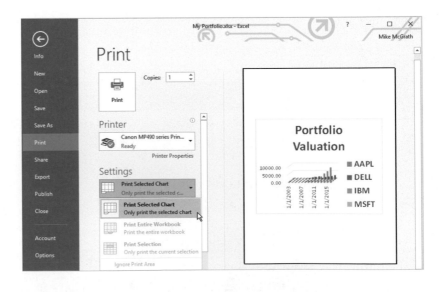

9 Macros in Excel

If there are tasks that you carry out frequently, you can define the actions required, as a macro. You can assign the macro to a key combination, or to an icon on the toolbar, to make it easy to reuse. However, you must make sure that security is in place to prevent abuse.

Beware

Macros are powerful, but they can be subject to misuse. Microsoft has included security checks and limitations in Excel to authenticate macros, and to help prevent them being introduced into your system and run without your knowledge.

Don't forget

To check which type of workbook you have open, tell Windows to reveal the file type (see page 37).

Beware

Enable all macros is not recommended as a permanent setting. Select a more restricted level as soon as you have finished creating or changing the macros stored in your active workbook.

Macros

Any task in Excel may be performed by a "macro". Macros are often used to carry out simple but repetitive tasks, such as entering your name and address, or inserting a standard piece of text. In other cases, macros may be used for complex and involved tasks, difficult to reproduce accurately without some kind of help.

To create a macro, carry out an example of the actions, with Excel recording the keystrokes involved as you complete the task. The sequence is stored as a macro in the **Visual Basic for Applications** (VBA) programming language. You can edit your recorded macro, or create new macros, using the Visual Basic Editor.

Macros can be very powerful, because they are able to run commands on your computer. For this reason, Microsoft Excel prevents the default Excel 2016 file format (file type **.xlsx**) from storing VBA macro code. Therefore, the recommended place for storing the macros you create is in your hidden **Personal Macro Workbook**, and this is the method used for the examples in the following pages. If you share macros, they need to be stored in the workbooks that use them. These workbooks must then be saved in the Excel 2016 macro-enabled file format (file type **.xlsm**). You may need to reset the security level, temporarily, to enable all macros, so that you can work on macros in the active workbook:

1 Select the **File** tab, **Options**, **Trust Center**, then click the **Trust Center Settings** and select **Macro Settings**

2 Check the setting to enable all macros, then click **OK**

Create Macros

To display the commands for recording and viewing macros:

1 Select the **View** tab, and click the arrow below the **Macros** button, in the **Macros** group

2 You can choose to view or record macros, and choose between relative or absolute cell references (a toggle setting)

These options are also available from the **Developer** tab, along with the **Macro Security** and **Visual Basic** commands. By default, this tab is not displayed. To add the **Developer** tab to the Ribbon:

1 Click the **File** tab, and then select **Options** (or press the keys **Alt F T**) and choose **Customize Ribbon**

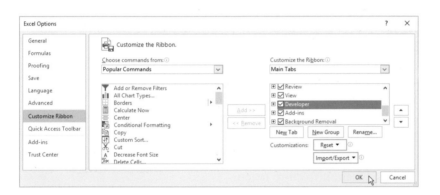

2 Click the **Developer** box in the **Main Tabs** section, and the **Developer** tab will be added to the Tab Bar

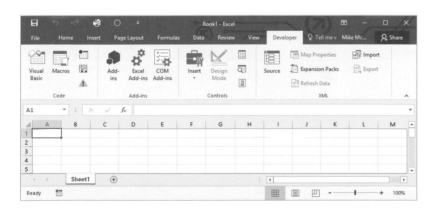

Selecting the **Macros** button, rather than the arrow, has the same effect as selecting the **View Macros** entry.

You can record, view, and edit macros, using commands from either the **View** tab or the **Developer** tab, but to create macros from scratch, or to change security settings, you will need to use the **Developer** tab.

Record a Macro

Assume that you need to add some standard disclaimer text to a number of workbooks. To create a macro for this:

1 Open a blank workbook, and click in cell A1

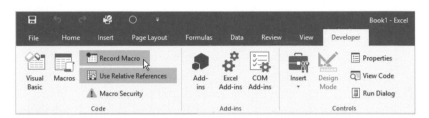

2 Select the **Developer** tab, then from the **Code** group click the **Use Relative References** button and the **Record Macro** button – to open the **Record Macro** dialog box

3 Enter a name for the macro, and specify a shortcut key, such as **Shift + D** (the **Ctrl** key is automatically added)

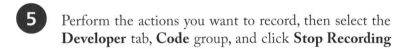

4 Select **Personal Macro Workbook** (the preferred location to store macros), add a description, then click **OK** to start the recording

5 Perform the actions you want to record, then select the **Developer** tab, **Code** group, and click **Stop Recording**

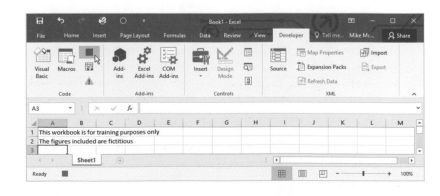

...cont'd

To check out the macro:

1 Click in a different cell, C4 for example, then press the **Shift + Ctrl + D** shortcut to try out the macro

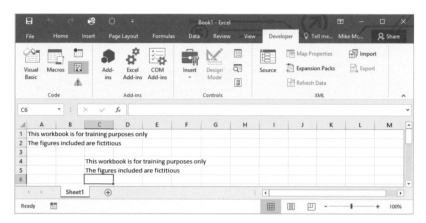

If there are problems with the macro, you may be able to use the **Visual Basic Editor** to make the changes that are needed (see page 148).

2 The text is entered into the worksheet, in the active cell

The start location changes, because the macro was created with relative references. However, if you click in any specific cells while the macro is being recorded, those references will be honored.

When you have finished checking the macro, close the workbook:

1 Click the **File** tab, and select **Close**

2 Select **Don't Save** when asked if you want to save changes

The relative reference applies to the macro, as the initial cell was selected before macro recording was started.

The macro itself will be retained in the **Personal Macro Workbook**. This will be saved at the end of the Excel session (see page 144).

Active Workbooks Macros

If you selected to store the recorded macro in the active workbook, you must save that workbook as file type **.xlsm**. You will also need to reset the level of macro security (see page 140).

When you close the active workbook, the macros it contains will no longer be available in that Excel session, unless you save it – as described on page 144.

Apply the Macro

1 Open a workbook that requires the disclaimer text, and select the location (e.g. My Personal Budget, cell A16)

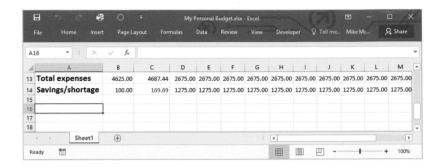

2 Press the shortcut **Shift + Ctrl + D** to run the macro

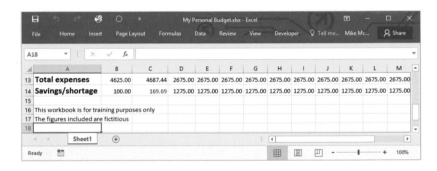

3 Save the worksheet (no need to change the file type)

4 When you end the Excel session, you can save your **Personal Macro Workbook**, and, with it, any macros that you have created during the session

View the Macro

1 Select the **View** tab, then, from the **Window** group, click the **Unhide** button

2 In the **Unhide** dialog box, select "Personal.xlsb", which is your **Personal Macro Workbook**, then click **OK**

3 From the **Developer** tab **Code** group, select **Macros**

4 Select the macro you want to review and click **Edit**, to display the code in the **Visual Basic Editor**

5 Select **File** and then **Save Personal.xlsb**, to save any changes. To finish, select **File** and then **Close and Return to Microsoft Excel**

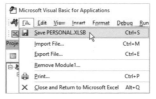

You can view and edit the macro. However, since it is stored in a hidden workbook, you must start by making the workbook visible.

You can make changes to the macro, e.g. revise the text that is entered into the cells, even if you don't know the VBA language.

When you've finished viewing or changing your macros, you should select **View**, **Hide**, to hide the **Personal Macro Workbook**.

Macro to Make a Table

1 Open a share history file, "YHOO.csv" for example

You can record a macro that carries out a more complex task, creating an Excel table from a Share history file for example.

2 Select **Developer, Use Relative References**, and then click **Record Macro**

3 Specify the macro name, shortcut, and description, then click **OK**, to start recording

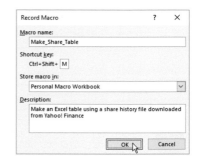

The keystroke steps in the process are as follows:

1 Go to cell A3 (the start of the data range):
Alt H FD G A3 Enter

You may find that it is better to use keystrokes, rather than mouse selections, when creating a macro. It is also useful to carry out a practice run, noting the keystrokes required, and then record the macro.

2 Select the whole data range (A3:G910 in this example) using the end and arrows keys:
ShiftDown (press and hold down Shift key)
End RightArrow
End DownArrow
ShiftUp (release Shift key)

...cont'd

Don't forget

This shows the data range selected, ready for creating the Excel table.

3 Create an Excel Table from the selected set of data:
Alt N T Enter

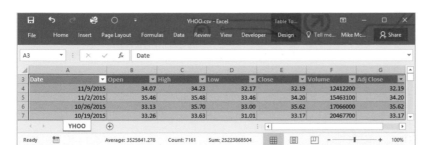

Don't forget

The table is created, but the date column is in descending order (unsuitable for a lookup table).

4 Go to cell A4 (the date field in first row of actual data):
Alt H FD G A4 Enter

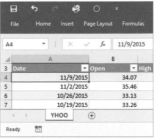

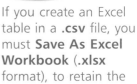

Beware

If you create an Excel table in a **.csv** file, you must **Save As Excel Workbook (.xlsx** format), to retain the table (see page 149).

5 Sort the column in ascending date sequence:
Alt A SA

6 Click **Developer, Stop Recording,** to complete the macro

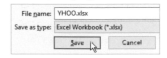

Edit the Macro

1 Unhide the **Personal Macro Workbook** (see page 145)

2 Select **Developer**, then **Macros**, from the **Code** group

Check the recorded macro, to see if any changes are needed.

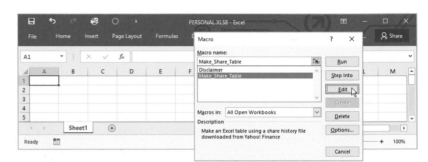

3 Select the "Make_Share_Table" macro, and click **Edit**, to display the code in the **Visual Basic Editor**

148

You should hide the **Personal Macro Workbook** when you have finished making changes to the macro.

Sections of the macro may be specific to the original workbook. In this case, there are references to the worksheet name. These can be replaced with the generic reference to **ActiveSheet**.

4 Select **Edit, Replace**, to replace "Worksheets("YHOO")" with "ActiveSheet", and then click the **Replace All** button

5 To save changes, select **File, Save Personal.xlsb**, then select **File, Close and Return to Microsoft Excel**

Use the Macro

1 Open another share history file ("ibm.csv", for example) that needs to be changed to an Excel table

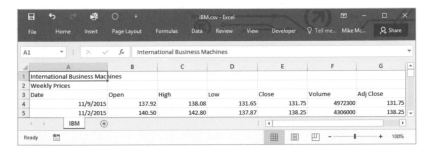

2 Press the macro shortcut key, **Shift + Ctrl + M**, and the data range is immediately converted to Excel table format

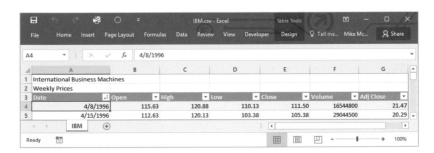

3 Save the worksheet as file type **Excel Workbook (.xlsx)**

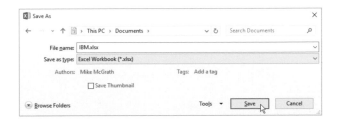

Repeat this for any other share history files, which can each be converted to Excel table format with a single click of the **Make_Share_Table** macro shortcut key.

Follow a similar procedure to create and test macros for any other tasks that you need to complete on a regular basis.

As written, the macro assumes that the worksheet will have data in rows 4 to 1025 (1996-2015). If there are fewer actual rows, the remainder will appear as empty table rows. Extra rows will be stored after the table.

The macro now refers to the **ActiveSheet**, so it converts the data range in the current worksheet, without regard to its name.

The macro remains in the **Personal Macro Workbook**, so the share workbooks do not need to be macro-enabled.

149

Create Macros with VBA

1 Display the **Developer** tab on the Ribbon (see page 141)

2 Select the **Developer** tab, and then select **Visual Basic**

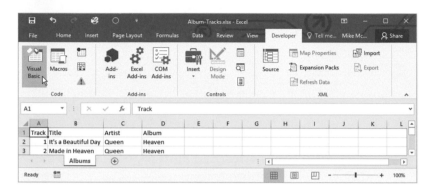

Hot tip

A list of Album Tracks is used here, to illustrate the use of Visual Basic to create a macro, in this case, to insert page breaks after each album.

Hot tip

You can discover more about Visual Basic programming in our companion book **Visual Basic in easy steps**.

Don't forget

This macro identifies the last non-blank row in the worksheet. It checks the values in column 4 (Album name), and inserts a page break whenever the name changes.

3 Click **VBAProject** for **Personal.xlsb**, and then select **Insert**, **Module**

4 In the code window for the module, type (or paste) the code for your macro

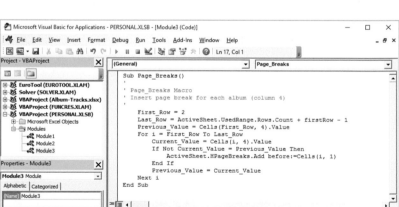

```vba
Sub Page_Breaks()
'
' Page_Breaks Macro
' Insert page break for each album (column 4)

    First_Row = 2
    Last_Row = ActiveSheet.UsedRange.Rows.Count + firstRow - 1
    Previous_Value = Cells(First_Row, 4).Value
    For i = First_Row To Last_Row
        Current_Value = Cells(i, 4).Value
        If Not Current_Value = Previous_Value Then
            ActiveSheet.HPageBreaks.Add before:=Cells(i, 1)
        End If
        Previous_Value = Current_Value
    Next i
End Sub
```

5 When you have entered and checked the macro code, select **File**, **Close and Return to Microsoft Excel**

You can search on the internet for sample Visual Basic macros, e.g. at **code.msdn.microsoft.com**

...cont'd

6 In the "Music_list" worksheet, click the **Page Break Preview** button on the status bar, to see the page setup

Page breaks occur at regular intervals, based on the number of lines, and independent of the albums themselves.

To apply page breaks based on albums:

1 Click the **Developer** tab **Macros** button

2 Select the **Page_Breaks** macro, and click **Run**

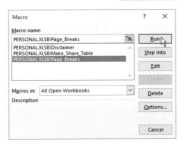

3 Manual page breaks are inserted at every change of album in the worksheet data range

The **Page_Breaks** macro is now stored in the **Personal Macro Workbook**, ready for use when required.

151

Save the workbook, to retain the new page breaks, or just print the pages required and close it without saving. The page breaks can be reinserted at any time, by re-running the macro.

4 Select **Page Layout**, **Print Titles**, and set **Rows to repeat at top** to replicate the headings on every page

Add Macros to the Toolbar

If you specified a **Ctrl** or **Shift + Ctrl** shortcut when you created your macro, you can run the macro by pressing the appropriate key combination. You can also run the macro by clicking the **Macros** button, from the **View** tab or the **Developer** tab. To make macros more accessible, you can add the **View Macros** option to the Quick Access Toolbar:

You could also right-click the **Macros** button, and select **Add to Quick Access Toolbar**.

1 Select **File**, **Options**, and select **Quick Access Toolbar**, then **Popular Commands** in **Choose commands from**

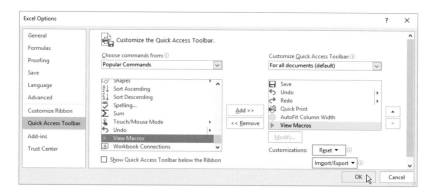

2 Click **View Macros**, click **Add**, and click **OK**. **View Macros** now appears on the Quick Access Toolbar

If you want to add or change the shortcut key for a macro, select it by using the Macros button, and then click the Options button.

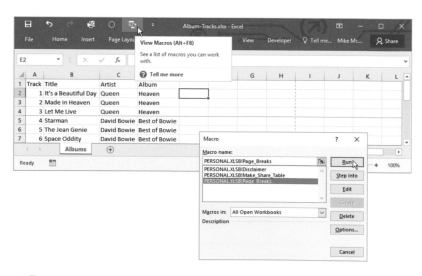

3 To run a macro, click the **View Macros** button on the toolbar, select the macro that you want, and click **Run**

...cont'd

Alternatively, you can add macros as individual icons on the Quick Access Toolbar. To do this:

1 Open Excel **Options**, select **Quick Access Toolbar**, then **Macros** in **Choose commands from**

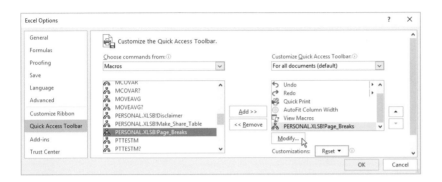

2 Scroll down to the particular macros, select each one in turn, and click **Add**

3 Each macro will have the same icon. You can click **Modify**, and select a different icon

4 The icons for the macros are added to the Quick Access Toolbar

Macros can also be associated with graphics, or hot spots on the worksheet.

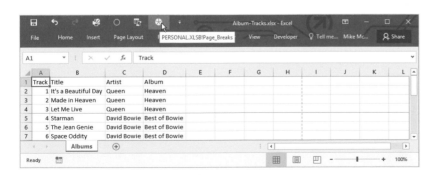

5 The tooltip shows the name of the macro, which runs immediately when you select its icon

Debug Macros

If you are having a problem with a macro, or if you are just curious to see how it works, you can run it one step at a time:

Open a worksheet for which the macro was written, before selecting the **Step Into** option.

1 Select **Macros** from **Developer** (or from **View**), choose the macro you want to run, and click **Step Into**

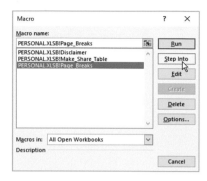

2 Press **F8** repeatedly to run through the code, one step at a time

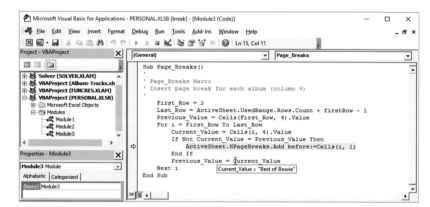

3 Hold the mouse over a variable, to see its current value

The breakpoint is the macro statement at which execution will automatically stop. The breakpoints you set will not be saved with the code when you exit.

4 Select **Debug**, to see the other testing options available, such as setting breakpoints

5 Press **F5** to continue to the next breakpoint (or to complete the macro, if no breakpoints are set)

6 To finish, select **File, Close and Return to Microsoft Excel**

154

10 Templates and Scenarios

For the most frequent uses of Excel, you'll find ready-made templates to give you a head start. There are more Excel resources at Microsoft Office Support and other websites. Excel also has special problem-solving tools.

Templates

You can save effort, and you may discover new aspects of Excel, if you base your new workbooks on available templates.

1 Click the **File** tab, and then click **New** (or press **Ctrl + N**), to see the blank workbook and other available templates

2 Review the example templates, or select a category such as "Loan" to see more templates

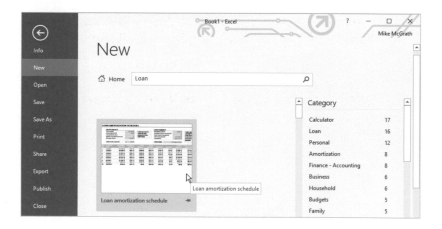

156

3 Select the template you want to use, "Loan amortization schedule" for example, and click **Create**

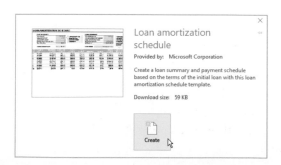

4 The input boxes are predefined with data, so that you can check out the way the workbook operates

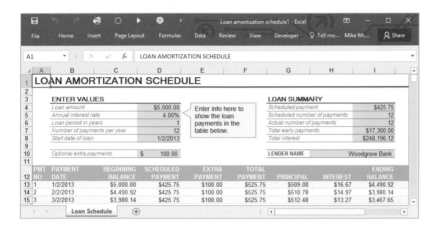

Hot tip

Review the data, and then make changes to the values, to see the effect. For example, change the payments per annum from 12 to 6.

5 Adjust the values, and the worksheet is extended by the number of payments, and displays the calculated amounts

6 To view the formulas behind the calculations, press **Ctrl + `** (or select **Show Formulas** on the **Formulas** tab)

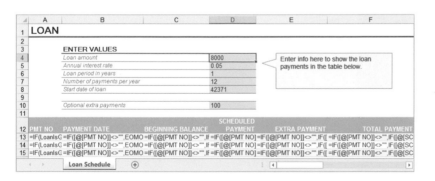

Don't forget

To keep the results, you need to save the workbook – the default name is the template name, with a number appended.

7 Select the **Formulas** tab and click the **Name Manager** button (or press **Ctrl + F3**), to see the names defined in the workbook, with values and references

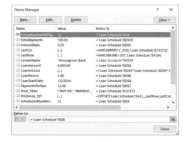

Online Templates

To help in creating a workbook for a particular purpose, you can amend an existing template and save the revised copy in your **Custom Office Templates** library for later use:

1 Select **File**, **New**, and click **Search for online templates**, then enter a search term, e.g. "exercise", and click the magnifier

2 Matching templates will be listed, and a series of related subcategories offered, to help focus on the topic

3 Scroll down and you will see that related templates from your other Office applications may also be detected

4 Choose a template, to **Create** and **Save** a workbook (see page 156)

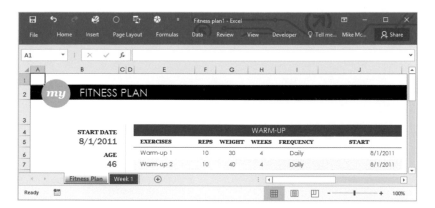

If the template contains macros or VB code, you will need to save it as an **Excel Macro-Enabled Template (*.xltm)**.

5 Select **File, Save As,** select the **Custom Office Templates** folder and choose the type of **Excel Template (*.xltx)**

6 Select **File, New, Personal** to view your templates

You can also save an Excel Workbook as a template to use as the basis for other workbooks. Such templates are also saved in the **Personal** area.

More Excel Resources

The internet is a prolific source of advice and guidance for Excel users at all levels. Here are some websites that may prove useful:

A search on Google.com with Excel-related search terms will result in millions of matches, so it may be easier to start from a more focused website such as Microsoft Office Support.

1 Open your web browser and visit **support.office.com**

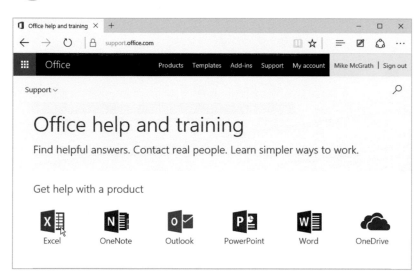

2 Select the Excel icon from the Office applications to find tutorials and tips for using Excel

The actual links and content for the Office web pages change over time, but you should expect to find links similar to those shown.

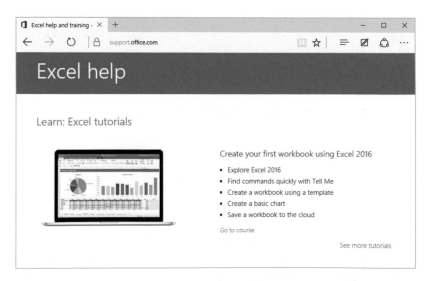

3 Click the **See more tutorials** link, then select **Excel 2016 training** to discover some training courses

4 Scroll to the end of the **Excel help** page then click the **Ask the community** link to ask any Excel questions you may have

Ask the community
Post, discuss and find answers

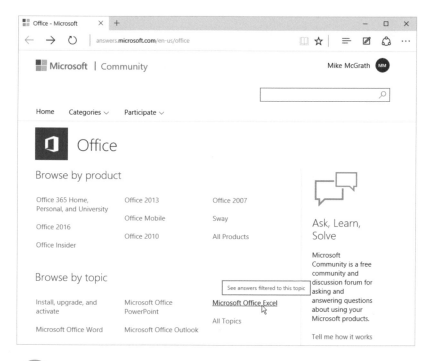

There is every possibility that your Excel question may have been answered previously on the community forum – use the Search box before repeating the question.

5 Microsoft MVPs (most valued professionals) can also provide useful information. Go to **mvp.microsoft.com**

6 Select **Find an MVP**, then enter the **Keyword** "Excel", and your **Country or region**, for a list of local specialists

You'll find that many forum references relate to Excel 2010, 2007 or other versions. These will often be just as applicable when you are running Excel 2016.

What-If Analysis

A **What-If Analysis** involves the process of changing values in cells, to see how those changes affect the outcome on the worksheet. A set of values that represent a particular outcome is known as a scenario. To create a scenario:

Sometimes you can set up your worksheet so that several outcomes are visible at once (as in the PMT example on page 93). You can get a similar effect by using a **What-If Analysis**, and defining scenarios.

1 Open the worksheet, and enter details for a loan; a 25-year mortgage, for example

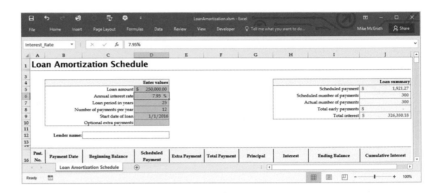

162

In Excel 2016 you can easily create a new worksheet to forecast data trends using the **Forecast Sheet** option on the **Data** tab.

2 Select the **Data** tab, and, from the **Data Tools** group, click **What-If Analysis**, then choose **Scenario Manager**

3 Click **Add**, type a scenario name (e.g. "X000"), enter the address references for the cells that you may want to change, and then click **OK**

In this case, the scenarios explore the effects of making extra payments, with the first scenario having an extra payment of zero.

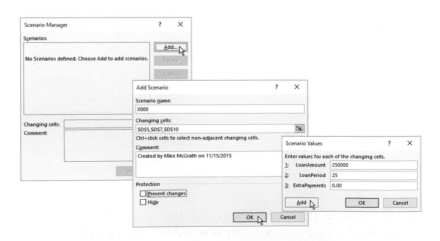

...cont'd

4 Change cells from their initial values, as required. In this case, adjusting the value of **Scheduled_Extra_Payments**

5 Repeat steps 3 & 4 for each scenario, clicking **Add** then **OK**, incrementing each by 50 (i.e. "X050"... "X350" and 50.00...350.00) finally, clicking **OK** after the last scenario

Additional input cells (**Loan_Amount** and **Loan_Years**) have been selected. They have been left unchanged for these scenarios, but give the option for other scenarios in a future analysis.

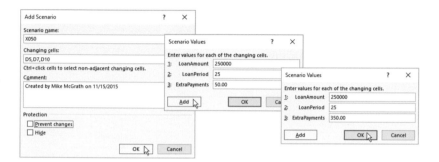

6 Select one of the scenarios, e.g. "X200", and click **Show** to display the associated results on the worksheet

7 Select **Close**, to exit the **Scenario Manager** and return to the worksheet

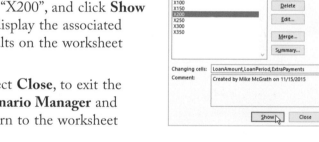

163

You can click **Edit** to make changes, or corrections to a scenario, or click **Delete** to remove unwanted scenarios.

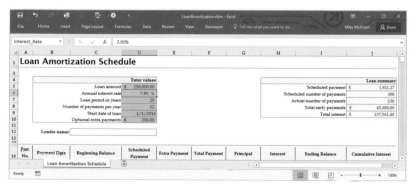

The results from the scenario that was last shown will be displayed. If no scenario was left selected in the **Scenario Manager,** the original worksheet values will be shown.

Summary Reports

To create a scenario summary report, showing all the possible outcomes on one worksheet:

1 On the **Data** tab, in the **Data Tools** group, click **What-If Analysis**, click **Scenario Manager**, and then click **Summary**

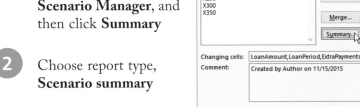

2 Choose report type, **Scenario summary**

3 Enter the references for the cells that you want to track (cells with values modified by the changes in scenario values), in this case J7 (actual number of payments) and J9 (total interest)

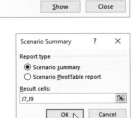

4 The outcomes for each of the scenarios are calculated, and the results placed on a new worksheet named "Scenario Summary". The **Changing Cells** section displays the values for each scenario of the cells that were selected on creation of the scenario. The **Result Cells** section shows the cell payments and **Total_Interest** when the summary report was created. The **Current Values** column shows the original values, before the scenarios were defined

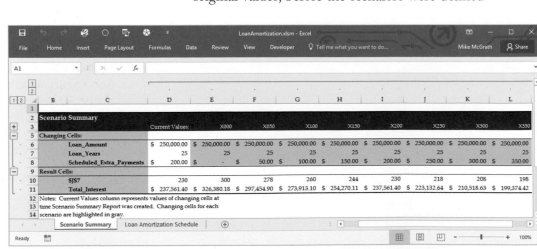

...cont'd

The results can also be presented as a **Scenario PivotTable** report:

1 Open the **Scenario Manager**, click **Summary**, choose **Scenario PivotTable report**, and enter the references for the result cells

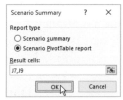

2 The results are shown in a table on a separate worksheet

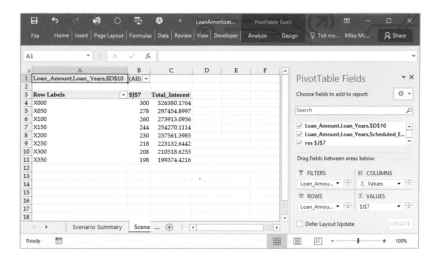

3 Select **PivotTable Tools**, **Analyze** tab, then select **PivotChart** from the **Tools** group, choose the type of chart, e.g. **Line** chart, and then click **OK**

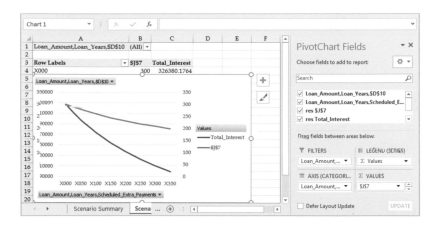

Beware

You must switch back to the **Loan Amortization Schedule** worksheet, before opening the **Scenario Manager**.

Hot tip

To generate a **Scenario PivotTable report**, it is always necessary to specify the relevant result cells you desire.

Don't forget

You can adjust the **Axis Options** to display a **Secondary Vertical Value Axis** as shown here, and you can select **Design**, **Move Chart**, and place the **PivotChart** on a separate worksheet.

Goal Seek

If you know the result that you want from an analysis, but not the input values the worksheet needs to get that result, you can use the **Goal Seek** feature. For example, you can use **Goal Seek** in the "Loan Amortization" worksheet, to determine the extra payment required to keep total interest below $150,000:

1 Select **Data**, then **What-If Analysis** from **Data Tools**, and then **Goal Seek**

2 For **Set cell**, enter the reference for the cell with the target value (cell J9, for "Total interest")

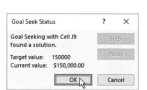

3 In the box for the **To value**, type the result you want (i.e. 150000)

4 In the box for **By changing cell**, enter the reference for the cell that contains the value you want to adjust (D10, for "Optional extra payments")

5 The value in D10 is rapidly varied, and the worksheet continually recalculated, until the target value of interest is reached

6 Click **OK** to return to the worksheet, at the target value

166

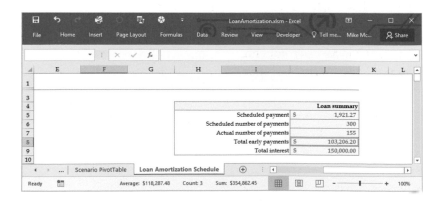

7 Save the results as another scenario, for later reference

Optimization

Goal Seek allows you to solve problems where you want to find the value of a single input, to generate the desired result. It is of no help when you need to find the best values for several inputs. For this, you require an optimizer, a software tool that helps you find the best way to allocate resources. These could be raw materials, machine time, people time, money, or anything that is in limited supply. The best or optimal solution will perhaps be the one that maximizes profit, or minimizes cost, or meets some other requirement. All kinds of situations can be tackled in this way, including allocating finance, scheduling production, blending raw materials, routing goods, and loading transportation.

Excel includes an add-in optimizer, called **Solver**. You may need to install this (see page 103) if it doesn't appear on your system. To illustrate **Solver**, we'll examine a product mix problem.

Sample Solver Problem

Imagine that your hobby is textiles, and that you produce craft goods (ponchos, scarves, and gloves). There's a craft fair coming up, and you plan to use your existing inventory of materials (warp, weft, and braid) and your available time (for the loom, and to finish goods). You want to know the mix of products that will maximize profits, given the inventory and time available. These include 800 hanks of warp, 600 hanks of weft, 50 lengths of braid, 300 hours of loom time, and 200 hours of finishing time.

To produce a poncho, you will need 8 units of warp, 7 of weft, 1 of braid, 6 for loom, and 2 for finish. For a scarf, the values are 3 warp, 2 weft, 0 braid, 1 loom, and 1 finish. For a pair of gloves, they are 1 warp, 0 weft, 0 braid, 0 loom, and 4 finish.

You make the assumption that your profit is $25 per poncho, $10 per scarf, and $8 per pair of gloves.

You remember that you need four of each item as samples, to show the visitors to the fair. Also, you recall that usually half the scarves are sold in sets with gloves.

Excel 2016 lets you easily grab data from many sources using the **Get & Transform** group options on the **Data** tab.

Project Worksheet

The craft fair optimization information (see page 167) can be expressed in a worksheet, with underlying formulas as follows:

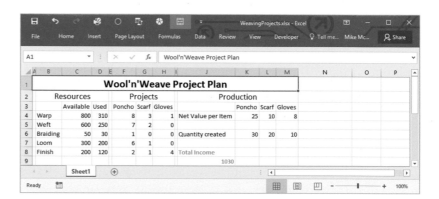

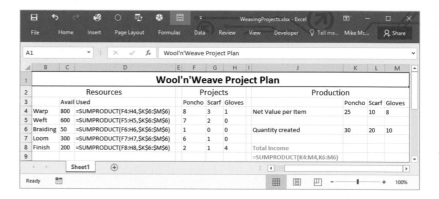

The worksheet captures the information about resources available, and the amounts needed for any specified level of production.

Some constraints are specified in the problem description, while others may be implicit (e.g. the requirement for integer (and positive) values of production).

Sample values for the production quantities have been inserted, just to check that the worksheet operates as expected. Excel **Solver** will be used to compute the optimum quantities. These limitations or constraints that must be taken into account:

1 You cannot exceed the available resources

2 There must be at least 4 of each product (samples for the craft show)

3 There must be whole numbers of products (integers)

4 There must be a pair of gloves each, for at least half the scarves (so that sets can be offered for sale)

Solver

To calculate the optimum solution for the craft fair problem:

1 Click the cell J9, which contains the target value "Total Income", then select the **Data** tab, and click **Solver** in the **Analyze** group

2 Check the **Max** option. Then, click the **By Changing Variable Cells** box, and use the collapse/expand buttons to select the product quantities cells (K6:M6)

Solver will use the currently selected cell as the target, unless you replace this reference with another cell.

3 Click the **Add** button, and select cells to specify that resources used must be less than or equal to those available

4 Click **Add**, and select cells to specify that quantities produced must be greater than or equal to 4

Click **Add**, to define the next constraint, or click **OK** to return to the **Solver Parameters** dialog box.

5 Add the constraint that quantities must be integers

...cont'd

6 Specify that the quantity of gloves must be at least half that of scarves, then click **OK**

7 Click **Solve**, and the results are calculated and displayed

8 If **Solver** finds a solution, click **Keep Solver Solution**, clear **Return to Solver Parameters Dialog**, select a report if desired, then click **OK**, to return to the workbook

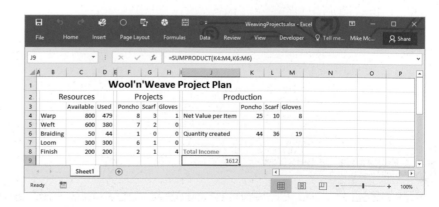

11 Links and Connections

Excel lets you make external references to other workbooks, or to web pages that contain data needed for your active worksheet. Your worksheet is updated automatically, if the source data changes. You can also share your data as an Office document, or as a PDF.

Link to Workbooks

Sometimes, you may want to refer to the data in one workbook, from another separate workbook. You may, for example, want to provide an alternative view of the data in a worksheet, or to merge data from individual workbooks, to create a summary workbook. You can refer to the contents of cells in another workbook by creating external references (also known as links).

References may be to a cell or to a range, though it is usually better to refer to a defined name in the other workbook.

To establish defined names in a source workbook:

1 Open a source workbook, **North.xlsx** for example

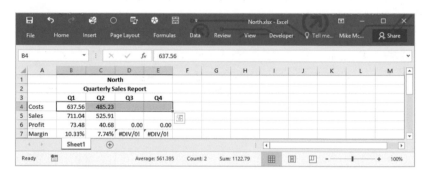

Hot tip

Workbook links are very useful when you need to combine information from several workbooks, that may be created in different locations, or on different systems.

172

Don't forget

This shows the sales by quarter, for one region, with the first two quarters entered. The calculations for margin (profit/sales) for the remaining quarters show zero divide errors, since the associated sales values are zero.

2 Select a range of cells, B4:E4 (the costs), for example

3 Select the **Formulas** tab, then click **Define Name**, from the **Defined Names** group

4 Specify the name (or accept the suggested name, based on the adjacent label "Costs"), then click **OK**

5 Repeat the **Define Name** process for the ranges of "Sales" (cells B5:E5) and "Profit" (cells B6:E6)

6 Select the **Formulas** tab, and click **Name Manager**, in the
Defined Names group, to see all the name definitions

Hot tip

The names will have the
same cell references for
the associated ranges,
as those shown for the
North workbook.

7 Save the "North" workbook to record the ranges names
that have been defined

8 Repeat this for the other source workbooks ("South",
"East", and "West"), defining the range names "Costs",
"Sales", and "Profit" in each, then save and close them

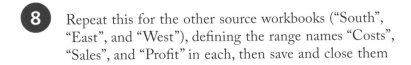

Don't forget

The benefit of links
is that, when source
workbooks change, you
won't have to make
changes manually to the
destination workbooks
that refer to those
sources.

173

Create External References

1 Open the source workbooks that contain the cells you want to refer to (e.g. "North", "South", "East", "West")

2 Open the workbook that will contain the external references (in the example, it is called **Overall.xlsx**)

You can incorporate the external reference into a function or formula, as you might with any cell reference.

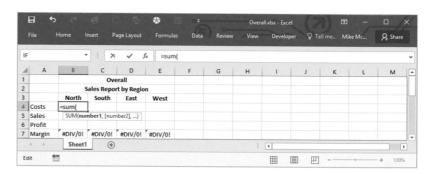

3 Select the cell in which you want to create the first of the external references (e.g. B4) and type (for example) **=sum(**

4 Select the **View** tab, and, in the **Windows** group, click **Switch Windows**, then click the source workbook to make it active (if necessary, select the worksheet that contains the cells that you want to link to)

5 Press **F3**, and select the defined name for the range of cells, e.g. "Costs", click **OK**, and then press **Enter**

When you paste **Costs** into the **Overall** worksheet it is the total costs from the **North** worksheet **Costs** row.

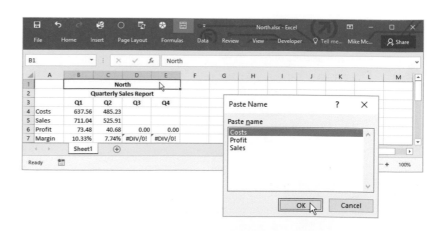

6 Similarly, enter a formula in B5 to sum "Sales", and enter a formula in B6 to sum "Profit"

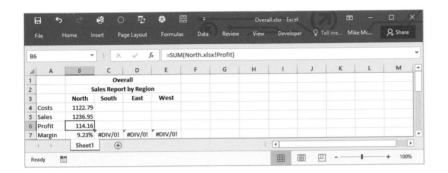

Hot tip

You can copy the formula for **Costs**, and then change the defined name to **Sales** or **Profit**.

You could refer to source workbook cells directly:

1 Click in cell B8, and type **=count(**

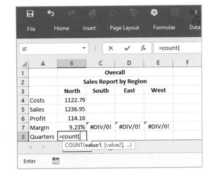

2 Switch to "North", and select the cell range B7:E7

Don't forget

This function counts the number of cells containing numbers (thus ignoring the incomplete quarters, where the **Margin** shows **#DIV/0!** – Divide by Zero).

3 Press **Enter** to complete the reference and formula

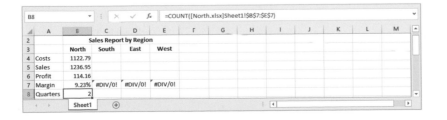

175

Styles of Reference

While the source workbooks are open, the links to defined names take the form:

North.xlsx!Costs

Where you refer to cells directly, the links take the form:

[North.xlsx]Sheet1!$B$7:$E$7

Note that the cell references could be relative or mixed, as well as absolute, as shown.

Close the source workbook, and you'll find that the external references are immediately expanded, to include a fully qualified link to the source workbook file:

Quotation marks will be applied to the workbook name, if it contains any spaces, e.g.**'Sales North.xlsx'!Costs**.

Hot tip

The references for **South**, **East**, and **West** have been incorporated. You can do this by selection, as with **North**, or you can just copy the formulas for **North**, and change the name appropriately.

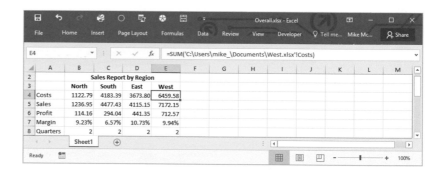

Links with direct cell references also show the file path and name:

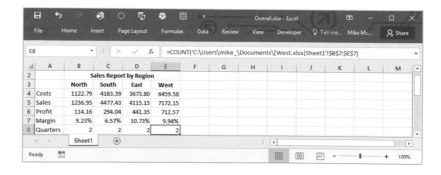

In each case, the path and file name will be enclosed in quotation marks, whether there are spaces included or not.

Source Workbook Changes

Assume that you receive new versions of the source workbooks (with the next quarter's data). You can control how and when these changes affect the destination workbook:

1 Open the destination workbook

2 By default you'll receive a warning message saying there are external links, and offering an option to apply updates

3 Select **Don't Update**, and the workbook opens, unchanged

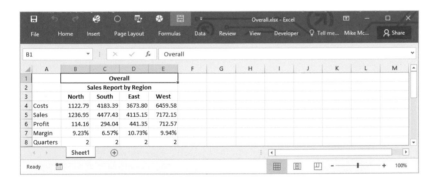

4 Select **File, Options,** click **Advanced** and review the settings for external links

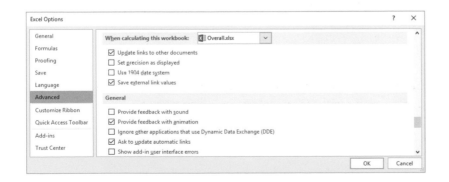

Leave source workbooks closed. When source and destination workbooks are open at the same time on the same computer, links will be updated automatically.

Select **Update**, and the source workbooks will be accessed and any changes will be applied when the destination workbook opens.

Do not use this option to turn off the prompt, or you will not be aware when workbooks get updated. Use the workbook-specific option (see page 179) instead.

Apply the Updates

1 Select the **Data** tab, then, in the **Connections** group, choose **Edit Links**

2 Select the links to refresh, and click **Update Values**

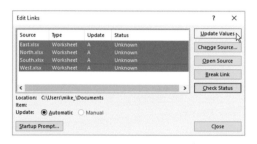

Don't forget

You can choose to only update selected entries, and you can use the **Check Status** button to see which entries still need to be applied.

Beware

Do not apply updates where you are unsure of the origin of the changes, or if you want to retain current values.

3 Data changes are applied, and the worksheet status is updated from "Unknown" to "OK"

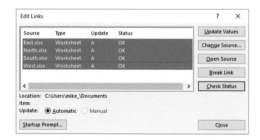

Hot tip

To see trends in **Costs**, select cell F4, click **Insert**, pick a **Sparklines** type, then select the data range (B4:E4).
Copy F4 to F5:F7 to see trends for overall **Sales**, **Profit**, and **Margin**.

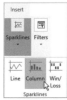

4 The updated information is added to the destination workbook, which now displays the data for three quarters

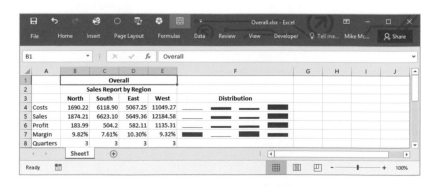

Turn Off the Prompt

If you are confident with the integrity of the external links, you can turn off the update prompt for a specific workbook. To do this:

1 Open the workbook and select **Edit Links** from the **Connections** group on the **Data** tab

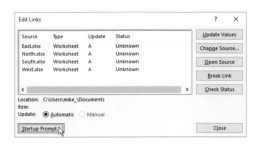

If you choose **Don't display the alert and don't update automatic links**, users of the workbook won't be aware when the data in the workbook becomes out of date.

2 Click the **Startup Prompt** button and choose **Don't display the alert and update links**, then click **OK**

3 Whenever you open that workbook in future, Excel will automatically check for updates and apply the latest values from the source workbooks

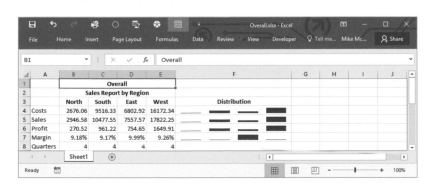

Save Workbook Online

You can store workbooks and other documents online, and access them via Office Online apps, or share them with other users.
To copy a workbook to OneDrive from within Excel:

1 Open a workbook, click the **File** tab, and select **Save As**

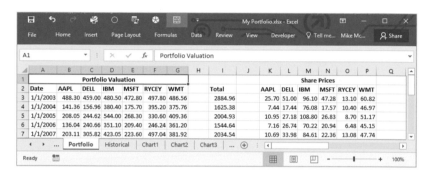

2 Select the OneDrive for the current user and click **Browse** to explore the OneDrive contents

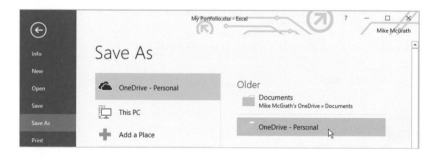

3 Select the OneDrive folder, e.g. "Projects" and click **Open**

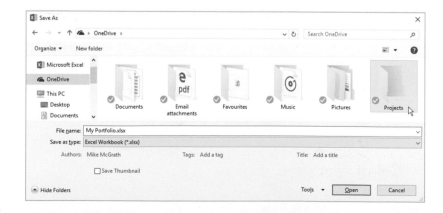

4 Amend the workbook name if required, and click **Save**

With the workbook on your OneDrive, you can now access it even on computers that do not have a copy of Excel 2016 installed.

1 Go online to **office.com** and sign in using the email address that is associated with your Microsoft Account

2 Scroll down and click the icon to access your OneDrive

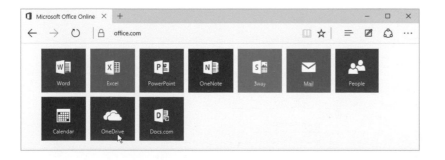

Once you have saved the workbook to your OneDrive, you should close it from within Excel if you are planning to open it from within your browser (see page 182).

At the Office Online website you can work with documents from Word, Excel, PowerPoint and OneNote, whether or not you have Office 2016 on your computer.

Using the Excel Online App

1 Having opened your OneDrive, click the folder that contains the workbook you want to view

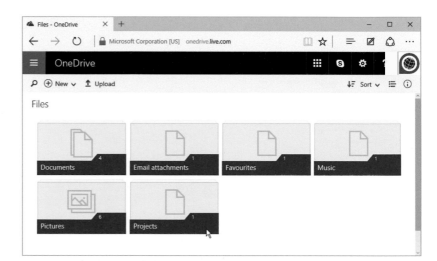

2 When the folder opens, right-click the workbook and select **Open in Excel Online**

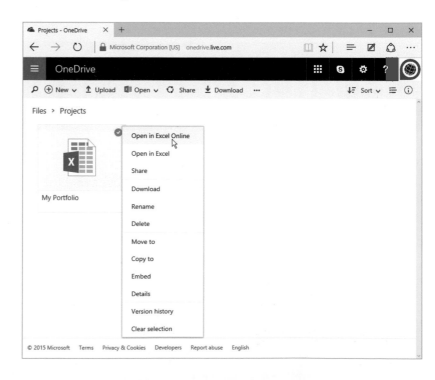

...cont'd

3 The workbook opens in your browser, for review and you can continue working on your workbook online

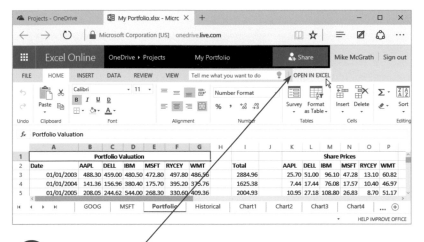

Someone else has this workbook locked

Unfortunately, the workbook needs to be closed or checked in before you can edit it. If everyone uses Excel Online, you can work on it at the same time.

4 Select **OPEN IN EXCEL** if you want to open the workbook in the full Excel 2016 app on your computer

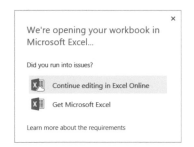

5 Confirm you wish to open the workbook on your computer, or choose to continue in Excel Online

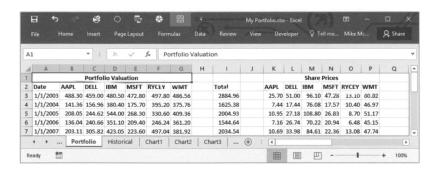

183

Excel in Word

To share data with others who don't have access to Excel or the Office Online apps, you can present the information in a Microsoft Office Word document (as illustrated here), or in a PowerPoint presentation.

You can paste the data as a table, retaining the original formatting, or using styles from the Word document, as shown. Alternatively, paste the data as a picture or tab-separated text. There are also options to maintain a link with the original worksheet.

To add data from an Excel worksheet to a Word document:

1 In Excel, select the worksheet data, and press **Ctrl + C** (or select **Home** and click **Copy,** from the **Clipboard** group)

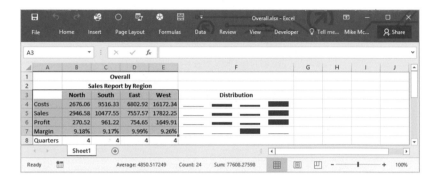

2 Click in the Word document, and press **Ctrl + V** (or select **Home** and click **Paste,** from the **Clipboard** group)

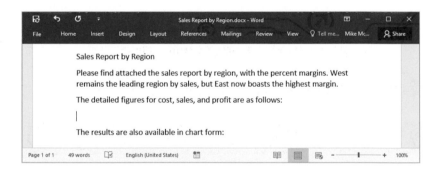

3 Click **Paste Options,** and select the type of paste you want

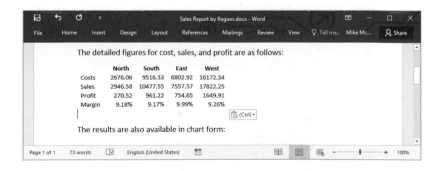

...cont'd

To copy an Excel chart to your Word document:

1 In Excel, select the chart on the worksheet or chart sheet, and press **Ctrl + C** (or select **Home, Copy**)

Apply any text styles or chart formatting required, before you copy the chart to the clipboard.

2 In the Word document, click where you want the chart, and press **Ctrl + V** (or select **Home, Paste**)

3 Click **Paste Options**, and select the type you want

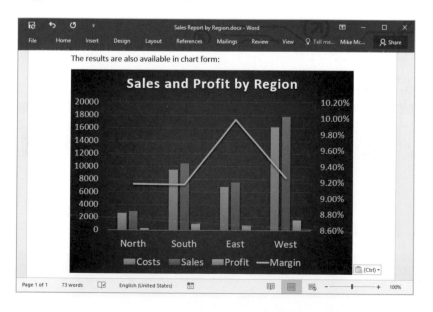

You can choose to simply paste the chart as a **Picture**. Alternatively, you may **Keep Source Formatting**, or **Use Destination Theme**, and **Embed Workbook** or **Link Data**.

Publish as PDF (or XPS)

To send data to others who do not have Excel or Word, you can publish the workbook in Adobe Acrobat PDF format, or XPS format. The recipient only need have any suitable viewing app, such as Acrobat Reader, Microsoft Reader, or XPS Viewer. To do this:

1 Open the workbook in Excel, click the **File** tab, and then click **Save As**

2 Set the **Save as type** drop-down box to PDF (or XPS)

Hot tip

Microsoft Reader in Windows 10 can read both PDF and XPS files. XPS Viewer can be used in previous versions.

Don't forget

You can publish the entire workbook, the active worksheet, or selected ranges of cells, as PDF or XPS documents.

3 Click the **Options** button, to set the scope, e.g. **Active sheet(s)** or **Entire workbook**, and click **OK**

4 Check **Open file after publishing**, then click **Save** to create and display the PDF (or XPS) file

Hot tip

If you save your workbooks as PDF (or XPS) files, you can be sure that the files you share retain exactly the data and format you intended.

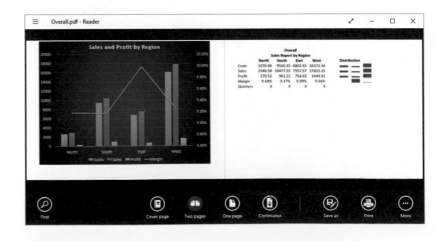

Index

U

V

W

X

Y

Z

Allosaurus

Brachiosaurus

Kentrosaurus

One extinct animal was Brachiosaurus. This was
a **dinosaur** that lived about 150 million years
ago. Other types of creatures lived at the same
time as Brachiosaurus. Nearly all the animals that
lived then have become extinct.

5

The home of Brachiosaurus

Brachiosaurus **fossils** have been found in rocks. Scientists called **geologists** study these rocks. The rocks can show what the area was like when Brachiosaurus lived there.

Some Brachiosaurus fossils were found in Africa in 1927.

Brachiosaurus lived in places where the land was
flat. There was plenty of water. The weather was
warm all year round. Some seasons were wet and
some seasons were dry.

The green valley

Scientists have found **fossil** plants in the same rocks as Brachiosaurus fossils. The fossil plants show them what plants grew when Brachiosaurus was living. Some of these plants were similar to those that grow today. Others were very different.

fossil of a plant

8

Brachiosaurus lived in open country. There were
many trees growing in small groups. Some were
pine and fir trees that looked quite like modern
trees but were much smaller. Some of the plants
that grew then are now **extinct**.

In the shadow of Brachiosaurus

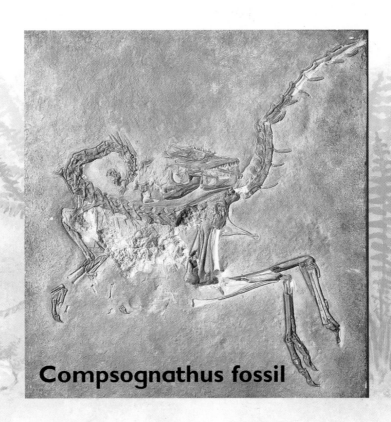

Compsognathus fossil

The **fossils** of beetles and other insects have also been found in the rocks. This shows they lived at the same time as Brachiosaurus. There are also fossils of small **mammals** that looked like **shrews**.

A tiny **dinosaur** called **Compsognathus** lived in the thick undergrowth. It hunted mammals, **lizards** and **insects**. Compsognathus was about 1 metre long. It weighed about the same as a large chicken.

What was Brachiosaurus?

Scientists study the **fossil skeletons** of Brachiosaurus. The fossils show that Brachiosaurus was a huge creature. It was about 23 metres long and may have weighed up to 80 tonnes!

Brachiosaurus was one of the largest animals ever to live on the Earth. Scientists believe it probably walked very slowly. They know that it ate plants, such as leaves from trees.

13

Growing up

Fossils of young **dinosaurs** similar to Brachiosaurus have been found. Scientists believe that Brachiosaurus was probably only one metre long when it first hatched. Perhaps Brachiosaurus hatched from eggs like these.

dinosaur egg fossils

It is possible that young Brachiosaurus hid from meat-eating dinosaurs in thick undergrowth. The undergrowth would also have provided plenty of food for the young. Young Brachiosaurus may also have travelled with adults as part of a **herd**.

The 'arm reptile'

The name Brachiosaurus means 'arm-reptile'. The **dinosaur** was given this name because its front legs are longer than its back legs. Most dinosaurs had longer back legs than front legs.

The long front legs of Brachiosaurus carried the weight of the long neck and head. Powerful shoulder **muscles** kept the dinosaur's head upright. Other muscles moved the legs.

17

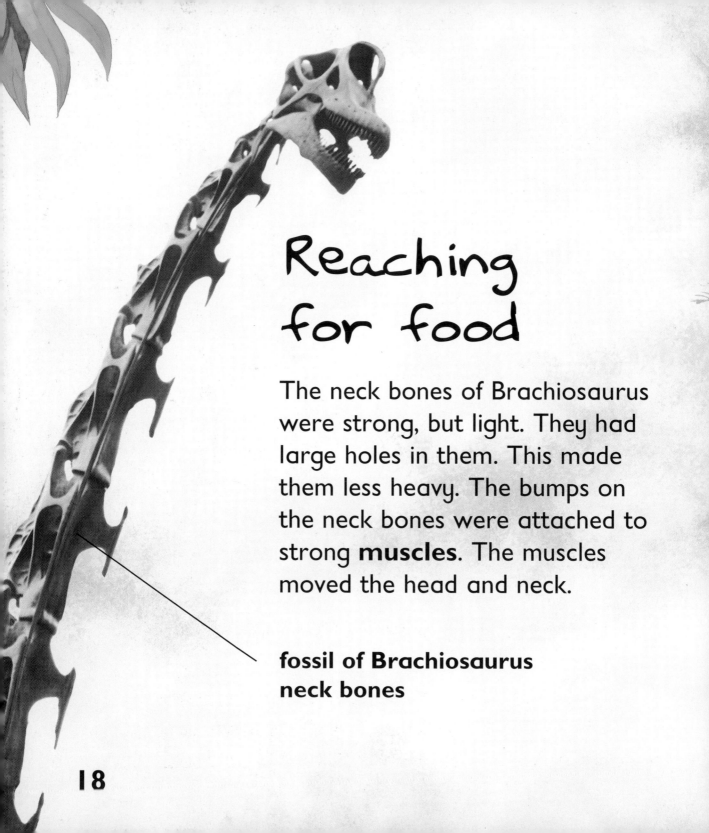

Reaching for food

The neck bones of Brachiosaurus were strong, but light. They had large holes in them. This made them less heavy. The bumps on the neck bones were attached to strong **muscles**. The muscles moved the head and neck.

fossil of Brachiosaurus neck bones

Fossil bones show that Brachiosaurus held its neck upright. This meant it could reach leaves and twigs at the tops of trees. Most dinosaurs could not reach this food. Brachiosaurus and a few other dinosaurs had it all to themselves.

19

Sharp teeth

Brachiosaurus teeth were large and strong. These teeth were good for stripping tough leaves from plants. Scientists have found the teeth are badly worn. This means Brachiosaurus bit through very tough plants.

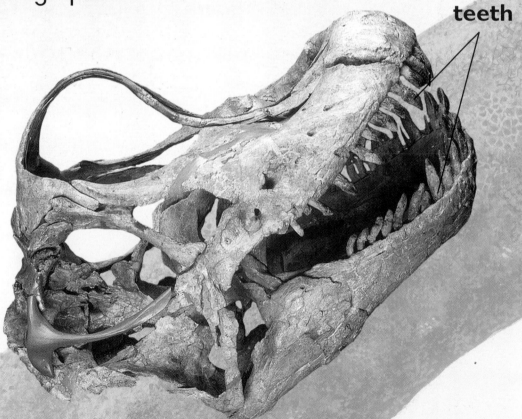

teeth

Brachiosaurus skull

Brachiosaurus probably ate by snapping its jaws shut on plants and then pulling. It would have bitten off chunks of leaves and twigs and swallowed them whole. Brachiosaurus did not chew its food.

Eating stones

Scientists who dig up Brachiosaurus and similar **fossils** occasionally find piles of stones nearby. These stones have been worn smooth. They are called 'gastroliths', which means 'stomach stones'.

Brachiosaurus sometimes swallowed stones. These
stones stayed in the **dinosaur's** stomach. They
pounded against the leaves eaten by the dinosaur.
This turned the plants into a mushy paste, which
could be easily **digested**.

23

Under attack!

Scientists have found the **fossils** of a large meat-eating **dinosaur**. They have named this dinosaur Allosaurus. Allosaurus was a hunter that lived at the same time as Brachiosaurus. It had sharp claws and teeth. It attacked and killed other dinosaurs.

sharp teeth

Allosaurus skull

24

Allosaurus was up to twelve metres long. Scientists think it might have attacked young Brachiosaurus that were small and easy to kill. If several Allosaurus worked together they might have been able to kill an **adult** Brachiosaurus.

Fighting back

Brachiosaurus had a large, sharp claw on its front foot. Some scientists think it used this claw to protect itself from attack. It might also have been used to stop Brachiosaurus from slipping.

claw

Perhaps Brachiosaurus tried to injure attackers
using its large claw. Or Brachiosaurus may have
tried to crush attackers by stomping on them.
Larger, older Brachiosaurus were less likely to
be attacked.

Around the world

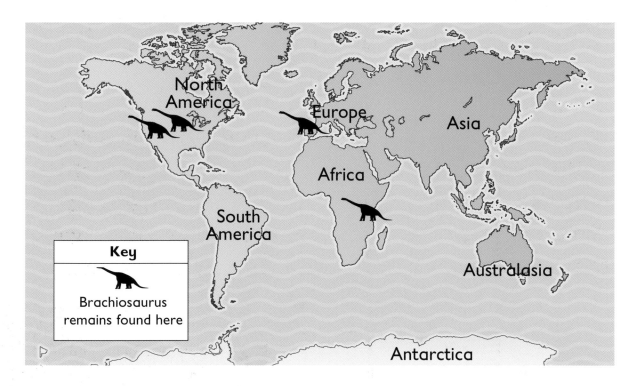

The **fossils** of Brachiosaurus have been found in
North America, East Africa and Western Europe.
At the time of Brachiosaurus these **continents**
were joined together. There was no Atlantic
Ocean. The dinosaurs could have moved from one
continent to the other.

When did Brachiosaurus live?

Brachiosaurus existed for just a few million years, about 150–140 million years ago (mya). They lived in the middle of the Age of the Dinosaurs, which scientists call the Mesozoic Era. Many other large dinosaurs with long necks and tails lived at about the same time. These are known as **sauropods**.

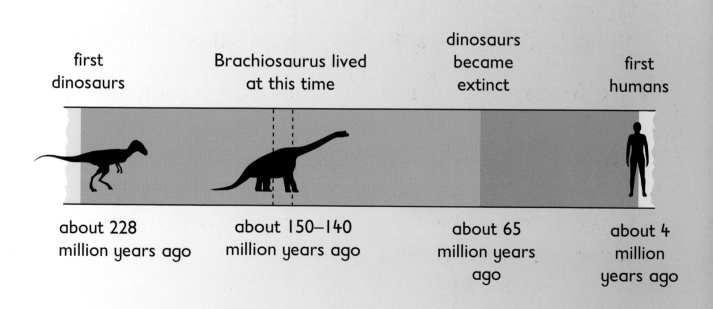

first dinosaurs

Brachiosaurus lived at this time

dinosaurs became extinct

first humans

about 228 million years ago

about 150–140 million years ago

about 65 million years ago

about 4 million years ago

Fact file

Brachiosaurus fact file	
Length:	about 23 metres
Height:	up to 14 metres
Weight:	up to 80 tonnes
Time:	Late Jurassic Period, about 150–140 million years ago
Place:	North America, Africa, Europe

How to say it

Allosaurus – al-oh-saw-rus
Brachiosaurus – brak-ee-oh-saw-rus
Compsognathus – komp-sogg-nay-thus
dinosaur – dine-oh-saw

Glossary

adult grown up

Compsognathus one of the smallest dinosaurs. It hunted mammals and other small animals.

continents large mass of land, such as Europe or Africa

digested food that has been broken into tiny pieces so it can be used by the body

dinosaurs reptiles that lived on Earth between 228 and 65 million years ago. Dinosaurs are extinct.

extinct an animal is extinct when there are none left alive

fossils remains of a plant or animal, usually found in rocks

geologist a scientist who studies rocks is called a geologist

herd group of animals living and travelling together

insect small creature with a hard outer covering and six legs

lizard small reptile with four legs

mammal animal with hair or fur. Mammals give birth to live young instead of laying eggs.

muscles parts of an animal's body that provide power to make it move

ocean very large area of sea

sauropods four-legged dinosaurs which ate plants and had long necks and tails

shrew type of small mammal with a long nose

skeleton bones that support the body of an animal

31

Find out more

These are some other books about dinosaurs:
Big Book of Dinosaurs, Angela Wilkes (Dorling Kindersley, 2001)
Brachiosaurus, Michael Goecke (Abdo Publishing, 2002)
Dinosaur Park, Nick Denchfield (Macmillan, 1998)

Look on these websites for more information:
www.bbc.co.uk/dinosaurs/fact_files/scrub/brachiosaurus.shtml
www.enchantedlearning.com/subjects/dinos/Brachiosaurus.shtml
www.oink.demon.co.uk/topics/dinosaur.htm

Index

Gone forever!

Sometimes all the animals of a particular type die. When this happens, the animal is said to have become **extinct**. Scientists study extinct animals by digging for **fossils**.

Contents

Some words are shown in bold, **like this**.
You can find out what they mean by looking in the Glossary.

www.heinemann.co.uk/library
Visit our website to find out more information about Heinemann Library books.

To order:

 Phone ++44 (0)1865 888066
Send a fax to ++44 (0)1865 314091
Visit the Heinemann Bookshop at www.heinemann.co.uk/library to browse our catalogue
and order online.

First published in Great Britain by Heinemann Library, Halley Court, Jordan Hill, Oxford OX2 8EJ, a part of Harcourt Education. Heinemann is a registered trademark of Harcourt Education Ltd.

© Harcourt Education Ltd 2003
First published in paperback in 2004
The moral right of the proprietor has been asserted.

Editorial: Andrew Farrow and Dan Nunn
Design: Ron Kamen and Paul Davies and Associates
Illustrations: James Field of Simon Girling and Associates
Picture Research: Rebecca Sodergren and Ginny Stroud-Lewis
Production: Viv Hichens
Originated by Ambassador Litho Ltd
Printed and bound in China by South China Printing Company

07 06 05 04 03   08 07 06 05 04
10 9 8 7 6 5 4 3 2 1   10 9 8 7 6 5 4 3 2 1
ISBN 0 431 16617 X   ISBN 0 431 16622 6
(hardback)   (paperback)

British Library Cataloguing in Publication Data

Matthews, Rupert
Brachiosaurus. - (Gone forever)
1. Brachiosaurus - Juvenile literature
I. Title
567.9'12

Acknowledgements

The Publishers are grateful to the following for permission to reproduce copyright material: AKG pp. 12, 16, 18, 26; FLPA p. 14 (Mark Newman); Museum für Naturkunde, Berlin p. 20; Natural History Museum, London pp. 4, 6, 8, 10, 22, 24.

Cover photo reproduced with permission of Museum für Naturkunde, Berlin.

Our thanks to Dr Angela Milner of the Natural History Museum, London for her assistance in the preparation of this book.

Every effort has been made to contact copyright holders of any material reproduced in this book. Any omissions will be rectified in subsequent printings if notice is given to the Publishers.

Disclaimer

All the Internet addresses (URLs) given in this book were valid at the time of going to press. However, due to the dynamic nature of the Internet, some addresses may have changed, or sites may have ceased to exist since publication. While the author and Publishers regret any inconvenience this may cause readers, no responsibility for any such changes can be accepted by either the author or the Publishers.

Gone Forever!
Brachiosaurus

Rupert Matthews

Heinemann
LIBRARY